REVISION WORKBOOK

Revenue Law

Fourth Edition

SARAH EFTHYMIOU
BA, JD, New York Attorney, Solicitor

OLD BAILEY PRESS

OLD BAILEY PRESS
at Holborn College, Woolwich Road,
Charlton, London, SE7 8LN

First published 1997
Fourth edition 2004

© Holborn College Ltd 2004

All Old Bailey Press publications enjoy copyright protection and the copyright belongs to Holborn College Ltd.

All rights reserved. No part of this publication may be reproduced or transmitted in any form or by any means, electronic, mechanical, photocopying, recording or otherwise, or stored in any retrieval system of any nature without either the written permission of the copyright holder, application for which should be made to the Old Bailey Press, or a licence permitting restricted copying in the United Kingdom issued by the Copyright Licensing Agency.

Any person who infringes the above in relation to this publication may be liable to criminal prosecution and civil claims for damages.

ISBN 1 85836 560 0

British Library Cataloguing-in-Publication.

A CIP Catalogue record for this book is available from the British Library.

Printed and bound in Great Britain.

Contents

Acknowledgement

Some questions used are taken or adapted from past University of London LLB (External) Degree examination papers and our thanks are extended to the University of London for their kind permission to use and publish the questions.

Caveat

The answers given are not approved or sanctioned by the University of London and are entirely our responsibility.

They are not intended as 'Model Answers', but rather as Suggested Solutions.

The answers have two fundamental purposes, namely:

a) to provide a detailed example of a suggested solution to an examination question; and

b) to assist students with their research into the subject and to further their understanding and appreciation of the subject.

Introduction

This Revision WorkBook has been designed specifically for those studying revenue law to undergraduate level. Its coverage is not confined to any one syllabus, but embraces all the major revenue law topics to be found in university examinations.

Each chapter contains a brief introduction explaining the scope and overall content of the topic covered in that chapter. There follows, in each case, a list of key points which will assist the student in studying and memorising essential material with which the student should be familiar in order to fully understand the topic.

Additionally in each chapter there is a key cases and statutes section which lists the most relevant cases and statutory provisions applicable to the topic in question. These are intended as an aid to revision, providing the student with a concise list of materials from which to begin revision.

Each chapter usually ends with several typical examination questions, together with general comments, skeleton solutions and suggested solutions. Wherever possible, the questions are drawn from the University of London external revenue law papers, with recent questions being included where possible. However, it is inevitable that, in compiling a list of questions by topic order rather than chronologically, not only do the same questions crop up over and over again in different guises, but there are gaps where questions have never been set at all.

Undoubtedly, the main feature of this Revision WorkBook is the inclusion of as many past examination questions as possible. While the use of past questions as a revision aid is certainly not new, it is hoped that the combination of actual past questions from the University of London LLB external course and specially written questions, where there are gaps in examination coverage, will be of assistance to students in achieving a thorough and systematic revision of the subject.

Careful use of the Revision WorkBook should enhance the student's understanding of revenue law and, hopefully, enable you to deal with as wide a range of subject matter as anyone might find in a revenue law examination, while at the same time allowing you to practise examination techniques while working through the book.

Studying Revenue Law

Revenue law involves a great deal of statutory material as well as a considerable volume of case law. It is of paramount importance for the student to become familiar with the legislation and this can only be achieved through constant use of the Taxes Acts throughout the course of study. It is not necessary to learn the statutory provisions verbatim at degree level, but merely to know where to find the appropriate section and to understand its meaning.

The common law is also essential as it provides an invaluable interpretation of the statutory material.

Diligent study of the subject is required from the very beginning since the basic structure of the UK tax system must be understood in order to be able to grasp the more complex aspects later on.

Revision and Examination Technique

Revision Technique

Planning a revision timetable

In planning your revision timetable make sure you do not finish the syllabus too early. You should avoid leaving revision so late that you have to 'cram' – but constant revision of the same topic leads to stagnation.

Plan ahead, however, and try to make your plans increasingly detailed as you approach the examination date.

Allocate enough time for each topic to be studied. But note that it is better to devise a realistic timetable, to which you have a reasonable chance of keeping, rather than a wildly optimistic schedule which you will probably abandon at the first opportunity!

The syllabus and its topics

One of your first tasks when you began your course was to ensure that you thoroughly understood your syllabus. Check now to see if you can write down the topics it comprises from memory. You will see that the chapters of this WorkBook are each devoted to a syllabus topic. This will help you decide which are the key chapters relative to your revision programme, though you should allow some time for glancing through the other chapters.

The topic and its key points

Again working from memory, analyse what you consider to be the key points of any topic that you have selected for particular revision. Seeing what you can recall, unaided, will help you to understand and firmly memorise the concepts involved.

Using the WorkBook

Relevant questions are provided for each topic in this book. Naturally, as typical examples of examination questions, they do not normally relate to one topic only. But the questions in each chapter will relate to the subject matter of the chapter to a degree. You can choose your method of consulting the questions and solutions, but here are some suggestions (strategies 1–3). Each of them pre-supposes that you have read through the author's notes on key points and key cases and statutes, and any other preliminary matter, at the beginning of the chapter. Once again, you now need to practise working from memory, for that is the challenge you are preparing yourself for. As a rule of procedure constantly test yourself once revision starts, both orally and in writing.

Strategy 1

Strategy 1 is planned for the purpose of quick revision. First read your chosen question carefully and then jot down in abbreviated notes what you consider to be the main points at issue. Similarly, note the cases and statutes that occur to you as being relevant for citation purposes. Allow yourself sufficient time to cover what you feel to be relevant. Then study the author's skeleton solution and skim-read the suggested solution to see how they compare with your notes. When comparing consider carefully what the author has included (and concluded) and see whether that agrees with what you have written. Consider the points of variation also. Have you recognised the key issues? How relevant have you been? It is possible, of course, that you have referred to a recent case that is relevant, but which had not been reported when the WorkBook was prepared.

Strategy 2

Strategy 2 requires a nucleus of three hours in which to practise writing a set of examination answers in a limited time-span.

Select a number of questions (as many as are normally set in your subject in the examination you are studying for), each from a different chapter in the WorkBook, without consulting the solutions. Find a place to write where you will not be disturbed and try to arrange not to be interrupted for three hours. Write your solutions in the time allowed, noting any time needed to make up if you are interrupted.

After a rest, compare your answers with the suggested solutions in the WorkBook. There will be considerable variation in style, of course, but the bare facts should not be too dissimilar. Evaluate your answer critically. Be 'searching', but develop a positive approach to deciding how you would tackle each question on another occasion.

Strategy 3

You are unlikely to be able to do more than one three hour examination, but occasionally set yourself a single question. Vary the 'time allowed' by imagining it to be one of the questions that you must answer in three hours and allow yourself a limited preparation and writing time. Try one question that you feel to be difficult and an easier question on another occasion, for example.

Misuse of suggested solutions

Don't try to learn by rote. In particular, don't try to reproduce the suggested solutions by heart. Learn to express the basic concepts in your own words.

Keeping up-to-date

Keep up-to-date. While examiners do not require familiarity with changes in the law during the three months prior to the examination, it obviously creates a good impression if you can show you are acquainted with any recent changes. Make a habit of looking through one of the leading journals – *Modern Law Review, Law Quarterly Review* or the *New Law Journal*, for example – and cumulative indices to law reports, such as the *All England Law Reports* or *Weekly Law Reports*, or indeed the daily law reports in *The Times*. The *Law Society's Gazette* and the *Legal Executive Journal* are helpful sources, plus any specialist journal(s) for the subject you are studying.

Examination Skills

Examiners are human too!

The process of answering an examination question involves a communication between you and the person who set it. If you were speaking face to face with the person, you would choose your verbal points and arguments carefully in your reply. When writing, it is all too easy to forget the human being who is awaiting the reply and simply write out what one knows in the area of the subject! Bear in mind it is a person whose question you are responding to, throughout your essay. This will help you to avoid being irrelevant or long-winded.

The essay question

Candidates are sometimes tempted to choose to answer essay questions because they 'seem' easier. But the examiner is looking for thoughtful work and will not give good marks for superficial answers.

The essay-type of question may be either purely factual, in asking you to explain the meaning of a certain doctrine or principle, or it may ask you to discuss a certain proposition, usually derived from a quotation. In either case, the approach to the answer is the same. A clear programme must be devised to give the examiner the meaning or significance of the doctrine, principle or proposition and its origin in common law, equity or statute, and cases which illustrate its application to the branch of law concerned. Essay questions offer a good way to obtain marks if you have thought carefully about a topic, since it is up to you to impose the structure (unlike the problem questions where the problem imposes its own structure). You are then free to speculate and show imagination.

The problem question

The problem-type question requires a different approach. You may well be asked to advise a client or merely discuss the problems raised in the question. In either case, the most important factor is to take great care in reading the question. By its nature, the question will be longer than the essay-type question and you will have a number of facts to digest. Time spent in analysing the question may well save time later, when you are endeavouring to impress on the examiner the considerable extent of your basic legal knowledge. The quantity of knowledge is itself a trap and you must always keep within the boundaries of the question in hand. It is very tempting to show the examiner the extent of your knowledge of your subject, but if this is outside the question, it is time lost and no marks earned. It is inevitable that some areas which you have studied and revised will not be the subject of questions, but under no circumstances attempt to adapt a question to a stronger area of knowledge at the expense of relevance.

When you are satisfied that you have grasped the full significance of the problem-type question, set out the fundamental principles involved.

You will then go on to identify the fundamental problem (or problems) posed by the question. This should be followed by a consideration of the law which is relevant to the problem. The source of the law, together with the cases which will be of assistance in solving the problem, must then be considered in detail.

Very good problem questions are quite likely to have alternative answers, and in advising a party you should be aware that alternative arguments may be available. Each stage of your answer, in this case, will be based on the argument or arguments considered in the previous stage, forming a conditional sequence.

If, however, you only identify one fundamental problem, do not waste time worrying that you cannot think of an alternative – there may very well be only that one answer.

The examiner will then wish to see how you use your legal knowledge to formulate a case and how you apply that formula to the problem which is the subject of the question. It is this positive approach which can make answering a problem question a high mark earner for the student who has fully understood the question and clearly argued their case on the established law.

Examination checklist

a) Read the instructions at the head of the examination carefully. While last-minute changes are unlikely – such as the introduction of a compulsory question or an increase in the number of questions asked – it has been known to happen.

b) Read the questions carefully. Analyse problem questions – work out what the examiner wants.

c) Plan your answer before you start to write.

d) Check that you understand the rubric before you start to write. Do not 'discuss', for example, if you are specifically asked to 'compare and contrast'.

e) Answer the correct number of questions. If you fail to answer one out of four questions set you lose 25 per cent of your marks!

Style and structure

Try to be clear and concise. Fundamentally this amounts to using paragraphs to denote the sections of your essay, and writing simple, straightforward sentences as much as possible. The sentence you have just read has 22 words – when a sentence reaches 50 words it becomes difficult for a reader to follow.

Do not be inhibited by the word 'structure' (traditionally defined as giving an essay a beginning, a middle and an end). A good structure will be the natural consequence of setting out your arguments and the supporting evidence in a logical order. Set the scene briefly in your opening paragraph. Provide a clear conclusion in your final paragraph.

Table of Cases

Table of Statutes and Other Materials

Chapter 1

Introduction

Definition of 'tax' per the *Shorter Oxford English Dictionary* – 'a compulsory contribution to the support of the government, levied on persons, property, income, commodities, transactions etc'.

Taxes charged in the UK

TAX	NATURE OF TAX	WHO PAYS THE TAX
Income tax	Tax on income	Individuals/Trustees/ Personal Representatives
		Partnerships
		Non-resident companies
Corporation tax	Tax on income and on capital transactions	Companies
Capital gains tax	Tax on capital transactions	Individuals/Trustees/Personal Representatives/Partnerships (in respect of chargeable gains) NB the capital gains of companies are charged under corporation tax
Inheritance tax	Tax on lifetime transfers of capital and on capital left at death	Individuals and their personal representatives and trustees
Value added tax	Tax on supplies of goods or services and on acquisition of goods on importation from EU countries	Anyone who makes taxable supplies beyond the limits for registration

Year of assessment

For individuals, partnerships and other non-corporate taxpayers the year of assessment is the income tax year from 6 April to the following 5 April. For companies the year is the 'financial year' which runs from 1 April. Financial year 2004 begins on 1 April 2004. The rates of tax are set for each income tax year or financial year. ss1 and 6 ICTA 1988.

Chapter 2

The Taxation of Income

2.1   **Introduction**

2.2   **Key points**

2.3   **Key cases and statutes**

2.4   **Question and suggested solution**

2.1 Introduction

Persons (other than corporate bodies and others charged to corporation tax) are charged to income tax on income according to the rules set out for each category of income falling within the Schedules A to F (except that Schedules B and C no longer exist, having been abolished by FA 1988 and FA 1996 respectively). The Schedules owe their origins to being schedules A to E (F added later) to the Taxes Act 1842 – though the current provisions are now sections of the main Income and Corporation Tax Act 1988: see ss15–20. (Schedules to Acts are of course now numbered.)

Individuals are subject to tax, with minor exceptions, on their worldwide income if 'resident' in the UK. For business income, the same rules apply to the calculation of taxable profits for individuals and partnerships. The schedular system also applies to income chargeable to corporation tax – only the mode of assessing differs.

2.2 Key points

Primary legislation

ACT	SCOPE OF ACT
Income and Corporation Taxes Act (ICTA 1988)	Income taxation of all corporate 1988 and non-corporate bodies
Taxes Management Act 1970 (TMA 1970)	Administration of income taxation
Annual Finance Acts (FA 200x)	To introduce new law and amend existing Tax Acts, confirming the announcements made by the Chancellor of the Exchequer in his annual Budget Speech

Capital Allowances Act 2001 (CAA 2001)	Allowances given against income in respect of certain capital items
Inheritance Tax Act 1984 (IHTA 1984)	Capital remaining upon death and some lifetime transfers of capital
Taxation of Chargeable Gains Act 1992 (TCGA 1992)	Computation (all taxpayers) of and taxation (non-corporate taxpayers) of capital gains. Companies charged to corporation tax on gains as computed under the Act.
Value Added Tax Act 1994 (VATA 1994)	Administration and collection of VAT Issued under the powers in sections of the Primary Acts

Secondary legislation

These include regulations/statutory instruments.

See for example the 'PAYE Regulations' issued as the Income Tax (Employments) Regulations 1993 (SI 1993/744) made under the provisions of ss203 and 204 ICTA 1988 which contain the detailed rules for collecting tax under schedule E on employment income.

Case law

The cases interpret the legislation and as such are indispensable to the student and practitioner.

Years of assessment

The fiscal year, or year of assessment, for most taxation purposes runs from 6 April of one year to 5 April of the next, and tax is levied on income arising in any given year of assessment.

The rules for each schedule determine how much income is to be treated as being assessable for each tax year by allocating the income of the relevant basis period (eg the income of the previous year) to that year of assessment.

The schedular system (post-FA 1994 provisions)

Note: the normal basis of assessment under the cases of Schedule D was switched to the 'current year' basis between 1994 for new businesses and sources and became fully operative from 1996–97 onwards for all purposes. The schedules apply both for income tax and for corporation tax purposes. However, between April 1995 and April 1998, two separate bases applied in computing income for Schedule A purposes for income tax and corporation tax purposes: see Chapter 4.

Each schedule covers different sources of income with its own rules for assessment and computation of tax due. The schedules are mutually exclusive: *Fry* v *Salisbury House Estate Ltd* [1930] AC 432. See *Bye* v *Coren* [1986] STC 393 – the Revenue are not prevented from making alternative protective assessments but a double charge assessment is to be cancelled: s32 TMA 1970.

See also *IRC* v *Wilkinson* [1992] STC 454.

Table of Schedules
(All references in the table are to ICTA 1988)

Note: the following table should be read in conjunction with Notes 1 and 2 at the end of the table, in connection with the changes to the basis of assessment of income under Schedule A and Schedule D.

Schedule	Income assessable	Deductions allowed	Normal basis of assessment
A (See Note 1) Up to 1994–95	Rents etc from land (s15(1))	All reasonable expenses (eg repairs) but *not* improvements (ss25–28)	Rent due less expenses *paid* in tax year (s15(2) and ss21–22)
From 1995–96	Profits or gains from United Kingdom land (s15 via FA 1995 s39 and Schedule 6)	Deduction rules as for Schedule D Case I (s21, s74 via FA 1995 s39(2) and Schedule 6) Interest allowable as deduction 1995–96 onwards (s355(1) deleted by FA 1995 s42)	Profits or gains arising in the tax year (s15 via FA 1995 s39 and Schedule 6)
D Case I	Profits from trade: including those arising from trading purpose loan relationships (s18)	All expenses incurred wholly and exclusively for the purposes of the trade or profession save for those specifically disallowed by statute (s74(1)(a))	Profits of accounting period ending in year of assessment (s60–s64) (see Note 2)
D Case II	Profits of a profession or vocation (s18)	As with Schedule D Case I (s74(1)(a))	As with Schedule D Case I (s60–s64) (see Note 2)

Schedule	Income assessable	Deductions allowed	Normal basis of assessment
D Case III	Interest annuities and other annual payments (s18(3), s66(1)). Profits or gains from non-trading loan relationships s18(3A) Profits from Public Revenue dividends payable in the United Kingdom s18(3)(c)	None	Income arising in tax year (s64) (see Note 2) Profits arising in tax year
D Case IV	Income from foreign securities (s18(3), s66(1)) Income from foreign possessions (eg trades carried on wholly abroad) (s18(3))	None Depends on type of income. If rent, as Schedule A; if business profits, as Schedule D Cases I and II (s65(2), s65(1)(a))	Income arising in tax year (s65, s66(1)) (see Note 2) D Case V Income arising in tax year (s65(1)) (see Note 2)
D Case VI	Any annual profits or gains not caught by any other Schedule or Case (s18(3))	Depends on type of income	Income of current tax year (s69)
E	Earnings from an office or employment (see Note 3)		
E Case I	Employee resident and ordinarily resident (s19, s131)	In each of Cases I, II and III, all travelling expenses wholly and exclusively incurred in the performance of the duties of the office or employment and all other expenses wholly exclusively and necessarily so incurred (s198)	(I) Emoluments received in the tax year (s202A)
E Case II	Employee either not resident, or, if resident, not ordinarily resident (s19, s131)		(II) Emoluments for United Kingdom duties received in the tax year (s202A, s132, s192)

Schedule	Income assessable	Deductions allowed	Normal basis of assessment
E Case III	Employee resident, in respect of certain income not caught by Cases I or II (s19, s131)		(III) Emoluments received in the United Kingdom in the tax year (s202A, s132)
F	Dividends and other distributions by United Kingdom companies (s20)	None	On dividends plus tax credit received in tax year (s20(1) para 2)

Notes

a) The changes to the Schedule A system of tax from 1995–96 applied only for income tax purposes. The old rules continued to apply until 1 April 1998 for corporation tax purposes. See Chapter 4 for further details of the changes.

b) FA 1994 contained provisions in ss200–208 which by the year of assessment 1996–97 changed the normal basis of assessment under Schedule D Cases I to V inclusive from profits or income of the previous year to those of the current year as well as introducing a system of self-assessment (see Chapter 23). However, new businesses commencing from 6 April 1994 became subject to the new current year basis from the start. (See Chapter 5 for further details.)

c) The charge to tax under Schedule E is not confined to income falling within the three cases. Part V (ss131–207) ICTA 1988 contains provisions further to s19, including in particular the charge to tax on payments under s148. (See *Nichols v Gibson* [1996] STC 1008, discussed in Chapter 7, section 7.2)

d) See *Fry v Salisbury House Estate Ltd* [1930] AC 432 (above) re exclusive nature of the schedules.

Exemptions from income tax

These include:

a) interest from National Savings Certificates (s46 ICTA 1988);

b) the first £70 of interest from a National Savings Bank ordinary account (s325 ICTA 1988);

c) scholarship and grant income (s331 ICTA 1988);

d) SAYE terminal bonuses (s326 ICTA 1988);

e) interest or bonuses payable on tax exempt special savings accounts (TESSAs) – s326A ICTA 1988,

f) dividends payable into an approved personal equity plan (PEPs);

g) interest and dividends earned in Individual Savings Accounts (ISAs);

h) interest payable on personal injuries awards (s329A ICTA 1988).

Persons exempt from income tax

a) the Crown (but from 6 April 1993 the Queen became taxable on her personal income, gains and lifetime transfers);

b) charities, on non-trading income and trading income applied for charitable purposes (s505 ICTA 1988);

c) approved pension funds, on non-trading income. See *Clarke* v *British Telecom Pension Scheme Trustees* [1998] STC 1075, where the sub-underwriting of shares issues in return for commissions was held to be taxable trading income.

2.3 Key cases and statutes

- *Bye* v *Coren* [1986] STC 393
  Income taxation – schedular system – alternative assessments – cancellation of double charge

- *Fry* v *Salisbury House Estate Ltd* [1930] AC 432
  Income taxation – schedular system – mutually exclusive

- *IRC* v *Wilkinson* [1992] STC 454
  Income taxation – schedular system – multiple assessments

- Income and Corporation Taxes Act 1988

- Taxes Management Act 1970

2.4 Question and suggested solution

'Many serious consequences still follow from the fact that the UK income tax system is a "schedular" one. In the modern world many of these consequences are both unattractive and unnecessary.'

To what extent, if at all, do you agree with this criticism of the UK income tax system? Illustrate your answer with examples from decided cases.

University of London LLB Examination
(for External Students) Revenue Law June 1997 Q4

General Comment

The schedules under which tax is charged, even to this day, date back to the early nineteenth century. Its system of classification and imposition of separate charging rules within each classification led to a complex system which has not always kept pace with the changing commercial world. Fortunately, recent radical reforms have improved the relevance of the rules to modern times while still retaining the basic framework of the schedular system.

Skeleton Solution

Schedular system: origins and history – sources of income: lack of definition of income – inconclusive ability of courts to determine comprehensive nature of 'income' – greater statutory detail: less cause for litigation in the courts – exclusive nature of schedules: *Fry v Salisbury Estate Ltd* and *Leeming v Jones* – benefit from recent changes to schedular system.

Suggested Solution

In order to understand the problems associated with the schedular system of income taxation in the United Kingdom, one needs to examine the origins of the system. It takes its present form from the structure of the ancient Finance Act of 1803. This replaced the original Act which introduced income tax in 1799. Surprisingly, when viewed by modern standards, the most unpopular part of the requirements of the 1799 Act was the compulsory making of a tax return disclosing the total income of the taxpayer: see *Attorney-General* v *London County Council* [1901] AC 26. This was rigorously opposed as constituting an infringement of civil liberties. The remedy contained in the 1803 Act was to require separate returns of income under distinct categories or schedules, each return being made to a separate tax authority responsible for assessment and collection of tax under each schedule. The schedules at that time were A, B, C, D and E, corresponding to their equivalents in recent times. When one considers that the principal cause which gave rise to the schedular system has long since been disregarded, it remains an enigma that the system itself has survived almost intact.

This system of categorisation of what is chargeable to income tax gave rise to the 'source' based system of income tax which survives today. It reflects the charge under each schedule according to the source of income or profit which falls within the scope of that schedule. One suspects that this is essentially why no attempt was made to define the concept 'income' in the Income Tax Acts for income tax purposes. In view of the separate returns which would be required according to various sources following the 1803 Act, little or no purpose has been served in requiring returns of 'income' in isolation from the source from which it was derived. The lack of a definition of what constitutes 'income' is viewed as causing the myriad of cases brought before the courts in an attempt to define the scope of the charge under each schedule. As it is, case law has provided guidance but not exhaustively defined the categories of income which fall to be taxed within the various schedules. The extent to which this has occurred or been necessary varies according to the individual schedule and to some extent reflects the detail or lack of detail in the statutes as to which specific types of income are chargeable under a particular schedule. The legislation under Schedule A, for example, is reasonably precise as to what types of receipt or income are liable for assessment under it. Section 15(1) ICTA 1988 imposes a charge on 'annual profits or gains' but goes on to specify 'rents and other receipts' in s15(2), while s15(3) further determines what 'other receipts' will include. The margin for error is lessened as a result. By contrast, the provisions of s18(1) ICTA 1988 relating to the charge under Schedule D are very much vaguer, in listing 'property ... any trade, profession or vocation ... interest of money, annuities and other annual profits or gains' as the main sources of charge. The majority of these terms, as can be seen, are less specific. It has therefore been the role of the courts to align individual activities with these general provisions. By comparison with the number of cases which have considered the definition of 'trading', 'trade', 'profession' and 'annual payments', the number of cases under Schedule A has been extremely low. It would appear, therefore, that the more precise the statute in defining the terms of its remit, the less scope for uncertainty. Cases still arriving before the courts at the present time are an indication that uncertainty still remains. This uncertainty might be argued as the most serious consequence of the schedular system as presently operated – certainty being the long-held kingpin of a tax system.

Each of the schedules contain the parameters which determine whether or not an item of income, profit or gain will be subject to income tax under the rules of that particular schedule. If it falls within it, then it is taxable under that schedule and under no other. If it does not fall within any schedule then it is not chargeable to income tax at all. This principle was upheld in the case of *Fry* v *Salisbury House Estate Ltd* [1930] AC 432, which confirmed that the schedules are mutually exclusive. If there is a categorisable source of income, then there is a potential charge to income tax. Without that categorisable source, there is no schedule under which an income tax charge may be imposed. See *Leeming* v *Jones* (1930) 15 TC 333 and referred to in *Memec* v *IRC* [1996] STC 1336.

The Revenue are not free to select under which schedule they will tax the income. It has to be assessed according to its source and the rules of the relevant schedule. Income tax is levied and can be levied only under the various schedules. Other than that no income tax charge may be imposed without specific statutory provision – the only examples of which in the income tax legislation are the charges under s349(1) and (2) ICTA 1988. Under these provisions an income tax is imposed on certain annual payments, including interest.

Despite the divergence of sources from which an income tax charge may arise, it remains one single tax, as stressed by Lord Macnaghten in *Attorney-General* v *London County Council*:

> 'It is one tax, not a collection of taxes essentially distinct ... The standard of assessment varies according to the nature of the source from which the taxable income is derived. That is all ... In every case the tax is a tax on income, whatever may be the standard by which the income is measured.'

The fact remains that the system is not based upon a definition of the types of income to be charged to income tax but instead relies on identifying the sources of income. Whether that requires the retention of a schedular system which contains separate rules for the computation of income from the various sources is a matter of some conjecture. The effect is more likely to be a divergence of opinion as to what constitutes a receipt of an income nature and, if this were to be defined by statute, it is unlikely to be able to embrace all the potential types of income which real commercial transactions are capable of generating. The main criticisms of the schedular system have largely been dealt with through the recent abolition of the previous year basis of assessment and the ending of the need for special computational rules in the opening and closing years of a source of income. On balance, therefore, without these features, the schedular system probably does present a more effective system by embodying each source's rules for computing income within separately defined areas of the legislation. Such an approach recognises that although the courts have been unable over the decades to define comprehensively what is 'income' for income tax purposes, it is beyond the scope of precise legislation to do so. This reflects the realities of the distinctions necessary for pure income – for example, an interest receipt and profit-based income such as arising from letting of property, both of which are equally within the ambit of the same income tax.

Chapter 3

Total Income

3.1   **Introduction**

3.2   **Key points**

3.3   **Key statute**

3.4   **Question and suggested solution**

3.1 Introduction

For the purposes of tax, income is anything which falls within the scope of the schedules.

Earned/unearned income

Definition of earned income s883(4)–(6) ICTA 1988 includes: income within Schedule E and Schedule D Cases I and II and certain taxable state benefits eg maternity pay: s150 ICTA 1988.

For taxpayers not liable at a higher rate, 'Savings income' is taxed at lower rate only: s1 ICTA 1988. From 6 April 1999 dividends are taxed at the appropriate Schedule F rate: s1B ICTA 1988, introduced by s31(5) F(No 2)A 1997.

Total income

Wherever referred to in the Income Tax Acts 'total income' takes the meaning given to it by s835 ICTA 1988. Basically it means all income less all allowable deductions. NB: personal allowances are not a deduction in arriving at total income but are a deduction from total income in providing the figure of taxable income or chargeable income.

3.2 Key points

Rates of tax

For 2003–04 three principle rates of income tax apply:

for income from £1 to £1,960, lower rate tax of 10 per cent applies;

for income from £1,961 to £30,500, basic rate tax of 22 per cent applies;

for any income exceeding £30,501, higher rate tax of 40 per cent applies.

The Schedule F rates from April 1999, referred to above are as follows:

a) Schedule F Ordinary rate – 10 per cent – s1B(2) ICTA 1988 – inserted by s31 F(No 2)A 1997 – applicable to taxpayers not liable at higher rate;

b) Schedule F Upper rate – 32.5 per cent – s1B(2) ICTA 1988 – inserted by s31 F(No 2)A 1997 – applicable to taxpayers liable at higher rate;

c) Schedule F Trust rate – 25 per cent – s686(1A) ICTA 1988 – inserted by s32 F(No 2)A 1997 – applicable to trustees.

Trustees of discretionary trusts are also liable to tax on income other than dividends at the 'rate applicable to trusts' – currently 34 per cent – s686 ICTA 1988.

Computation of total income and taxable income

Earned income	£	£
Schedule D Case I		X
(inclusive of deductions for capital allowances)		
Schedule E	X	
Less: expenses	(X)	
		X
		X
Investment and savings income		
Schedule A	X	
UK Dividends (gross)	X	
Bank interest (gross)	X	
Building society interest (gross)	X	
	X	
Less: charges on income paid gross		
	(X)	
		X
TOTAL INCOME (per s835 ICTA 1988)		X
Less: personal allowances		(X)
TAXABLE INCOME		X (See Note below)
Tax payable 10 per cent on first £1,960 (2003–04)		X
22 per cent on next £28,539 (2003–04)		X
40 per cent on remainder		X
		X

Less:

a) 10% tax relief on married couples allowance   £257   X

b) tax paid at source (eg building society
    and bank interest, dividends)   X(X)

    Income tax liability   X

Note: if 'taxable income' does not exceed upper limit of basic rate band, tax is calculated on non-savings income at lower and basic rates, then all savings income is taxed at 22 per cent (in addition to the normal lower rate band). If total income exceeds upper limit of basic rate band, tax is calculated on non-savings income at lower and basic rates, then all savings income up to the remainder of the basic rate band is taxed at 22 per cent, then at 40 per cent on the amount by which total income exceeds the basic rate band. Effectively, the savings income is treated as the top slice of the taxpayer's income.

Relief for loan interest paid: ss353–379 ICTA 1988

Loans for the purchase of land: ss354–357C ICTA 1988

1995–96 and subsequent years – let property

Historically, relief for interest on the purchase or improvement of property was only available if either:

a) the land was the only or main residence of the borrower or of a dependent relative: *Frost* v *Feltham* [1981] STC 115; or

b) the land was let at a commercial rent for more than 26 weeks and was available for letting or being repaired for the rest of the time.

As stated in the table of schedules and in the notes to that table in Chapter 2, profits from letting of property for those liable to income tax, are calculated in the same way as business profits – s39(2) FA 1995 et seq, refers to the 'Schedule A business'. Hitherto no interest relief on property loans was available for income tax purposes unless it satisfied the 'main residence' (or 'commercial' let) conditions in s355(1) ICTA 1988, mentioned above. That relief, where due, was given against total income and not, as now, as a deduction in calculating the taxable income from the letting. (See Chapter 4.)

The tax relief for interest on a mortgage over a private residence has been abolished by FA 1999.

Other types of interest relief

a) Loans to acquire an interest in a close company (s360 ICTA 1988);

b) Loans to acquire an interest in a co-operative (s361 ICTA 1988);

c) Loans to acquire an interest in a partnership (s362 ICTA 1988);

d) Loans to acquire plant and machinery (s359 ICTA 1988);

e) Loans to pay IHT (s364 ICTA 1988);

f) Loans to purchase life annuities secured on land (s365 ICTA 1988);

g) Interest on loans for business purposes, including a 'Schedule A business', may be treated as a business expense (in the absence of exclusions under s74 ICTA 1988);

h) Relief is also available for interest paid on a loan for the purchase of a car which is used for the purposes of an employment: s359(4). The relief would be proportionate to the business use of the car.

Charges on income

Certain payments made by an individual may be deducted from total income – these are called charges on income. Note that s36 FA1988 greatly reduced payments which may be treated as charges on income. Covenanted payments to charities are no longer covered by s347A ICTA 1988 and, instead, fall within ss25–26 FA 1990, as amended by FA 2000.

Personal reliefs

Every individual is entitled to at least one personal relief which is deductible from total income. Under s278 ICTA 1988, the entitlement to personal allowances is normally restricted to individuals who are residents of the United Kingdom. Certain double taxation agreements between the United Kingdom and other countries provide for personal allowances to be made available to non residents who are taxable in the other country.

Section 145 FA 1996 extended the entitlement to personal allowances to nationals of all of the member states of the European Economic Area, irrespective of whether they are resident in that member state or not.

The reliefs available are as follows:

a) Reliefs in respect of children:

    i) Working Families Tax Credit;

    ii) Children's Tax Credit (s257AA ICTA 1988);

b) Married Couple's Allowance (now available only on an age-related basis);

c) Additional Personal Allowance (s259 ICTA 1988);

d) Widow's Bereavement Allowance (s262 ICTA 1988);

e) Reliefs for Blind Persons (s265(1) and (2) ICTA 1988);

f) Age Allowances (s272(2) and (5) ICTA 1988).

Enterprise Investment Scheme (EIS) and Venture Capital Trust reliefs (VCT)

A deduction may be made from income for qualifying investments into new shares in unquoted trading companies, but the tax relief is restricted to 20 per cent of the amount invested, subject to a maximum investment of £150,000 in a tax year: ss289–290 ICTA 1988. Similar relief applies for investment in quoted Venture Capital Trusts (VCTs) (maximum investment £100,000 in any one tax year): Sch 15B ICTA 1988. Up to £25,000 of the amount invested in an EIS company in the first six months of a tax year may be carried back to obtain tax relief in the previous income tax year.

3.3 Key statute

- Income and Corporation Taxes Act 1988, ss353–379 and 883(4)–(6)

3.4 Question and suggested solution

Fanny has to make the following payments in the near future. She is confused as to whether she should make the payments gross or net of income tax.

a) £500 to Gabrielle, who lives in Spain. The £500 is interest on a loan made to Fanny by Gabrielle recently;

b) £500, again by way of interest on a loan, to Hernando. Hernando was born in Spain but has become a UK resident. The loan, the capital sum of which is £5,000 and which was made on 1 May 1997, is intended to last for ten months only.

In addition, Fanny receives income by way of interest from the Loamshire Bank. They have recently paid her £250 interest under deduction of lower rate tax.

Finally, Fanny is a member of a class of discretionary objects under a trust created by her late father. Recently the trustees paid her £10,000 by way of an appointment of capital and £5,000 by way of an appointment of income.

Advise Fanny on the income tax consequences of all these facts.

University of London LLB Examination
(for External Students) Revenue Law 1997 Q5

General Comment

This question illustrates the principles of taxing income at its source or via the originator of the payment on whom the responsibility for taxing the payment lies. This largely relieves the Inland Revenue from the onus of pursuing a recipient who is beyond its jurisdiction.

Skeleton Solution

Obligation to deduct tax under s349(2)(c) – rate of tax: s4(1A) – usual place of abode outside the UK – obligation to account for tax deducted: s350(1).

Suggested Solution

Note: all references are to the Income and Corporation Taxes Act (ICTA) 1988 unless stated otherwise.

Gabrielle

Fanny has a liability to make a payment of interest to Gabrielle who is resident in Spain. The question of whether she should make the payment gross or net of income tax is specifically covered by the provisions of s349(2)(c). This section determines that a payment of interest which is being made to a person whose usual place of abode is outside the United Kingdom should be made net of income at the prescribed rate. For this purpose the rate of tax to be deducted is the lower rate of tax of 20 per cent as provided for in s4(1A), since the income would be treated as 'savings income' in the hand of the recipient and therefore is 'income to which section 1A applies'. It is assumed for the purpose of the example that Gabrielle is not residing in Spain merely temporarily, but that Spain is where she usually resides. Fanny will need to account to the Inland Revenue for the tax so deducted, but if she is a taxpayer it will be regarded as having been paid out of income already taxed and no separate direct payment of tax requires to be made: s350(1).

Hernando

Payment of interest to Hernando as a former non-resident who has become resident in the UK might also be subject to the need to deduct tax at the lower rate as noted above. The provisions governing the need to deduct tax under s349(2)(c) relate to any recipient of the interest whose usual place of abode is outside the United Kingdom. Fanny would therefore normally be well advised to verify Hernando's UK residence status before making payment of the interest, in order to determine whether Hernando is only temporarily resident in the UK or whether his usual place of abode is outside the UK. If he is still 'ordinarily resident' abroad, then the deduction mechanism should normally apply. However, as the loan is intended to be with interest for only ten months, then it is not 'yearly interest' and is therefore not within the scope of the s349(2)(c) deduction provisions. She may therefore safely make the payment gross.

Interest on bank account

Interest received by Fanny on her bank account has had tax at the lower rate of income tax already deducted. This is generally to avoid tax being directly assessed on each individual recipient. Section 1A determines that all tax on 'income from savings', as defined there, will be subject to tax at the lower rate only, with the exception of those taxpayers whose income renders them liable to tax at the higher rate. Only if Fanny is in this category will she be required to pay any extra tax at 40 per cent, less the tax at 20 per cent already deducted, leaving her to an additional £50 on her £250 interest received.

Trust capital and income

Introductory Note: the payment of £10,000 to Fanny by the trustees of her father's discretionary trust by way of appointment of capital suggests an 'advancement', as the capital has left the trust. (An 'appointment' usually indicates funds being set aside within the trust for reversion to the beneficiary while the beneficiary continues to benefit from the income arising from the 'sub-trust' created by the appointment: see Lord Romiley MR in *Re Gosset's Settlement* (1854) 19 Beav 529.) This suggested solution is prepared on that assumption.

The payment of £10,000 by way of advancement will have a number of consequences for Fanny. Trust income of discretionary trusts is subject to tax in the hands of the trustees under ss686–687. Income received by the trustees is subject under s686 to tax at the special 'rate applicable to trusts', currently 34 per cent. Income distributed to beneficiaries is grossed up at this rate and is regarded as having suffered tax at 34 per cent of the gross amount – ie a distribution of £66 to a discretionary beneficiary is treated as £100 income of the beneficiary with tax of £34 already paid. Equally, where trustees make a payment to any person in the exercise of a discretion exercisable by them or any other person, then if the sum paid is income of the recipient (but would not be his income apart from the payment) the payment is treated as being made net of tax at the rate applicable to trusts for the year in which payment is made. Tax at the rate applicable to trusts is assessable on the trustees; they can set-off against this any tax at the same rate which they have been charged in respect of income arising to the trustees.

A payment of capital will be subject to this rule if it is taxable as income in the hands of the beneficiary. Thus, if trustees are obliged to pay an annuity to a beneficiary but have insufficient income to pay the full amount and pay the shortfall out of capital, the whole of the annuity is still taxable as income in the hands of the beneficiary: *Brodie's Will Trustees* v *IRC* (1933) 17 TC 432. On the basis of *Cunard's Trustees* v *IRC* (1946) 27 TC 122 the Inland Revenue sought to charge beneficiaries to income tax on any recurring expenses made by trustees on behalf of beneficiaries if the purpose of expenditure was an income purpose (eg payment of school fees). However, following the case of *Stevenson* v *Wishart* [1987] STC 266 it is now necessary to have regard to the nature of the trust or power exercised; in that case the trustees expended capital in defraying nursing home expenses – this was held to be a capital receipt in the hands of the beneficiary. The advancement of capital to Fanny would appear to have no such disguised income element to it and would therefore not be subject to income tax.

As discussed above, the payment of income to the beneficiary of a discretionary trust gives rise to the treatment of the amount as having suffered tax at the rate applicable to trusts. Fanny's receipt of £5,000 income will therefore be grossed up at 34 per cent and she will therefore be treated as having taxable income of £5,000 x 100 ÷ (100 – 34) = £7,575 on which tax of £2,575 has been paid. Depending upon her personal rate of tax she will be able to recover the excess over basic rate, or will have to pay an additional 6 per cent x £7,575 if she is a higher rate taxpayer.

Chapter 4

Schedule A

4.1   **Introduction**

4.2   **Key points**

4.3   **Key cases and statute**

4.1 Introduction

Under the current (post 1995–96) rules, Schedule A taxes income from land and from furnished or unfurnished lettings in the UK. Foreign lettings are taxable under Schedule D Case V but are calculated as for UK Schedule A business income – see ss65(2A) and 65A ICTA 1988. The taxpayer cannot opt to have such income treated as a trading receipt: *Griffiths* v *Jackson and Pearman* [1983] STC 184. However, furnished holiday lettings falling within ss503–505 ICTA 1988 may be treated as earned income; this is advantageous in that roll-over relief and retirement relief for capital gains tax purposes may be granted in respect of such lettings. Income from these 'commercial lettings of furnished holiday accommodation' is taxed as a Schedule A business but is treated for all other income tax purposes as a Schedule D Case I trade: s503(1)(a) ICTA 1988.

Finance Act 1995 changes – the 'Schedule A business' – for income tax purposes

Fundamental changes to the Schedule A rules were introduced by FA 1995 with effect from 6 April 1995. These rules applied initially for income tax purposes only, until the corporation tax rules followed suit from 1 April 1998 (see below). By ss39–42 FA 1995 and Schedule 6, all income from property, including furnished lettings and premiums, is assessed as a 'Schedule A business' with rules for income and expenditure the same as for Schedule D business income. Deductions (including interest relief currently governed by ss353–358 ICTA 1988) need to satisfy only the 'wholly and exclusively' and other tests of s74 ICTA 1988 to be allowable and income tax will be paid on the profits as calculated for other business purposes – the accruals basis replacing the current rule of assessing income, ie rents, premiums, etc, to which one becomes entitled in the year of assessment. Interest relief, which previously was restricted under s354 to loans to purchase property, is due for all relevant business borrowing – such as maintenance and repairs.

Corporation tax

From 1 April 1998, s38 Finance Act 1998 introduces FA 1998 Sch 5 which incorporates the changes required to the previous rules in ICTA 1988. From 1 April 1998, the computation of property income of companies follows the 'Schedule A Business' rules. The effect of this is to apply the normal Schedule D Case I computation of profits principles both as regards income to be included and expenditure to be deducted from it.

4.2 Key points

Scope and basis of the charge under Schedule A

Section 15 ICTA 1988 charges tax on:

> 'The annual profits or gains arising from any business carried on for the exploitation, as a source of rents or other receipts, of any estate, interest or rights in or over land in the United Kingdom.'

For income tax purposes tax is charged – see s21(2) ICTA 1988 – on the full amount of the profits or gains arising in the year of assessment. Therefore one applies the normal accruals basis of apportioning rents etc to the accounting period to which they wholly or partly relate. For corporation tax, s12(1) applies the same basis of assessment.

a) Sections 21A and 21B ICTA 1988 require the profits of a Schedule A business to be calculated in accordance with the rules which apply for Schedule D Case I.

b) Section 65A ICTA 1988 provides for overseas property income to be assessed to income tax under Schedule D Case V, but the profits are to be calculated in accordance with Schedule A business rules.

c) Section 70A ICTA 1988 provides for overseas property income to be assessed to corporation tax under Schedule D Case V, but the profits are to be calculated in accordance with Schedule A business rules.

Non-receipt of rent

Relief for rent not received will follow the same test set out in s74(1)(j) ICTA 1988 for other trade bad debts.

Allowable deductions

As mentioned above, Schedule A treats the income as arising from a business under Schedule D Case I. Deductions from the rents, including interest, are therefore governed by the 'wholly and exclusively' principles which apply for Schedule D businesses: see s74 ICTA 1988 and Chapter 5.

The normal rules of s74 ICTA 1988 and decided case law apply for the purpose of the expenditure but an exception is made for companies' interest payments (see below).

Other Schedule D provisions (eg treatment of post-cessation receipts) continue to apply under the Schedule A business rules – s21A(2)–(4) ICTA 1988.

Corporation tax variations

Some rules are varied for corporation tax purposes, the principal one being the deductibility of interest payments, for which corporation tax has a special regime for all trade and non-trade purposes: see Chapter 15. The provisions of the Finance Act 1996, which deal with interest and other associated receipts from what are referred to in these provisions as 'loan relationships', will determine whether and when an interest payment on borrowings associated with property may be deducted. Similarly, the other special rules for companies' foreign exchange gains and losses under FA 1993 apply to property related foreign exchange gains and losses associated with foreign currency borrowings.

The treatment of Schedule A business losses also differs from income tax (see below).

Losses – income tax

The new rules remove some of the restrictions on the use of losses arising from the renting of property. Under the previous rules losses were segregated according to the type of lease under which the property was let and distinguished between those under which the landlord fulfilled the obligation to repair the property and those under which the tenant was obliged to carry out the repairs. The revised rules for treatment of Schedule A losses for income tax purposes are as follows:

a) Losses, are freely transferable between properties let on a commercial basis. An allowable loss cannot arise from properties not let on a commercial basis, eg at a nominal rent to a relative: s384(1).

b) Losses may be carried forward to be set off against the Schedule A business income of the next or (in the absence of income in the next year) against the next year and so on: s379A(1).

c) Losses may be set against the general income of the year of the loss or of the next year following: s379A(3).

d) Losses arising from letting of overseas property (referred to as an 'overseas property business' follow the same treatment for income tax purposes as losses from of UK property: s379B ICTA 1988.

e) Loss relief claims may also include capital allowances for furnished holiday lettings: s503(2)(a) ICTA 1988. Where allowable losses do arise they may be set off against general income of the year of the loss or against general income in the year preceding that in which the loss was made: s380(1).

f) Losses arising through expenditure and the maintenance or repair of agricultural land or buildings may be set against general income in the same manner as that explained above in relation to capital allowances: s379A(8).

Losses – corporation tax

Where Schedule A expenditure exceeds Schedule A income, losses may be dealt with for corporation tax purposes as follows:

a) Losses are only relieved to the extent that the business is carried on with a view to profit: s392A(5).

b) Schedule A business losses are set off against the company's total profits of the same accounting period: s392A(1).

c) To the extent to which the loss is not relieved in the same accounting period, it may be carried forward to the next period, providing the schedule A business continues to be carried on: s392A(2).

d) Losses of companies arising from the carrying on of an 'overseas property business' are more restricted in their use than similar losses for income tax purposes. For corporation tax purposes, s392B determines that such losses can be relieved only by carry forward against profits arising from the 'overseas property business'.

e) Unused losses which arose under the old Schedule D Case VI treatment may be carried forward and used against income arising under the new Schedule A business rules: see Sch 5 para 7 FA 1998 for corporation tax.

Premiums ss34–39 ICTA 1988

Section 34: Where a premium is paid for a lease of less than 50 years, a part of the premium will be treated as rent and so fall within the charge under Schedule A.

'Premium' includes any sum payable to either the immediate or superior landlord or any connected person: s24 ICTA 1988.

The amount of the premium which is treated as rent is calculated as follows:

Premium less [(n-1) x 2 per cent of premium]

where n = number of years of lease.

The longer the lease, the lower the amount of the premium that will be treated as rent. The remainder of the premium is capital.

For leases of over 50 years, the whole premium is treated as capital.

Anti-avoidance provisions

a) If the lease is unlikely to run its full term the shorter term is used in the calculation in the paragraph above.

b) If the lease is likely to exceed the term stated, the longer term is used: s38 ICTA 1988.

c) If the tenant is required by the lease to pay for capital improvements during the term, the landlord is treated as having received a premium equal to the difference between the value of his reversionary interest immediately after the start of the lease and that without such provision.

d) Receipts by the landlord in respect of commutation of rent, or variation or waiver of terms in the lease are treated as premiums in the year of receipt with certain discounting provisions: s34(1) ICTA 1988.

e) Section 35 ICTA 1988 prevents assignment of lease by the landlord to an associate at an undervalue (ie without any premium) and subsequent re-assignment by the associate to the tenant at full market value by taxing the associate in respect of the amount that the landlord could have charged.

Top slicing relief

This reduces the effective rate of tax payable on that portion of a premium which is to be treated as rent.

Note: for leases of under 50 years, capital gains tax is payable on that part of the premium which is not to be treated as rent: Sch 8 paras 5–7A TCGA 1992.

For leases of over 50 years, capital gains tax is payable on the whole amount.

Assessment and payments

Schedule A is assessed on a current year basis and is now payable under the income tax self-assessment scheme, on 31 January during the year of assessment with any balancing payment due on the following 31 January. Corporation tax payments follow the normal due date of nine months after the end of the accounting period: see Chapter 15.

Capital allowances

Section 211 FA 1994 changed the basis on which relief for capital allowances for income tax purposes, including Schedule A businesses is given, in most cases from 1997–98 onwards. Instead of being given as an allowance against the profit being taxed, capital allowances are now a trading expense to be deducted in calculating the actual amount of income or profit assessable.

Income from overseas property and overseas landlords

The changes to Schedule A, introduced in 1995–96, do not affect the method of assessing income from overseas property. This remains as a Schedule D Case V source of income but computation of the income now follows the Schedule A business rules: see ss65(2A) and 65A ICTA 1988. The same applies for corporation tax purposes from 1 April 1998: s70A ICTA 1988.

Where the property is owned by a non-resident, tax will be collected either by withholding it from the rent paid by the tenant or letting agent to the landlord, or by self assessment where the non-resident landlord has received approval from the Inland Revenue for the submission of self-assessment returns

Where there is an obligation to deduct tax from the rents, this arises under the Taxation of Income from Land (Non-Resident Landlords) Regulations 1995 (SI 1995/2902). The letting agent or, where there is no letting agent the tenant, is obliged to deduct tax from the payment of rent and make payment to the Inland Revenue. The amount to be paid over is tax at the basic rate of 23 per cent of the rent payable less a deduction for expenses, providing those expenses are deductible under the Schedule A rules.

4.3 Key cases and statute

- *CIR* v *John Lewis Properties plc* [2003] STC 117
  Assignment of rentals for five-year period – whether income with Schedule A

- *McClure* v *Petre* [1988] STC 749
  Fees for use of land

- *Tenbry Investments Ltd* v *Peugeot Talbot Motor Co Ltd* [1992] STC 791
  Non-recovery of tax not withheld from non-resident on future payment of rent

- Income and Corporation Taxes Act 1988, ss15 and 22

Chapter 5

Schedule D, Cases I and II: Profits of a Trade, Profession or Vocation

5.1   Introduction

5.2   Key points

5.3   Key cases and statute

5.4   Questions and suggested solutions

5.1 Introduction

Schedule D Cases I and II cover profits from a trade, profession or vocation. Thus the Schedule D taxpayer will be self employed. A company's trading profits are within Schedule D Case I but are assessable to corporation tax. The ordinary rules of Case I computation apply to companies.

The Finance Act 1994 contained provisions which by 1996–97 year of assessment changed the normal basis of assessment under Schedule D cases I and II from profits of the previous year to the current year's profits as well as introducing a system of self-assessment: see Chapter 23. However, new businesses commencing from 6 April 1994 became subject to the new current year basis from the start.

5.2 Key points

Scope of the charge: s18 ICTA 1988

Section 18 taxes the annual profits or gains from a trade carried on by a resident in the UK or elsewhere (Case I) and from a profession or vocation (Case II).

Differences between Cases I and II

Generally the same principles apply to both cases, but the following should be remembered:

a) A single transaction can be a trade (Case I) but cannot be a profession or vocation (Case II).

b) Certain capital allowances (industrial buildings allowances) are applicable to trades only.

c) The rule in *Sharkey* v *Wernher* applies only to trades.

Trade, profession and vocation

'Profession'

a) No statutory definition.

b) *IRC* v *Maxse* [1919] 1 KB 647: 'an occupation requiring either purely intellectual skill or manual skill controlled by the intellectual skill of the operator – eg solicitors, barristers, doctors, surgeons.'

'Vocation'

a) No statutory definition.

b) *Partridge* v *Mallandaine* (1886) 2 TC 179: 'analogous to a calling ... the way in which a person passes his life' – eg self-employed bookmakers, jockeys and authors.

c) *Wain* v *Cameron* [1995] STC 555 considered whether an author's drafts, working papers and manuscripts (but not including copyrights to any works) had been disposed of as part of the proceeds of Professor Wain's activities as an author. It was held that these were part of the fruits of these activities, irrespective of the fact that when he created them it was not contemplated or known that a source for selling them for profit would arise.

'Trade'

a) No statutory definition, although per s832(1) ICTA 1988 'it includes every trade, manufacture, adventure or concern in the nature of trade'.

The decision as to whether a trade is being carried on and whether a transaction is an 'adventure in the nature of a trade' is a question based on facts and one which itself becomes a question of fact to be decided by the Commissioners hearing the appeal, against whose decision there is no further avenue of appeal: see s56 TMA 1970. The only exception to this rule would be on the basis of the decision in *Edwards* v *Bairstow & Harrison* (see Chapter 23, section 23.2).

b) See *Ransom* v *Higgs* (1974) 50 TC 1: 'Trade normally involves the exchange of goods or services for reward ...': Lord Wilberforce.

c) The badges of trade: the Radcliffe Commission 1955

   i) The subject matter of the transaction: see *Martin* v *Lowry* [1927] AC 312; *Rutledge* v *IRC* (1929) 14 TC 490; and *Marson* v *Morton* [1986] STC 463.

   ii) Length of ownership: see *IRC* v *Rheinhold* (1953) 34 TC 389.

   iii) Frequency of similar transactions: see *Pickford* v *Quirke* (1927) 13 TC 251; *Leach* v *Pogson* (1962) 40 TC 585; and *Clarke* v *British Telecom Pension Scheme Trustees*

[1998] STC 1075, where the sub-underwriting of shares issues in return for commissions was held to be taxable.

iv) Supplementary work done on the property: see *Cape Brandy Syndicate* v *IRC* [1921] 2 KB 403 and *IRC* v *Livingston* (1927) 11 TC 538.

v) The reason for the sale: see *Simmons* v *IRC* [1980] STC 350.

vi) Motive: see *Wisdom* v *Chamberlain* (1968) 45 TC 92 and *Ensign Tankers (Leasing) Ltd* v *Stokes* [1992] STC 226; [1992] WLR 469, where a tax avoidance element in the structure was held not to invalidate the genuine trading activity.

Special cases

Mutual trading

a) *Ransom* v *Higgs*: Lord Wilberforce: 'trade presupposes a customer'. Hence the maxim 'no man may trade with himself'.

b) See also *Carlisle and Silloth Golf Club* v *Smith* (1913) 6 TC 198; *New York Life Insurance Co* v *Styles* (1889) 2 TC 460; and *Fletcher* v *IRC* [1972] AC 414.

Illegal trading

a) Illegality of the trade does not prevent the charge to tax under Schedule D, Case I.

b) See: *Martin* v *Nash* (1932) 16 TC 532 and *IRC* v *Aken* [1990] STC 497.

Farming and market gardening

Section 53 ICTA 1988 such activities will be treated as a trade.

Computation of profits falling within s19

a) 'Annual' means arising in any given year (not necessarily recurrent).

b) 'Profits or gains' are calculated as revenue receipts less revenue deductions.

'True and fair view' introduced as the standard basis of accounting for profits: s42 FA 1998.

Deductions must follow normal accounting principles – *Gallagher* v *Jones; Threlfall* v *Jones* [1993] STC 537 – and relate to the accounting period in question.

Courts have supported the taxpayer rather than the Inland Revenue where two or more 'acceptable accounting practices' exist.

Johnston v *Britannia Airways Ltd* [1994] STC 763: the decision supported the precept that sound accounting principles were best placed to determine how items of expenditure were to be provided for – in this case by way of current provision for future engine overhauls.

See also *Herbert Smith* v *Honour* [1999] STC 173.

c) The three historical bases of computation

    I) Earnings basis (used by most traders) – imposed as statutory for most businesses – s42 FA 1998 – for accounting periods beginning after (not on or after) 6 April 1999.

    ii) Cash basis (used by barristers) – under s43 FA 1998 barristers (and no other professionals) are allowed to retain the cash basis for the first seven years of their practice, at which point they must resort to the 'true and fair view' accounting basis.

    iii) Bills delivered (used by solicitors and accountants) – the s42 FA 1998 'true and fair view' provision applies equally to trades, professions and vocations and disapplies the cash basis (with limited exception) and bills delivered basis of computing profits.

    iv) The new provisions apply to accounting periods beginning after (not on or after) 6 April 1999.

d) 'Revenue receipts' are receipts of an income as opposed to those of a capital nature. What constitutes a revenue receipt will depend on the nature of the business. See also 'revenue or capital' expenses below.

    For case law focus on the 'tree or the fruit' distinction in deciding what gives rise to a capital or revenue receipt: see *Vallambrosa Rubber Co Ltd* v *Farmer* [1910] 5 TC 529. The tree is the enduring element of the asset (capital) and the fruit is the recurring (revenue) product from it.

e) Special cases

    i) Payments for restriction of activities: see *Higgs* v *Olivier* (1952) 33 TC 143 and *IRC* v *Biggar* [1982] STC 677.

    ii) Compensation for sterilisation of assets: see *Glenboig Union Fireclay Co Ltd* v *IRC* (1921) 12 TC 427; *Burmah Steamship Co Ltd* v *IRC* (1931) 16 TC 67; and *Lang* v *Rice* [1984] STC 172.

    iii) Compensation for cancelling business contracts: see *Van Den Berghs* v *Clark* [1935] AC 431; *Kelsall Parsons & Co* v *IRC* (1938) 21 TC 608; and *Rolfe* v *Nagel* [1982] STC 53.

    iv) Compensation for loss of income

    See *Deeny & Ors* v *Gooda Walker Ltd (In Voluntary Liquidation) & Ors* [1996] STC 299, where the plaintiffs were awarded damages against the managing and members agents of various Lloyd's underwriting syndicates (Gooda Walker Ltd and Others). This case did not directly concern the Inland Revenue, since it did not involve the collection of tax comprised in assessments made by them on a taxpayer, but they consented to be joined as a third party to the case, in view of the importance of the tax matters at issue between the Names and their agents. The issue was whether, in determining the amount of damages to be ordered to be paid to the Names, a reduction should be made to reflect what the agents claimed was a tax-exempt sum for the Names and that Lord Hoffmann, approving the dicta of Diplock LJ in *London and Thames Haven Oil Wharves Ltd* v *Attwooll* (1966) 43 TC 491 at 495, confirmed that the receipt of a sum by a trader as compensation for the failure to receive what would have been a revenue receipt of his trade was sufficient to demonstrate that the compensation was itself a receipt of the business. The source of the award was therefore the business conducted by the Names. See s184(1) FA 1993 for the definition of 'underwriting business'.

Valuation of trading stock

Trading stock

a) At the end of an accounting period unsold trading stock must be brought in as a receipt.

b) At the start of the next accounting period, the same stock must be brought in as an expense.

c) *IRC* v *Cock Russell & Co Ltd* (1949) 29 TC 387: the values used therein may be cost or market value, whichever is the most advantageous to the trader, provided the same value is chosen for each of the two accounting periods.

Work in progress

The move to a compulsory 'true and fair view' accounting method for the calculation of Schedule D Case I and II profits will have the effect of making the inclusion of work in progress obligatory in annual accounts: s42 FA 1998.

a) The same accounting procedure as for trading stock must be used at the year end and commencement of the next year.

b) There are two methods of valuation:

    i) direct cost method eg labour costs;

    ii) on-cost method, eg indirect overheads such as heat and light plus direct costs.

c) See *Duple Motor Bodies* v *Ostime* (1961) 39 TC 537.

d) The Revenue prefer the on-cost method.

Valuation on a discontinuance

See ss100–102 ICTA 1988.

The rule in Sharkey v Wernher

a) Where an item of trading stock is disposed of otherwise than in the ordinary course of business, the taxpayer must account for it as trading receipt at market value at the date of disposal.

b) The rule applies where a trader makes gifts or sales at an undervalue or takes trading stock for his own personal use.

c) See also *Mason v Innes* (1967) 44 TC 326 (the rule applies to trades only); *Petrotim Securities Ltd v Ayres* (1963) 41 TC 389; and *Jacgilden v Castle* (1969) 45 TC 685.

Section 770 ICTA 1988

Prevents *Sharkey* v *Wernher* style transactions between multi-national corporations.

Trading expenses

Trading expenditure is only deductible if:

a) it is of a revenue and not a capital nature (s74(1)(f));

b) it is not prohibited by s74 or s577 ICTA 1988.

Revenue and capital expenses

See *Vallambrosa Rubber Co Ltd v Farmer* (1910) 5 TC 529; *British Insulated & Helsby Cables Ltd v Atherton* (1926) 10 TC 155; *Tucker v Granada Motorway Services Ltd* [1979] STC 393; and *Lawson v Johnson Matthey plc* [1991] STC 259.

In *Vodafone Cellular Ltd v Shaw* [1997] STC 734 the Court of Appeal held (reversing the decision of the High Court) that expenditure to discharge an onerous trading agreement (which following the decision in *Van den Berghs Ltd v Clark* [1935] AC 431; 19 TC 390 was a revenue payment and receipt) was nevertheless for the benefit of the trade of the company meeting the payment (the payment having been paid for another company in the group) and therefore was held to be deductible under ICTA 1988 s74 'for the purposes of the trade'.

Capital expenses may nevertheless fall within the capital allowances system: see Chapter 6

Section 74 ICTA 1988

a) Section 74(1)(a): Revenue expenses must be wholly and exclusively for the purpose of the trade.

See *Bowden v Russell & Russell* (1965) 42 TC 301; *Mallalieu v Drummond* [1983] STC 665; *Watkis v Ashford, Sparkes & Harward* [1985] STC 451; *MacKinlay v Arthur Young McClelland Moores* [1990] STC 898; *Stone & Temple Ltd v Waters* [1995] STC 1 (payment to protect investment was held to be on capital account); and *Vodafone Cellular Ltd* v *Shaw* [1997] STC 734 ('the trade' in 'the purposes of the trade' means the trade of the company meeting and claiming the expense, but the purpose of the payment should not be confused with its effects. A benefit for (or effect on) a group of companies does not diminish the 'wholly and exclusively' nature of the payment).

b) Personal expenditure: s74(1)(b): see *MacKinlay* v *Arthur Young McClelland Moores & Co* [1990] STC 898 (disallowance of partner's removal expenses).

c) Travelling expenses: see *Newsom* v *Robertson* (1952) 33 TC 452 and *Horton* v *Young* (1971) 47 TC 60.

d) Rent: see s74(1)(c).

e) Improvements and repairs: s74(1)(d). See *Law Shipping Co Ltd* v *IRC* (1924) 12 TC 621 and *Odeon Associated Theatres* v *Jones* (1971) 48 TC 257.

f) Damages: see *Strong* v *Woodifield* (1906) 5 TC 215 and *Knight* v *Parry* [1973] STC 56.

g) Compensation payments: see *Mitchell* v *Nobles* (1927) 11 TC 372; *O'Keefe* v *Southport Printers Ltd* [1984] STC 443; and *Whitehead* v *Tubbs* [1984] STC 1.

h) Bad debts: s74(1)(j)

When using the earnings or 'true and fair view' basis, bad debts are only deductible when shown to be bad and if later paid off must be treated as a revenue receipt in the year of payment.

i) Interest – for income tax, interest other than annual interest is allowed as a deduction in computing the profits of the business, subject to s74 ICTA 1988. Annual interest (ie interest on a debt which is capable of lasting for more than 12 months) is allowed as a charge against income – s353 – providing it is of the kind which falls within ss354 et seq. Interest on a business overdraft is not treated as annual interest: s353(3)(a).

j) Interest: s74(1)(n)

Interest paid to a non-UK resident on a business loan is a deductible expense only if paid at a reasonable commercial rate.

k) Interest: s353(3)

The 'commercial rate' restriction also applies to interest allowed as a charge on income, irrespective of the residence of the recipient.

l) Companies' interest payments

For companies all interest deductions are now governed by the 'loan relationships' (also referred to as the 'corporate debt' provisions introduced by ss80–102 and Schs 8–15 FA 1996 – see s337A ICTA 1988 and Chapter 15).

Section 577 ICTA 1988

Entertainment expenses are generally not deductible unless they are:

a) for the entertainment of bona fide members of staff;

b) small gifts carrying conspicuous advertisements.

The basis of assessment

General: s60 ICTA 1988

a) The normal basis of assessment from 1996–97 onwards is the current year's profits: s60 ICTA 1988. Thus, tax in a given year of assessment is paid on the profits and gains of the accounting period ending in that year of assessment.

b) Special rules apply to the opening and closing years of a trade.

Opening years: ss60–61 ICTA 1988

s61(1)	Year 1:	tax is paid on actual profits from the date of commencement to the following 5 April: eg profit of first months xx, where

$$x = \frac{\text{number of months}}{12} \text{ from}$$

commencement to next 5 April

If the business happens to have commenced on 6 April, then the profits of the first year's accounts to 5 April will be assessed.

s61(2)	Year 2:	tax is paid on the profits of the first 12 months. Where the accounts ending in the second year of assessment are not for a 12 month period which began at the commencement of the business, then the profits are normally apportioned so that the second year's assessment does represent profits of the first 12 months.

Overlap relief

The profits which are assessed twice in these opening years are what is now called 'overlap' and 'overlap relief' is given either when assessing the closing years when a business ceases or when there is a change of accounting date: s63A ICTA 1988.

Closing year: s63 ICTA 1988

Section 63(a): if discontinued in year 2, profits from the previous 6 April to date of cessation are assessed.

Section 63(b): if discontinued in any other year, profits of the period from the end of the previous year's basis period are assessed. (See example below.)

Example under the current year basis

Assume the results of a business ceasing to trade on 31 October 2004 with profits for years ending 5 July 2002 to 2004 £21,000, £15,000 and 30,000 respectively and to 31 October £4,800.

The assessments would be:

> *Final year (2003–2004)*
> (Basis period 6 July 2003 to 31 Oct 2004)
> Year to 5 July 2004   £30,000
> 6 July to 31 Oct 2004   £4,800
> Total Assessment: 34,800   (less any overlap relief
>   brought forward)
>
> *Penultimate year (2002–2003)*
> Year to 5 July 2003   £15,000
>
> *Ante-penultimate year (2001–2002)*
> Year to 5 July 2002   £21,000

Section 113 ICTA 1988

Any change in ownership of the trade is generally deemed a discontinuance and commencement of the trade.

Note: if one of a chain of supermarkets is sold by the owner, that will not be a discontinuance since the trader is still running supermarkets. It is merely a contraction of the trade.

Edmunds v Coleman [1997] STC 1406 involved a change of a freelance part-time business to full-time and whether a new business had commenced. The court held that the mere increase in intensity of the activities was not sufficient to determine that a business had been discontinued and a new business had commenced.

Losses

a) Losses arise if allowable trading expenditure exceeds trading receipts, and in the year of assessment following a loss-making accounting year no charge to tax will arise.

b) Provisions exist to offset losses against other profits.

  i) Section 380 ICTA 1988

   Provided that the losses were incurred from a trade carried on on a commercial basis, they may be set off against the taxpayer's income in that year under other schedules; see *Butt v Haxby* [1983] STC 239.

Section 72 FA 1991 extends s380 to a trader's capital gains. If a trader has surplus trading losses which cannot be set off against his other income under s380, then the trader may elect to have the trading loss treated as a loss for CGT purposes, but only to the extent that the trader has capital gains for the year. Thus trading losses may not be turned into capital losses to be rolled forward. Surplus trading losses may however be rolled forward in the usual way.

ii) Section 385 ICTA 1988

Provided that the trade is continued, any losses unrelieved under s380 may be carried forward and offset against future profits of the same trade. The 'same' trade is important: see *Rolls Royce Motors Ltd v Bamford* [1976] STC 162.

iii) Section 388 ICTA 1988

If the trade is discontinued, unrelieved losses may be set off against any profits of the three years preceding the final year of assessment. (Profits of the most recent year will be used first.)

iv) Section 386 ICTA 1988

If the trade is incorporated, unrelieved losses may be set off against income from the taxpayer's shares in the new company.

Post cessation receipts: ss103–104 ICTA 1988

Post cessation receipts will be charged to tax under Schedule D Case VI, since the source of income under Schedule D Cases I or II will no longer exist.

5.3 Key cases and statute

- *Mallalieu v Drummond* [1983] STC 665
  Deduction of business expenditure with ancillary personal advantage

- *Ransom v Higgs* (1974) 50 TC 1
  Badges of trade

- *Sharkey v Wernher* [1956] AC 58
  Disposing of stock in trade otherwise than in the course of trade

- Income and Corporation Taxes Act 1988, ss18, 74, 103–104, 380–388 and 770A

5.4 Questions and suggested solutions

QUESTION ONE

D runs and owns a restaurant. Advise him of the likely income tax consequences of the following facts which have arisen in 1999–2000.

a) D paid his landlord £5,000 to amend the terms of the lease between L and D so that the annual rent payable by D in respect of the restaurant premises would decrease by £1,250 per anum.

b) D took stock to a value of £250 from the restaurant in order to prepare a party for his daughter, E.

c) D received £10,000 by way of compensation from Coal Co plc, a coal mining company, whose mining operations beneath the car park adjacent to the restaurant have rendered the car park unusable by D's customers for three years.

d) D spends £1,500 on travel between his home and the restaurant and between his suppliers and the restaurant.

University of London LLB Examination
(for External Students) Revenue Law June 2000 Q4

General Comment

This question illustrates when and how expenses are deducted under s74 ICTA 1988.

Skeleton Solution

Deductible expenditure: s74 ICTA – capital/income distinction: *Tucker* v *Granada* – identification of trading receipts: *Sharkey* v *Wernher* – travelling expenses.

Suggested Solution

Note: all references are to the Income and Corporation Taxes Act (ICTA) 1988 unless stated otherwise.

D is self-employed and is therefore assessable under Schedule D on his net profits. He is allowed to deduct deductible expenditure in computing his net profits. The rules for deducting allowable expenditure are provided in s74. There are five basic requirements for an expense to be deductible:

a) that it be incurred for a business purpose;

b) that it be incurred only for a business purpose;

c) that it be incurred for the purpose of earning a profit;

d) that it be a revenue or recurrent expense, and not a capital one;

e) that it be not expressly disallowed by s74 or any other section.

The basis of assessment for Schedule D Case I and II is the new, modified current year basis (s60) and a trader will normally be obliged to render his or her accounts on an earnings basis (rather than on a cash basis or a bills delivered basis).

a) Expenditure, to be deductible, must be revenue expenditure, not capital expenditure. In *Tucker* v *Granada Motorway Services Ltd* [1979] STC 393 the House of Lords held that the nature of the payment was not be judged by the subjective test of the intentions of those who actually made the payment, but by the nature and effect of the payment made and the benefits the payer received in turn. The £5,000 payment made by D was a single payment and had the effect of lowering his annual rent payable. Therefore, it is more likely that the payment would be viewed as a capital rather than a revenue expenditure, and not be deductible.

b) The rule in *Sharkey* v *Wernher* [1956] AC 58 provides that where a trader disposes of part of his stock in trade otherwise than in the course of his trade, in particular for his own use, enjoyment or recreation, he must bring the market value of the stock so utilised as a trading receipt. The only way of avoiding the application of *Sharkey* is to be able to justify the apparently non-commercial use of the trading stock on some actual commercial ground. There does not appear to be such justification here as D took the stock in order to prepare for a family party. Therefore, D will have to bring in the full £250 as a trading receipt and, having already deducted the cost of the stock through his purchases and other business expenses, he will have to pay tax on the theoretical profit element as required by the *Sharkey* v *Wernher* principle.

c) The treatment of the £10,000 compensation payment will depend on whether it is viewed as a capital receipt or income receipt. In *Glenboig Union Fireclay Co Ltd* v *IRC* (1921) 12 TC 427 the House of Lords held that compensation received when the taxpayer's fields could not longer be used was a capital receipt on the ground that the compensation was for the 'sterilisation and destruction' of its capital asset. Compensation for the loss of profits which would otherwise have been made is itself to be treated as a trading receipt, as established in *Lang* v *Rice* [1984] STC 172. Here the £10,000 compensation payment is likely to fall outside the ambit of *Glenboig* because the interference with D's business was temporary and therefore did not amount to a sterilisation or destruction of D's capital asset. It is likely that the payment will be viewed as an income rather than a capital receipt.

d) The cost of travelling on business is a deductible expense under s74. A distinction is drawn, however, between travelling to work which is not deductible (*Newsom* v *Robertson* (1952) 33 TC 452) and travelling in the course of one's work which is. Travelling from one place of business to another is also generally deductible: *Sargent* v *Barnes* [1978] STC 322. Therefore, the costs of D's travel between the suppliers and the restaurant are probably deductible; the remaining expenses are probably not.

QUESTION TWO

Compare and contrast the expenses deductible for income tax purposes under Schedule D Case I and II with Schedule E.

University of London LLB Examination
(for External Students) Revenue Law June 1996 Q3

General Comment

This question explores the different treatment accorded by Schedule D Case I and II and Schedule E to deductible expenses.

Skeleton Solution

Schedule D rules: s74; operates by excluding expenditure from deduction – s74 has two limb approach: 'wholly and exclusively' and 'for the purpose of the business' – Schedule E rules: s198; three limb approach; 'wholly and exclusively', 'necessarily' and 'in the performance of the duties of the employment' – dual purpose expenditure: *Bowden* v *Russell & Russell*; *Mallalieu* v *Drummond* – travelling between locations: *Ricketts* v *Colquhoun* – relevant to the employment but not 'in the performance of the duties' – *Humbles* v *Brookes*: teacher attending lectures to improve knowledge of the subject which he taught – *Smith* v *Abbott* and *Fitzpatrick* v *IRC*: journalists purchasing periodicals and newspapers in order to be better prepared for their work as employees – both disallowed.

Suggested Solution

Note: all references are to the Income and Corporation Taxes Act (ICTA) 1988 unless stated otherwise.

Schedule D expenditure

The principle rules governing the deduction of expenses for the purposes of Schedule D Cases I and II are set out in s74. The general rule is set out in s74(1)(a) which provides, although in the form of negative wording, for the deduction of expenditure laid out 'wholly and exclusively ... for the purposes of the trade, profession or vocation'. There is, therefore, a dual requirement that the expenditure be both for the purpose of the trade and, if that is so, then the expenditure must be laid out wholly and exclusively for that purpose. Having set out these primary requirements, the remainder of s74(1) proceeds to exclude various items of expenditure, notably those laid out for the personal upkeep of the trader or his family and the expenditure of a capital nature. It follows that only expenditure of a revenue nature may be deducted, and the exclusion of personal expenditure is to some extent superfluous since the general requirement of being for the purposes of the trade, as well as being wholly and exclusively for that purpose, would seem to eliminate the possibility of deducting expenditure laid out for personal upkeep.

Schedule E expenses

The rules for deduction of expenses for Schedule E purposes are governed by s198. In general the rules follow the same two-limb approach of s74 for Schedule D purposes in that there is a requirement that the expenditure has to be laid out 'in the performance of the duties of the employment', and at the same time the expense also has to be laid out not only 'wholly and exclusively' for that purpose, but with an additional requirement over the Schedule D rules that the expenditure also has to be 'necessarily incurred' before it can be deducted. This additional requirement is the primary difference between the rules for the deduction of expenses under Schedule D purposes and those deductible under Schedule E.

Wholly and exclusively

In determining whether the expenditure meets the two requirements, a distinction can be drawn in that 'wholly' refers merely to the quantum of the expenditure, whereas 'exclusively' refers more to the motive behind the expense. By way of illustration, if expenditure were incurred in the provision of petrol in a car, half of which is used for business purposes and the remainder for private purposes, one half may be deducted in the profit and loss account as the whole of that amount was incurred and used exclusively for business purposes.

By way of contrast however, for expenditure where the conduct of business is mixed with a holiday the full amount of the expenditure would be disallowed for tax purposes since none of it could be related wholly or exclusively for the purposes of the business: *Bowden* v *Russell & Russell* (1965) 42 TC 301.

In the case of *Mallalieu* v *Drummond* [1983] STC 665 where expenditure was incurred by a female barrister on clothes for wear in court in compliance with guidelines laid down by the Bar Council, the claim was rejected by the House of Lords on the grounds that, when purchasing clothes, the motive must involve a combination of both business and personal requirement.

The contrast between the two sets of rules under Schedule D and Schedule E can be seen in *Ricketts* v *Colquhoun* [1926] AC 1 where a barrister with a secondary Schedule E post was denied the cost of travelling between chambers and the other location. This illustrates the more stringent requirement, which the House of Lords confirmed in this case, that each and every occupant of the particular office or employment would necessarily be obliged to incur the expense before it is allowed.

A further illustration is in respect of expenses incurred in order to perform the job better, as in *Humbles* v *Brookes* (1962) 40 TC 500, where a teacher attending lectures to improve knowledge of the subject which he taught was disallowed. Similarly, in the cases of journalists purchasing periodicals and newspapers in order to be better prepared for their work as employees (*Smith* v *Abbott* and *Fitzpatrick* v *IRC* [1994] STC 237), the expense was disallowed by the House of Lords. By contrast, the purchase of technical periodicals for the purpose of Schedule D would be an allowable expense.

This highlights the difference between the 'for the purposes of the trade', and 'in the performance of the duties of the employment'. Other expenses such as travelling and expenditure of a voluntary nature (for example, a trader choosing to support a local activity which may benefit his trade), may pass the Schedule D s74 test but fail the Schedule E test of s198, particularly in relation to it not being incurred while carrying out the actual duties of the employment.

QUESTION THREE

Andrew and Barbara are neighbours. Andrew is employed by Papers plc as a journalist at an annual salary of £50,000. Barbara is a self employed freelance journalist whose profits average £25,000 per annum.

Andrew is provided with the use of a 2,000 cc car. He uses the car to drive to work, for business purposes and for private purposes. Papers plc permit Andrew to have the car serviced at a garage near Papers' office and Papers pays the bill for the servicing. Andrew regularly purchases newspapers and magazines in connection with his work. He reads them at home in the evenings and weekends. In 1993–94 these cost him £500 which was re-imbursed to him by Papers. During the year Andrew attended a prestigious conference for journalists. The conference fee was £200 and his living expenses during the conference were £300. He paid these himself.

Barbara works from her office at home. She uses her own car for business purposes and spends money on petrol, road tax, insurance and servicing. She attended the same conference as Andrew and she also purchased newspapers and magazines which cost her £400.

Both Andrew and Barbara leave their young children with the same childminder. They each pay her £1,000. Advise on the income tax consequences of the above facts.

University of London LLB Examination
(for External Students) Revenue Law June 1994 Q2

General Comment

This question illustrates the principles of taxing emoluments and employee benefits.

Skeleton Solution

Andrew

Schedule E taxable emoluments: ss19(1) and 131 ICTA 1988 and cash-convertible payments; *Tennant* v *Smith* – employees earning over £8,500 pa: additional emoluments and benefits; ss153 et seq – expenses reimbursed: additional emoluments under s153(1); not if under £8,500 pa; *Pook* v *Owen* – use of car: cash equivalent benefit under s157 and Schedule 6 for private use element and s155(1) re repairs – deductible expenses: s198 and *Smith* v *Abbott*; *Fitzpatrick* v *IRC*; newspaper and conference expenses subject to 'necessity' and other tests of s198 – child-minding: not an expense in the performance of the duties of employment.

Barbara

Schedule D deductions: governed by s74 – use of home as office: s74(1)(c) – car expenses: s74(1)(a) – newspaper expenditure: less restrictive than Schedule E equivalent – conference expenses: business deduction – child-minding: domestic expense; fails s74(1)(b) test.

Suggested Solution

Note: all references are to the Income and Corporation Taxes Act (ICTA) 1988 unless stated otherwise.

Andrew

Employees are subject, under s19(1), to tax under Schedule E on the 'emoluments' arising from the employment. Section 131 provides that emoluments includes not only salaries but all perquisites and profits whatsoever. This brings into account all benefits arising from the employment. Benefits which are convertible into cash are also emoluments for all employees according to the decision in *Tennant* v *Smith* [1892] AC 150 where a bank manager escaped tax on a benefit which offered no cash opportunity to him. Benefits without an opportunity to convert into cash are specially legislated for in s154(1) et seq by setting out their 'cash equivalent' and apply only to employees earning more than £8,500 per annum. In addition, for these employees, emoluments include the reimbursement of expenses – s153(1) – whereas for those below that earnings threshold such reimbursement is not an emolument: *Pook* v *Owen* (1971) 45 TC 571, as held by the House of Lords.

Andrew's emoluments will include, therefore, the benefit of the use of the company car for private purposes, which brings a benefit chargeable as laid down in s157. The amount chargeable to tax is the cash equivalent laid down in Schedule 6, according on the type of car. The costs of repair do not provide an additional benefit since s155(1) deems the cash equivalent benefit to include all costs connected with the provision of the car, except that provision of a driver will be charged additionally.

If Andrew were using his own car and the firm met the garage bill direct the employer would then be assuming a liability incurred by the employee and this would be an additional emolument under *Nicoll* v *Austin* (1935) 19 TC 531.

The reimbursement of expenses is an emolument of the employment of anyone earning over £8,500 per annum (s153(1)), but s198 permits the deduction of expenses wholly, exclusively and necessarily incurred in the performance of the duties of the employment. The reading of newspapers might be considered to satisfy these tests but in *Smith* v *Abbott* and *Fitzpatrick* v *IRC* [1994] STC 237 the House of Lords ruled that various journalists had not incurred such expenditure necessarily nor in the performance of the duties of the employment and therefore disallowed any deduction under s198, whereas the lower courts had favoured the taxpayers' claim that the duties of the employment dictated that the expense be incurred. The cases re-emphasised that expense to put an employee in a position to carry out the duties will not qualify; the expense must be one incurred in the performance and not for the purpose of the duties of the employment. For this reason Andrew will not be able to claim the expense of attending a journalists' conference whereas if such cost were met directly by his employer he would not be taxed on it. It is generally viewed that if an expense is necessary, the employer will meet the expense.

Barbara

Although Andrew and his neighbour Barbara are both in the same profession Barbara is not an employee and will be assessable under Schedule D on her profits. The test for the deductibility of expenses in calculating her profits is that all business expenses are deductible except those which are denied by s74. The fundamental difference between these provisions and those of s198, which will apply to Andrew, is that he must satisfy three criteria for the expense to be allowed, whereas Barbara will need to satisfy only two. Schedule D taxpayers may deduct all expenses 'wholly and exclusively' incurred for the purposes of the business whereas employees' expenditure must also be 'necessarily' incurred for it to qualify. Based on this, Barbara will be able to deduct the cost of attending the same conference as Andrew since her criteria under s74 is that the expense is (a) for the purpose of the business, (b) it is wholly for that purpose, and (c) it is exclusively for that purpose. By the same reasoning she will succeed in her claim to deduct the costs of newspapers purchased for the purpose of her profession, since she is not subject to the *Smith* v *Abbott* decision.

Barbara's claim for a deduction of maintaining an office at home will satisfy s74(1)(c) and be deductible and the costs of running her car will qualify under s74(1)(a) to the extent of the proportion incurred on business mileage. The ownership of a car for both business and private purposes might be thought to infringe the 'wholly and exclusively' test of s74. However it would be impractical to have a separate vehicle for each type of journey and it can be argued that a journey wholly for business purposes is incurring separate expense mile by mile on both capital and running costs.

The cost of child-minding incurred by both Andrew and Barbara will not succeed since, in his case, the expense is not incurred in performing the duties of the employment but to put him in a position to perform the duties. If Andrew's employer were to provide such facilities in premises at work which satisfy s155A then he would not be taxed on the cost of providing that benefit. For Barbara, the allowance is ruled out by s74(1)(b) on the ground that no domestic expense may be deducted.

QUESTION FOUR

'Try as you will, the word trade is one of those common English words which do not lend themselves readily to definition but that all of us think that we understand well enough. We can recognise a trade when we see it, and also an adventure in the nature of trade. But we are hard pressed to define it.' Per Lord Denning in *Griffiths v Harrison*.

In light of the above quotation consider, with examples to illustrate your answer, the factors which the courts take into account in recognising a trade.

University of London LLB Examination
(for External Students) Revenue Law June 1996 Q1

General Comment

This question explores the meaning of the word 'trade', focusing particularly on the concept of 'badges of trade'.

Skeleton Solution

'Trade' not defined by ICTA: extended meaning under s832 – includes 'trade, manufacture, adventure or concern in the nature of trade' – single or repetetive actions not conclusive – courts have ruled not on meaning of trade, but whether a particular set of facts amount to trade – question of trading is a determination of fact, within the ambit of the Commissioners – courts can only disturb the Commissioners' findings on the basis of unreasonable and unsustainable decision: *Edwards* v *Bairstow and Harrison* – concept of 'badges of trade' was first referred to in the 1955 Report of the Royal Commission on income tax: subject matter, period of ownership, frequency, supplementary work on assets, circumstances of sale and motive.

Suggested Solution

Note: all references are to the Income and Corporation Taxes Act (ICTA) 1988 unless stated otherwise.

The concept of 'trade' is not defined in the Income Tax Acts, which leaves the determination of its meaning to be interpreted by the courts. The matter is further complicated by the fact that s832(1) provides that when interpreting the term 'trade', it also includes any 'trade, manufacture, adventure or concern in the nature of trade'. Therefore, in determining whether the profit or gain arising from specific transactions falls to be taxed under Schedule D Case I, both limbs of this term need to be considered. It is possible that where a trade as such is not being carried on – in the ordinary meaning of the word – that what has transpired is a transaction in the form of an adventure, etc, in the nature of a trade. While in some cases before the courts, the concept of a repetition of dealings has denoted a trade, the absence of such repetition has not prevented single transactions from being treated as within Schedule D Case I, on the grounds of being regarded as falling within the second limb of the s832 provision.

Since differing trades are certain to have a variety of forms of organisation and modus operandi, no single set of rules would settle the problem of defining what is a trade for the purposes of taxing the profits arising from a transaction or series of transactions.

The courts therefore have of necessity considered a number of circumstances found within the facts of successive cases, and have laid down guidelines or 'badges of trade', to which regard might be paid either to any one or any combination of the badges of trade, in order to determine the nature of a transaction. In the end, the approach taken has been not to define 'what is a trade?', but rather to determine whether a particular deal amounts to a trading transaction or an adventure, etc, in the nature of a trade. In the final analysis, this leads to no point of law upon which reliance can be placed, and the question of whether or not the trade exists becomes a matter of determining a point of fact, against which of course there is no appeal from the Commissioner's decision unless such a decision had been arrived at unreasonably, adopting the principle in *Edwards* v *Bairstow and Harrison* [1956] AC 14.

The collective term 'badges of trade', was first referred to in the 1955 Report of the Royal Commission on income tax, which inter alia examined the various decisions of the courts in this area. The report of the Commission, and the six badges of trade referred to in it, have been widely quoted and relied upon by the courts in determining whether judgments of the Commissioners as to the carrying on of a trade, etc, could be substantiated.

In the early cases before the courts, the issue was that if the profit or gain was not from a trading transaction, it was by default a capital receipt, and therefore at that time free of tax, because capital gains tax was not introduced until 1965. The courts were then concerned with distinguishing between capital employed in the business being committed to trading stock and the business realising the employed capital through the disposal of the stock, as opposed to capital not committed to stock and realised in other forms or transactions.

Badges of trade

The six established badges of trade which the courts might consider are:

a) The subject matter of the realisation.

b) The length of the period of ownership.

c) The frequency or number of similar transactions by the same person.

d) Supplementary work on or in connection with the property realised.

e) The circumstances that were responsible for the realisation.

f) Motive.

In the early case of *Leeming* v *Jones* (1930) 15 TC 333 Lord Buckmaster took the often-quoted view that 'accretion to capital' does not become income merely because the original capital was invested in the hope and expectation that it would rise in value.

In *Rutledge* v *IRC* (1929) 14 TC 490 it was held that a trading transaction had taken place since the vast quantity of paper purchased could not have been purchased for any other reason than for the making of a profit. It could not, for example, be held in order to produce an income nor as an asset providing personal enjoyment.

In *IRC v Reinhold* (1953) 34 TC 389 it was held that the intention to sell an asset some day at a profit, and in the meantime to hold it as an income-producing investment, was not sufficient to stamp the eventual sale as a trading transaction.

In *Pickford v Quirke* (1927) 13 TC 251 the taxpayer carried out four separate asset-stripping operations, by buying shares, liquidating the company and selling its assets to a new company. On each occasion he did so in combination with a different set of partners. He alone was held to be trading simply because of the repetition of the exercise, whereas his partners were held not to have been trading.

In an early case, *Cape Brandy Syndicate v IRC* [1921] 2 KB 403, the blending of brandy and subsequent recasking led the court to decide that the transaction was a trading one, due to the amount of work performed on the brandy before its resale. This was sufficient to elevate an otherwise isolated capital transaction into an adventure in the nature of a trade. Similarly, in *IRC v Livingston* (1927) 11 TC 538 carrying out work and adapting an asset into a different asset, where three tradesmen joined forces to purchase and convert a cargo vessel into a steam drifter which they then sold, was held to be trading in view of the supplementary work carried out on the vessel.

There may be occasions where a taxpayer can prove that he was an unwilling seller and therefore his reason for selling was not to realise a profit or carry on a trading transaction. In *Simmons v IRC* [1980] STC 350 the taxpayer bought properties for investment purposes with the intention of floating a public investment company. He subsequently found the market going against him, had to sell up and did so at a profit. The House of Lords decided that he was not trading and that a permanent investment may be sold in order to acquire another investment without giving rise to an operation of trade.

The Royal Commission noted that motive is never irrelevant in determining the outcome in cases of trading but may be inferred from surrounding circumstances where direct evidence of the seller's intentions cannot be confirmed. In *Overseas Containers (Finance) Limited v Stoker* [1989] STC 364 Sir Nicolas Browne-Wilkinson stressed that a trading transaction must have a commercial purpose and in *Ensign Tankers (Leasing) Limited v Stokes* [1992] 2 WLR 469 it was pointed out that the purpose of a transaction must not be confused with the motive of the taxpayer entering into it. In addition, in the *Ensign Tankers* case, Sir Nicolas Browne-Wilkinson pointed out that the established six badges of trade should not be regarded as restrictive, and proceeded to list a series of 11 points which the courts might wish to consider in appropriate circumstances.

It is clear, therefore, that Lord Denning's comment in *Griffiths v Harrison* [1963] AC 1, posed for discussion in this question, remains as true today as it was when first stated.

QUESTION FIVE

Richard has for many years run a restaurant in London of which he is the sole proprietor. He employs Steven as a waiter at a salary of £8,000 pa and Steven is provided with free meals in the restaurant. The cost of these to Richard is £300 but they would have cost a customer £900. Richard often eats his own meals in the restaurant and does not pay for them.

In January Richard decided to offer a special meal at a reduced price to customers. This special offer meant that Richard did not cover his expenses on the meals which he served.

One of Richard's customers hired the whole restaurant one evening for a birthday party. It was a most successful evening and a few days after the bill had been paid Richard received a watch from the customer with a note thanking Richard for his excellent personal service at the party.

During the year Richard replaced one of his refrigerators in the kitchen and also purchased an extra one as the restaurant was very busy.

Richard's son was awarded a PhD during the year and Richard was so excited that he took a crate of champagne from his stock and gave it to his son so that he could have a party to celebrate. The champagne had been purchased as part of Richard's stock in trade in 1989 for £10 per bottle. The current price in the restaurant would be £20 per bottle although the retail price would be £15 per bottle.

Advise Richard on the income tax implications of these facts.

University of London LLB Examination
(for External Students) Revenue Law June 1995 Q4

General Comment

This question illustrates the Schedule D and E implications of expenditure made in the course of running a business.

Skeleton Solution

Schedule D and E implications of payment of employee's salary – provision of meals for employee and for employer: s155(5) ICTA 1988; *Sharkey* v *Wernher* – sales at undervalue: no adjustment – capital expenditure: short life assets or part of pool of expenditure – son's party: s74(1)(b) ICTA 1988.

Suggested Solution

Note: all references are to the Income and Corporation Taxes Act (ICTA) 1988 unless stated otherwise.

Steven's salary

Richard employs Steven in his restaurant at a salary of £8,000. He may deduct this amount in calculating his taxable profits for Schedule D purposes. Steven's income tax position is that those benefits which are taxable only on those earning at least £8,500 per annum will be tax-free in Steven's hands, unless they amount to more than £500 per annum. If they do, they are augmented with his salary and deem him to be within the £8,500 or more per annum category.

Steven's meals

Certain benefits, however, are generally excepted from the main charge to tax. Employees in the £8,500 category may receive canteen meals tax-free if they are provided for all employees generally: s155(5) ICTA 1988. In addition, an extra-statutory concession ESC A74 exempts free or subsidised meals (not restricted to canteen meals as in s155) and meal voucher arrangements if they are available to all employees and are on a reasonable scale. For those within the catering and hotel trades this does not apply to meals taken while customers are being served, unless there is a 'staff only' area set aside for this purpose. If the arrangements for Steven can satisfy these conditions then there are no income tax implications for him. Irrespective of the implications for Steven, Richard may deduct the full cost of the meals in the calculation of his profits for Schedule D purposes.

Richard's meals

In contrast with Steven's tax-free position, Richard is effectively taxed on the meals which he consumes on the premises. This arises from the application of s74(1)(b) ICTA 1988 in preventing a deduction from profits for expenditure of a domestic nature. The cost which he incurred in supplying them would be the amount which he has to add for his profit for the year. If the principles decided in *Sharkey* v *Wernher* [1956] AC 58 were held to apply, Richard would have had to bring in the full £900 as a trading receipt and, having already deducted the costs of the meals through his purchases and other business expenses, he would have had to pay tax on the theoretical profit element as required by the *Sharkey* v *Wernher* principle. Although this principle normally does apply to stock appropriated for own use, it is not regarded as applying to meals taken in-house by proprietors of restaurants and hotels and their families. This is an interpretation confirmed by the Inland Revenue in an official release.

Sales at undervalue

A trader is entitled to sell his stock at whatever price he pleases, so long as he does so in the ordinary course of business. The Revenue cannot force a trader to sell at the maximum possible price, nor can he be taxed on profit foregone through trading in such circumstances. The anti-avoidance provisions for adjusting prices for undervalue trading are applicable only where the recipient is an associated person and a non-United Kingdom resident, so that a taxable profit is leaving the United Kingdom tax net by artificial arrangements: s770. However, trading at an undervalue in the ordinary course of business (and therefore not with associated non-resident persons), is not within the ambit of these provisions. The arrangement which Richard made for the hire of the restaurant will therefore result in a tax-deductible loss.

The later receipt of an unsolicited gift for personal services may not be taxable on Richard, since it could be argued that it does not relate to the business but to his personal attributes. However, it might equally be argued that it is akin to tipping, which is taxable. In the light of *Wing* v *O'Connell* (1926) 1 ITC 170 the expectation of such a receipt under what is regarded as common practice may be sufficient to render it taxable.

Expenditure on refrigerators

Richard's replacement of one refrigerator and purchase of an additional one is expenditure of a capital nature and therefore not deductible as an expense in calculating his profits (s74(1)(f)) but he may claim capital allowances under s24 Capital Allowances Act 1990. If the items have an expected life of less than five years allowances at the rate of 25 per cent of the cost may be claimed in the first year and 25 per cent of the balance left after deducting such allowances, for each subsequent year. When sold, any balance of allowance still due after deducting the sale price may be claimed or if the reverse position arose, the excess is taxed by way of recovery of excess allowances given during its use in the business. Alternatively, allowances may be claimed by adding the new items (less the sale price of the one sold) to the general pool of capital expenditure and recalculating allowances on the new pool of capital expenditure.

Party for son

The income tax position in relation to the celebration for Richard's son is most likely to be treated differently to that applied in respect of meals taken by him. The interpretation of *Sharkey* v *Wernher* can probably not be extended to cover a specific party of this nature, as opposed to family meals. The withdrawal of champagne from stock on this occasion will result in a tax charge on the profit element arrived at by bringing in the full market value of the wine. In this instance the value would correspond to the retail value rather than the full price charged in the restaurant.

QUESTION SIX

a) Explain the opening and closing year provisions applicable to traders assessed to income tax under Schedule D Case I.

b) Gordon, a self-employed financial consultant, draws up his account to 5 January each year. His accounts for the year to 5 January 2001 show an agreed loss of £15,000. Gordon also has substantial investment income.

Advise Gordon as to how he may use that loss to obtain tax relief in each of the following alternative situations:

i)   Gordon began trading in 1990 and has no plans to discontinue his business;

ıı) Gordon began trading on 6 January 2000;

iii) Gordon began trading in 1990 and ceased trading on 5 January 2001.

University of London LLB Examination
(for External Students) Revenue Law June 2001 Q3

General Comment

Since part (b) of this question covers a factual scenario very much like others in this Chapter, it is only part (a) that is of interest. This section of the question explores the basis of assessment for new businesses and those which have been permanently discontinued.

Skeleton Solution

Schedule D, Case I – ICTA ss60–61 – opening and closing year provisions.

Suggested Solution

Note: all references are to the Income and Corporation Tax Act (ICTA) 1988 unless stated otherwise.

The basis on which profits under Case I of Schedule D are assessed is the current year basis, laid down in s60, which in the normal case of an ongoing business means that the profits to be assessed are the profits of the 12 months' accounting period ending in that (ie 'current') income tax year. Adjustments are required for the first year of business and this is provided for in s61, so that the profits of the first accounting period are apportioned up to the 5 April following commencement and tax is charged on this amount.

For new businesses, the first year assessment is on the actual profits arising from the date of commencement to the following 5 April. For the second year of trading, a person is charged on the profits of his first 12 months. Where the accounts ending in the second year of assessment are not for a 12-month period which began at the commencement of the business, then the profits are normally apportioned so that the second year's assessment does represent profits of the first 12 months. Thereafter, the accounting profits of the period ending the relevant tax year provide the taxable profit.

When a business is permanently discontinued, the basis of assessment is that the profits for the account period ending in the previous tax year are added to the profits from the commencement of the current tax year up to the actual discontinuance date.

Chapter 6

Capital Allowances

6.1   Introduction

6.2   Key points

6.3   Key cases and statute

6.4   Questions and suggested solutions

6.1 Introduction

Capital allowances are a form of allowance on qualifying capital expenditure relating to plant and machinery, industrial buildings and other qualifying assets. They are available to trades, professions and employments. The allowances are intended to replace the accounting deduction for depreciation of capital assets, which being a capital item is barred from deduction against profits under s74 ICTA 1988.

6.2 Key points

a) Provisions exist under the Capital Allowances Act (CAA) 1990, amended by the Capital Allowances Act (CAA) 2001 to relieve certain forms of capital expenditure by means of a gradual depreciation of capital assets. In particular relief is given to plant and machinery, and certain industrial buildings. The relief given therein is deductible, usually over a period of some years from the profits of a trade, profession or vocation.

b) 'Plant and machinery'

   i)   There is no statutory definition but following s117 FA 1994, a new Schedule AA1 was introduced into the Capital Allowances Act 1990, now within ss21 and 22 CAA 2001, which excludes land, buildings and fixed structures from the definition of 'plant' other than those items which case law decisions have already held to be plant. These items are listed in the new schedule and will continue to qualify. Similarly items (eg expenditure on safety at football grounds) for which specific statutory provision is made will continue to qualify.

   ii) Classic definition: Lindley LJ in *Yarmouth* v *France* (1887) 19 QBD 647

        '... it includes whatever apparatus is used by a businessman for carrying on his business ... all goods and chattels, fixed or moveable, live or dead ... for permanent employment in his trade.' The *Yarmouth* v *France* principle excludes stock in trade from the meaning of 'plant' and, by inference, the business premises. The tests which it sets out are the most important factors adopted by the courts.

iii) The following cases are important decisions, primarily based on the application of the *Yarmouth* v *France* principle:

- *Hampton* v *Fortes Autogrill Ltd* [1980] STC 80 – false ceilings in the restaurant were held to be coverings for the premises' electrical and plumbing fittings and not to be providing a function of the trade.

- *Munby* v *Furlong* (1977) 50 TC 491 – initial expenditure on law books by a barrister were held to be 'plant' within the *Yarmouth* v *France* principle.

- *IRC* v *Barclay, Curle & Co Ltd* (1969) 45 TC 221 – a dry dock was held to be plant, being apparatus used in the trade and not just the setting in the which the trade was carried on.

- *Benson* v *Yard Arm Club Ltd* [1979] STC 266 – expenditure on the refurbishment of a ferry as a floating restaurant was held to be expenditure on the setting for the business and therefore not 'plant'.

- *Brown* v *Burnley Football & Athletic Club* [1980] STC 424 – expenditure on a football stand was also held to part of the setting or premises 'in which' and not 'through which' the business was carried on.

- *Wimpey International Ltd* v *Warland* [1989] STC 273 – part of the claim was successful on the basis that the expenditure on lighting provided the essential atmosphere for the carrying on of the business.

- *IRC* v *Scottish & Newcastle Breweries Ltd* [1982] STC 296 – expenditure on lightings and fittings was held to be 'plant' part of the atmosphere needed to attract the business customers and therefore not the premises 'in which' but the apparatus 'with which' the business was carried on.

- *Barclays Mercantile Business Finance Ltd* v *Mawson* (also known as: *ABC Ltd* v *M*) [2003] STC 66 – expenditure on a pipeline by a finance company which was leased back to the seler was held to be 'wholly and exclusively for the purpose of its trade of providing asset-based finance' and allowable expenditure.

iv) Two further cases illustrate the fine line between premises and apparatus or 'plant':

In *Gray* v *Seymours Garden Centre* [1995] STC 706, a glasshouse was held to be no more than part of the setting for selling plants, despite having some environmental attributes necessary to keep the plants in a saleable condition. The Court of Appeal approved Fox LJ's statement that 'the fact that a building in which a business is carried on is, by its construction, particularly well-suited to the business, or indeed was specially built for that purpose, does not make it plant.'

The decision in *Gray* v *Seymours Garden Centre* was applied in *Attwood* v *Anduff Car Wash Ltd* [1997] STC 1167, in which the company claimed capital allowances for car wash halls on a number of sites laid out to a specific design system under which four vehicles could be treated at any one time. It was held that the buildings provided only a housing for the car wash cleaning machinery and control equipment and that they were therefore not plant.

See also *Bradley* v *London Electricity plc* [1996] STC 1054, in which the structure of an electricity substation was held not to be plant.

Availability of capital allowances

a) Sole traders, partnerships and companies in respect of Schedule D, Cases I and II, profits or gains and furnished holiday lettings under Schedule A: see *Ensign Tankers (Leasing) Ltd* v *Stokes* [1992] STC 226 – whether trading for capital allowances purposes – FA 1971 s41(1) (now s22 CAA 1990).

b) Employees under Schedule E who purchase plant and machinery necessary for the proper performance of their duties: *White* v *Higginbottom* [1983] STC 143.

c) Landlords under Schedule A who provide plant or machinery to repair, maintain or manage the property per s32 ICTA 1988.

d) Most importantly, the expenditure on which allowances are claimed must result in the asset 'belonging' to the claimant – s24(1)(b) CAA 1990 – see *Stokes* v *Costain Property Investments Ltd* [1984] STC 204 and *Melluish* v *BMI (No 3) Ltd* [1995] STC 964, which concerned claims for allowances for leased assets located in local authority owned homes, which having become fixtures of the buildings, could not be said to belong to the lessors. However, the House of Lords also held that the local authorities, despite being a tax exempt body, could enter into an election under s53 CAA 1990, having the effect of giving the lessors allowances for post-1984 expenditure. Schedule 16 FA 1997 reversed the latter part of the decision, excluding non-taxable entities from s53 elections.

The allowances

a) Expenditure on plant and machinery qualifies for a writing down allowance (WDA) given annually at 25 per cent on the reducing balance of expenditure after deducting previous allowances: s24 CAA 1990. Long life assets (predicted life of more than 25 years) qualify for only 6 per cent straight line allowance, following s84 and Schedule 14 FA 1997.

First year allowances are made available as capital allowances on plant and machinery under Chapter 4 CAA 2001. 'Small and medium-sized' is defined by reference to the number of employees and the turnover of the business: s22A CAA 1990.

Long life assets (those with an expected life of 25 years or more) are excluded from the allowance. For expenditure incurred in the first 12 months the first year allowance is 40 per cent.

There are separate provisions for expenditure between 12 May 1998 and 11 May 2002 on assets for use in Northern Ireland.

b) Expenditure must be incurred wholly and exclusively for the purposes of the trade: s24(1)(a) CAA 1990.

c) Short life assets may be written off within a shorter period than normal: ss83–89 CAA 2001. Long life assets post-FA 1997 restricted to 6 per cent straight line allowance. (See above.)

d) All similar types of assets are pooled and the allowances are given to the pool rather than to separate assets: ss53–54 CAA 2001.

e) Upon disposal, disposal proceeds will be taken into account as per ss24 and 26 CAA 1990 to produce either a balancing allowance or balancing charge.

Industrial buildings

a) Definition: ss271 and 274 CAA 2001, and see *Bourne v Norwich Crematorium* 44 TC 165.

b) No initial allowances are available for expenditure incurred after 31 March 1986.

c) A writing down allowance (WDA) of 4 per cent of the original cost of construction is given for a total of 25 years after which time the expenditure is treated as completely written off.

d) Upon disposal, a balancing allowance or charge is made. If, however, the disposal value exceeds the original cost, the excess will be treated as a capital gain.

Method of giving the allowances

Capital allowances are now given in the same manner as trading expenses – as a deduction in calculating the profits of the trade: s140 CAA 1990 as amended by FA 1994 s211. They were given previously as a deduction from the assessable profit.

6.3 Key cases and statute

*   *Barclays Mercantile Business Finance Ltd* v *Mawson* (also know as *ABC Ltd v M*) [2003] STC 66
    Capital allowances – leaseback schemes

- *Bradley* v *London Electricity plc* [1996] STC 1054
  Capital allowances – plant and machinery – apportionment of expenditure

- *Yarmouth* v *France* (1887) 19 QBD 647
  Capital allowances – plant and machinery – test

- Capital Allowances Act 2001

6.4 Questions and suggested solutions

QUESTION ONE

Bona Art Gallery Ltd has just leased premises which they use as a new art gallery. They have converted the building by installing specialised air conditioning, subdued recessed lighting and moveable partitions. For their opening exhibition they have been loaned a very valuable sculpture. To house that sculpture, they have had to install a specially constructed glass pyramid which is attached to the floor in the centre of the gallery and has a sophisticated alarm system built into it. They will sell this pyramid when the loan of the sculpture comes to an end.

Advise Bona Art Gallery Ltd whether they may claim capital allowances as a result of any of these items of expenditure and, if so, how those allowances will affect their tax assessments.

University of London LLB Examination
(for External Students) Revenue Law June 2001 Q4

General Comment

This question illustrates the principles of capital allowances.

Skeleton Solution

Capital allowances: plant and machinery; *Yarmouth* v *France* – leased premises: 'belonging' requirement – calculation of allowance: short-life asset.

Suggested Solution

Relief for capital expenditure is given to plant and machinery, and certain industrial buildings. Schedule AA1 was introduced into the Capital Allowances Act (CAA) 1990, amended by Capital Allowances Act (CAA) 2001, which excludes land, buildings and fixed structures from the definition of 'plant' other than those already held to be plant in past cases. The classic definition of 'plant' found in *Yarmouth* v *France* (1887) 19 QBD 647 is 'whatever apparatus is used by a businessman for carrying on his business ... for permanent employment in his trade.' It is likely that all of the items procured by Bona would fall under this definition.

Although Bona is not the owner of the building, under ss51–59 CAA 1990 fixtures can be treated as belonging to a person other than the landlord. Here, items added in the conversion and the glass pyramid could be separated from the leased premises and therefore be treated as 'belonging' to Bona.

Bona would likely be able to claim capital allowances on all of these items of expenditure. Expenditure on plant and machinery qualifies for a writing down allowance (WDA) given annually at 25 per cent on the reducing balance of expenditure after deducting previous allowances: s24 CAA 1990. All similar types of assets are pooled and the allowances are given to the pool rather than to separate assets: ss53–54 CAA 2001. However, a taxpayer can elect within two years of acquiring an asset for that asset (short life asset) not to be placed within the general pool. Bona may chose to elect the pyramid to be a 'short life' asset.

QUESTION TWO

Bilbo owns and operates a roadside café and small amusement park. In May 2000 he converted one of his buildings into a butterfly house as an additional attraction. As part of the conversion he installed a specially controlled heating, lighting and humidity system designed to provide the correct atmospheric conditions for the butterflies. The humidity part of the system has to be renewed every four years. To allow visitors to walk through the butterfly house Bilbo has installed several mezzanine platforms and special doors.

Advise Bilbo as to whether he may claim allowances in respect of the butterfly conversion.

University of London LLB Examination
(for External Students) Revenue Law June 2004 Q4(b)

General Comment

This question explores the parameters of the deductions available Capital Allowances Act.

Skeleton Solution

Capital allowances: plant and machinery – *Yarmouth* v *France*.

Suggested Solution

The revenue laws provide a system of capital allowances so that expenses incurred in the acquisition of a capital asset deductible when determining trading profits. However, only certain types of capital expenditure qualify for allowances, and the size of the allowance depends on the type of capital expenditure incurred. Whether Bilbo may claim capital allowance in respect of the butterfly house conversion will depend on whether his expenditure was on 'plant' or 'machinery'.

There is no statutory definition of 'plant, but following s117 FA 1994 a new Schedule AA1 was introduced into CAA 1990, now within ss21 and 22 CAA 2001, which excludes from the definition of 'plant' land, buildings and fixed structures, other than those items which case law decisions have already held to be plant. For the most part, therefore, one has to look to decided cases for the meaning of 'plant' and 'machinery'.

The classic definition of 'plant is found in *Yarmouth* v *France* (1887) 19 QBD 647 (Divisional Court):

> '… in its ordinary sense, it includes whatever apparatus is used by a business man, for carrying on his business – not his stock in trade which he buys or makes for sale; but all goods and chattels, fixed or moveable, live or dead, which he keeps for permanent employment in his trade.'

The modern trend in the cases seems to be towards a finding that the expenditure is unlikely to be allowable if it is purely on premises or fixtures to premises which are not directly related to the particular type of business activity involved. Therefore, it is unlikely that Bilbo could claim capital allowances in respect of conversion of the building itself. However, as the specially controlled heating, lighting and humidity system is specifically related to the type of business activity involved, ie, maintaining conditions in which butterflies may live, it is likely that Bilbo could claim capital allowances in respect of these costs.

Chapter 7

Schedule E

7.1   Introduction

7.2   Key points

7.3   Key cases and statutes

7.4   Questions and suggested solutions

7.1 Introduction

Anybody who is employed in any way is likely to be charged to income tax under Schedule E. Therefore most of the working population in the UK are Schedule E taxpayers, as are those who receive pensions in respect of past employment. Tax is charged, by ICTA 1988 s202A, on a receipts basis under the Pay As You Earn (PAYE) system whereby the employer deducts tax from the employee's salary and passes it direct to the Inland Revenue.

PAYE can also be applied to non-cash payments so that the cash flow disadvantage to the Inland Revenue is nullified through earlier collection of tax on items previously chargeable to tax under Schedule E but for which a direct assessment after the end of the relevant tax year was required. Sections 125–130 FA 1994 introduced rules into s203 ICTA 1988 in the form of new ss203B–203K for payment of PAYE at the relevant time on payments by intermediaries of the employer, payments in respect of employees of a non-resident employer, proportionate payments for employees working abroad, payments to certain contractors, payment in the form of tradeable assets, non-cash vouchers, credit tokens and cash vouchers. In s65 FA 1998 these rules were extended to any 'readily convertible asset' and applies to any asset for which trading arrangements exist or are likely to exist to enable an employee or member of the employee's family to obtain an amount of money from the provision of the asset.

7.2 Key points

Scope of the charge

Section 19 ICTA 1988 taxes emoluments – as defined in s131(1) – from office or employment. There are three cases within the Schedule: Case I covers a taxpayer who is both resident and ordinarily resident in the UK, Cases II and III operate where a foreign element is involved. The charge under Schedule E is not restricted to items which fall into the three cases – see for example the charge under ss148 and 188 and *Nichols* v *Gibson* [1996] STC 1008.

Definitions

'Office'

a) No statutory definition.

b) Classic definition: see *Great Western Railway Co Ltd* v *Bater* [1920] 3 KB 266 and *McMillan* v *Guest* [1924] AC 561.

c) More recently: see *Edwards* v *Clinch* [1981] STC 617 and *McMenamin* v *Diggles* [1991] STC 419.

The position must be capable of continuance and of being held by successive incumbents.

'Employment'

See *Davies* v *Braithwaite* [1931] 2 KB 628 and *Fall* v *Hitchen* [1973] STC 66. See also *FS Consulting Ltd* v *McCaul* [2002] STC (SCD) 138.

Note distinction between:

a) a contract for services = Schedule D, Cases I and II; and

b) a contract of services = Schedule E.

See *Market Investigations Ltd* v *Minister of Social Security* [1968] 3 All ER 732. See also *Hall* v *Lorimer* [1994] STC 23 – an important decision regarding the employment status of a freelance vision mixer who worked for many different employers on short-term contracts each of a few days. He successfully claimed to be self-employed and therefore to be assessable to tax under the more liberal Schedule D regime for allowable expenditure.

It is possible both to hold a Schedule E employment and exercise a trade, profession or vocation under Schedule D, Cases I and II: *Mitchell and Edon* v *Ross* [1962] AC 814.

'Emoluments'

Section 131(1) ICTA 1988 states: 'Emoluments shall include all salaries, fees, wages, perquisites and profits whatsoever.' This includes the benefits which are convertible into money on *Tennant* v *Smith* principles – other taxable benefits have to be specifically legislated for – as in ss154–165 ICTA 1988.

Section 61 FA 1997 phases out the tax-free pay under an employer's profit-related pay scheme, reducing the maximum of £4,000 to £2,000 for schemes whose periods commence on or after 1 January 1998, then to £1,000 from 1 January 1999 with nor relief for periods commencing 1 January 2000 or thereafter.

'Therefrom'

In *Hochstrasser* v *Mayes* (1959) 38 TC 673 the House of Lords approved a dictum of Upjohn J that:

> '[The payment] must be something in the nature of a reward for services past, present and future.'

Also: see *Hamblett* v *Godfrey* [1987] STC 60; *Beecham Group Ltd* v *Fair* [1984] STC 15; and *Shilton* v *Wilmshurst* [1991] STC 88.

It can also be said that the employment must be causa causans of the benefit, not just the causa sine qua non.

Note: *Wicks* v *Firth* [1981] STC 28.

Section 131 does not apply where statutory provisions render a benefit taxable under Schedule E despite the employment being merely the causa sine qua non of the benefit.

The inducement cases

Where an employee receives a payment from an employer to induce him to forego something, the payment is likely to be treated as compensation (ie outside the scope of Schedule E) unless it can be shown that the payment was in return for services past, present or future.

See *Jarrold* v *Boustead* [1964] 3 All ER 76; *Pritchard* v *Arundale* (1972) 47 TC 680; and *Riley* v *Coglan* [1969] 1 All ER 314.

The variation cases

Where payment was made by an employer to an employee in return for a genuine variation in the employee's rights, and in relation to the termination of employment, the payments were held not to come within Schedule E.

See *Hunter* v *Dewhurst* (1932) 16 TC 605 and *Wales* v *Tilley* (1943) 25 TC 136, although they are now taxable under the provisions of ss148 and 188 ICTA 1988.

Voluntary payments by third parties

Such payments made to an employee will only be chargeable if made in return for services past, present or future made under that employee's contract of service, eg a tip given to a waiter will be an emolument.

See *Moorhouse* v *Dooland* (1955) 36 TC 1; *Blakiston* v *Cooper* [1909] STC 347; and *Shilton* v *Wilmshurst* [1991] STC 88.

See ss141(6B), 142(3B) and 155(7) ICTA 1988 for provision of benefits and vouchers etc by third parties.

Benefits in kind

These are non-cash payments which may or may not fall within the scope of 'emoluments therefrom'.

Employees may be divided into two categories:

a) those earning (including any benefits) less than £8,500 per annum;

b) those earning more than £8,500 per annum and all directors (except those excluded in s168 ICTA 1988).

In *Templeton* v *Jacobs* [1996] STC 991, a loft conversion for use as an office was contracted for in the tax year before the employment commenced but completed afterwards. The taxpayer contended that benefit in kind had been provided during the tax year 1990–91, which was before the commencement of his employment with the company. The court held that in order for a benefit to be regarded as 'provided' for the purposes of s154(1), the benefit had to be available to the taxpayer and until such times as the benefit was capable of being enjoyed by the taxpayer, there was no relevant benefit for s154 purposes.

Rules applying to all employees

a) *Tennant* v *Smith* [1892] AC 150 – 'the convertibility test'

Any benefit which is capable of being turned to pecuniary advantage by the employee will be treated as an emolument.

b) *Wilkins* v *Rogerson* (1961) 39 TC 344

The value of a benefit so convertible will be the amount into which it could be turned (usually its secondhand value).

Rules applying to directors and to employees earning £8,500 pa and above: ss153–168 ICTA 1988

Benefits given to employees in this category and directors will be treated as emoluments at the cash cost to the employer less any amount made good to the employer by the employee. Other statutory provisions exist for benefits not covered by ss153–168.

Benefits in kind which continue to be provided after the termination of the employment (eg the use of a car) are, with effect from 6 April 1998, to be taxed in the year in which the benefit is received and not in the year when the employment ceases: s148 ICTA 1988 as amended by s58 FA 1998. This rule also applies to benefits provided when there is a change in the terms of the employment.

The cash equivalent of benefits

ICTA 1988 s154(1) taxes the 'cash equivalent' of a benefit in kind as an emolument. The cash equivalent is defined in s156(1) as the 'cost of the benefit, less so much (if any) of it as is made good by the employee'. The meaning of 'cost of the benefit' was determined in *Pepper* v *Hart* (below).

Pepper v Hart [1992] STC 898

The 'cost of the benefit' is the specific extra cost incurred by the employer in providing the specific benefit for its employees. It is not the average cost of supplying the service etc from which the employees benefit – for example if it costs no extra to run a public service train from A to B by allowing employees of the rail company to travel on it, there is no 'cost of the benefit' and no liability under Schedule E. The extra cost is referred to as the 'marginal' cost. In *Pepper* v *Hart* the House of Lords decided that the extra cost of educating children of schoolmasters was not the fees charged for children of non-employees nor the average cost of running the school divided by the number of pupils, but the specific extra cost of providing places for those children. In this case, that cost had been 'made good' by a payment made by the schoolmasters and therefore no taxable benefit arose.

The rule in Nicoll v Austin (1935) 19 TC 531

Debts of an employee discharged by his employer shall be treated as emoluments.

Special types of benefits in kind

a) Section 155 ICTA 1988

   Any of the following benefits are not emoluments:

   i) business accommodation, supplies and services used in performing the duties of employment;

   ii) death or retirement benefits;

   iii) free or subsidised meals taken in a canteen provided for all staff.

b) Scholarships: s165 ICTA 1988

   i) Scholarships paid to a higher paid employee or to any member of his family are treated as an emolument of the employee unless no more than 25 per cent of payments from a scholarship fund are to employees of that employer, and the award is unconnected with the employment.

   ii) Section 165 reverses the decision in *Wicks* v *Firth* [1983] AC 214, which held that s331 exempted both the recipient of the scholarship and the employee from a charge to tax under Schedule E.

c) Car benefits provided for directors and higher paid employees: ss157–159 ICTA 1988

    i) Pool cars

These are not taxable as a benefit in kind so long as the conditions of s159 ICTA 1988 are satisfied.

    ii) Cars provided for private use: s157

Such cars are treated as emoluments, the value thereof being found in Part I, Schedule 6 ICTA 1988. From 6 April 2002, tax will relate to type and size of engine for cars registered after 1997: FA 2000, Schedule 11.

Where a car continues to be used after the employment has ceased, a benefit in kind will continue to arise in each of the years for which the benefit continues – s148 ICTA 1988 as amended by s68 FA 1998, for employments which cease after 5 April 1998.

'Private use': see s168(5)(f).

The values given in Schedule 6 cover all related benefits, eg insurance and repairs except fuel and the provision of a chauffeur.

    iii) Cash alternative to cars

Where an employee is offered a cash alternative to the provision of a car he was taxable on the cash amount instead of the scale benefit – under the principles of the decision in *Heaton* v *Bell* [1970] AC 728, since the benefit is 'convertible'. However FA 1995 s43 remedies the abuse of this principle which arose where low cash alternatives were offered. The provision takes the charge out of ICTA 1988 s19 as an emolument and since it is no longer 'otherwise taxable' (see the wording of ICTA 1988 s154(1)(b)), the benefit to be taxed is the normal scale charge.

    iv) Car fuel

Fuel provided for private use is an emolument of the value determinable from Tables A or B of s158 unless the whole cost of providing the fuel is made good to the employer.

d) Beneficial loans to directors and higher paid employees: ss160 and 161 ICTA 1988

Section 160 treats the difference between the interest paid and the interest payable at the Treasury's official interest rate as an emolument. Prior to 1994–95 where the interest benefit exceeded £300, tax was charged on the full amount but if less than £300 it was exempt (s161). From 1994–95 onwards no tax is charged where the loan does not exceed £5,000 (aggregating all relevant loans): s88 FA 1994 amending s161 ICTA 1988.

Where the taxable loan is for a qualifying purpose (eg purchase of main residence) the reduction in the tax payable in respect of the qualifying portion of the loan (eg

£30,000 for main residence purchase loans), must not exceed 20 per cent for 1994–95 and 15 per cent for 1995–96 to mirror the provisions for interest paid relief under s353 ICTA 1988 (see Chapter 3, section 3.2). Section 107 FA 1996 allows the aggregation of loans as an option in reporting the cash equivalent to be taxed under s160(1B) ICTA 1988.

e) Shares: s162 ICTA 1988

The difference between the market value at the date of issue and price paid by an employee in respect of shares is treated as an emolument.

Beneficial loans for the purchase of shares fall under s160.

Where the employer pays part of the purchase price of the shares, that sum is deemed an interest free loan to the employer: s160. The loan continues until the employee dies, sells the shares or reimburses his employer.

f) Unapproved share options

Where an employee is granted an option to acquire shares at a future date and which is not granted under an approved share scheme, there is no income tax charged at the time when the option is granted. This exemption is conditional upon the option having to be exercised within ten years and on the option being exercised, the income tax charge arises at that point and is based on the excess of the value of the shares obtained less the payment made by the employee for the shares and for the option, if anything.

The ten year rule was increased from seven years for options granted after 5 April 1998: s135 ICTA 1998, as amended by s49 FA 1998.

See *Wilcock* v *Eve* [1995] STC 18 concerning payment for the loss of an opportunity to exercise a share option.

Statutory benefit in kind provisions applicable to all employees

a) Living accommodation: s145 ICTA 1988

If living accommodation for an employee or his family is provided by reason of his employment, the value of such accommodation (as per s837) is an emolument unless:

i) it is necessary for the proper performance of his duties, eg caretakers;

ii) it is for the better performance of his duties and is customary, eg hotel staff;

iii) there would otherwise be a threat to his security;

iv) where the employment is with a local authority and a council house is provided on normal terms.

Section 106 Finance Act 1996 counters avoidance of the tax charge on the benefit of living accommodation. The ss145 and 146 charges applied only if the benefit was not chargeable to tax under s19 ICTA 1988. By utilising the decision in *Heaton v Bell* [1969] 46 TC 211 (HL), an option to take a cut in salary in return for living accommodation, would make the amount of salary cut (which would be nominal only) taxable under the normal rules of Schedule E, without any charge under ss145 or 146. Section 146A gives priority to the charge under ss145 and 146 before considering whether any other amount is to be treated as Schedule E emoluments.

b) Expensive living accommodation: s146 ICTA 1988

Where employee accommodation is caught by s145 and its cost and improvements exceed £75,000, the employee is taxed on the excess over £75,000 as if it were a beneficial loan as well as being taxed under s145, except that the rate in force at the start of the tax year is not varied.

c) Ancillary services: s163 ICTA 1988 (exempt job-related accommodation)

i) These include furniture, repairs and cleaning.

ii) Higher paid employees only are taxed on the cost to the employer of providing such services up to a maximum of 10 per cent of his emoluments less any sums made good to the employer.

d) Cash and non-cash vouchers and credit tokens: ss141–144 ICTA 1988

i) Non-cash vouchers: s141

A voucher exchangeable for goods or services, eg a transport season ticket. The employee is taxed on the cost of the voucher and the goods, money or services provided (not on the exchange value): s89 FA 1994 amending ss141–144 ICTA 1988.

ESC A2: Luncheon vouchers of a value of up to 15 pence a day escape tax.

ii) Cash vouchers

A voucher exchangeable for money. The employee is taxed on the expense incurred by the person at whose cost it is provided.

iii) Credit tokens: s142

These include credit cards. The employee is taxed on the cost to the employer or to the person at whose cost goods or services are obtained by use of the credit tokens.

Where car fuel is purchased with a credit token, s158 overrides s142.

In s65 FA 1998 the rules in s203F ICTA 1988 were extended to any 'readily convertible asset' and applies to any asset for which trading arrangements exist or are likely to exist to enable an employee or member of the employee's family to obtain an amount of money from the provision of the asset.

iv) Third parties

See ss141(6B), 142(3B) and 155(7) ICTA 1988 for provision of benefits and vouchers etc by third parties.

e) Removal expenses

Schedule 11A ICTA 1988 limits the amount of tax-free 'qualifying removal expenses' and 'qualifying removal benefits' to an aggregate amount currently set at £8,000: Sch 11A para 24. These include those associated with relocation of the employee and the disposal and acquisition of properties associated with the relocation.

Terminal payments: ss148 and 188 ICTA 1988

Section 148 is a catch-all provision covering any form of terminal payment although s188 exempts:

a) Termination payments due to death or injury of the employee.

b) Sums taxable under s73 FA 1988 (restrictive covenants).

c) Benefits under approved retirement benefits schemes. The Revenue have been known to challenge the pension scheme lump sum exemption where an employee returns to employment with the same company. The true legal position is therefore currently not free from doubt.

d) Payments otherwise taxable under Schedule E (caught by *Dale* v *De Soissons* (1950) 32 TC 118).

e) Certain payments for foreign services

Relief under s188(4)

In *Nichols* v *Gibson* [1996] STC 1008, a payment of compensation for loss of office which a former employee received in a year when he was no longer resident or ordinarily resident in the UK was held to be taxable under s148 ICTA 1988. This section imposed a charge to tax under Schedule E independently of the charge under s19. In other words the charge under Schedule E is not confined to what falls within the three cases of s19. The s148 charge includes past holders of an office or employment so that being non-resident by being absent from the UK from 1 April and remaining out of the UK for a whole tax year was not sufficient to avoid tax on the payment. The effect of s148 was that although the taxpayer was not within any of the three cases of Schedule E he was nevertheless taxable under Schedule E despite his residence status at the time of receipt.

Payments in respect of restrictive covenants: s313 ICTA 1988

These are treated as emoluments of the employee. On 4 April 1996 the Inland Revenue published a statement of practice (SP 3/96) confirming that sums paid in settlement of claims which the employee could have pursued in law would be regarded as having no value for the purpose of any charge under s313 ICTA 1988 (restrictive undertakings on termination of employment).

Allowable expenses: s198 ICTA 1988

The following are deductible under Schedule E:

a) expenses incurred wholly, exclusively and necessarily in performance of the duties of the office or employment;

b) travelling expenses necessarily incurred in the performance of the duties of office or employment (including keeping a horse for such purposes).

Travelling expenses

i) As a rule expenses incurred in going to and from work are not deductible. However, in certain cases, eg a travelling salesman, all travelling expenses are allowed. From 1997–98 onwards the additional cost of travelling from home direct to a site other than the normal place of employment is deductible: see s62 FA 1997, amending s198 ICTA 1988. The Finance Act 1998, however, went a stage further to provide that not only the 'additional' cost (ie over and above the normal daily home to office travel cost) but the entire cost of such 'triangular' travel situations was deductible, s198 ICTA 1988 being rewritten accordingly. See *Miners* v *Atkinson* below.

See *Ricketts* v *Colquhoun* [1926] AC 1; *Owen* v *Pook* (1971) 45 TC 571; *Taylor* v *Provan* [1974] STC 168; *Marsden* v *IRC* (1965) 42 TC 326; and *Smith* v *Stages* [1989] 1 All ER 833; *Kirkwood (Inspector of Taxes)* v *Evans* [2002] 1 WLR 1794.

In *Miners* v *Atkinson* [1997] STC 58 a director who incorporated a company from his home address could not deduct the cost of travel from there to clients' premises. In delivering her judgment Arden J relied on *Horton* v *Young* [1972] 1 Ch 157, *Pook* v *Owen* (1971) 45 TC 571 and *Taylor* v *Provan* [1974] STC 168 and although the special commissioner had found that the taxpayer worked from his home address, his duties as a director were not necessarily carried out from there. These findings of fact were not disturbed by the High Court decision but the case therefore fell on the 'necessarily' aspect of s198 not being satisfied. However the outcome of this case has been to precipitate the review of travelling expenses as mentioned above from 1997–98.

ii) Using own car for business travel

See Inland Revenue leaflet IR 125 regarding fixed tax-free mileage allowance in accordance with the scales set out in the Fixed Profit Car Scheme. Any reimbursement of amounts up to this scale will not be taxed under Schedule E, and if no reimbursement or reimbursement at less than the FPSC rate, is made and the expense satisfies the qualifying conditions in s198, the employee may deduct an amount equivalent to the scale set out under this scheme. Relief is also due for interest on loans to acquire a car used for business purposes, in proportion to the business use mileage.

Other expenses

These are more difficult to deduct than travelling expenses since the 'wholly, exclusively and necessarily' test must be satisfied.

See *Brown* v *Bullock* (1961) 40 TC 1; *Lupton* v *Potts* (1969) 45 TC 643; and *Lomax* v *Newton* (1953) 34 TC 558.

See two similar cases: *Smith* v *Abbott* and *Fitzpatrick* v *IRC*, both ultimately decided in the House of Lords ([1994] STC 237), where groups of journalists were denied a deduction under s198 ICTA 1998 for the cost of newspapers purchased and read in connection with their employment. The Court of Appeal had allowed the relief in the former case, whereas the latter had been unsuccessful. The House of Lords decided that the commissioners had erred in law in their interpretation of 'in the performance of the duties' and ruled that the expenses were incurred to enable the journalists to perform the duties of their employment better and were not incurred in the actual performance of those duties.

7.3 Key cases and statutes

- *Davies* v *Braithwait* [1931] 2 KB 628
  Definition of employment

- *Fall* v *Hitchin* [1973] STC 66
  Definition of employment

- *FS Consulting Ltd* v *McCaul* [2002] STC (SCD) 138
  Definition of employment

- *Great Western Railway Co Ltd* v *Bater* [1920] 3 KB 266
  Definition of office

- *Hochstrasser* v *Mayes* (1959) 38 TC 673
  Payment must be in nature of reward for services

- *McMillan* v *Guest* [1924] AC 561
  Definition of office

- *Pepper* v *Hart* [1992] STC 898
  Cost of benefit – specific extra cost incurred by employer for specific benefit

- *Templeton* v *Jacobs* [1996] STC 991
  Benefits in kind – benefit must be available to taxpayer

- *Tennant* v *Smith* [1892] AC 150
  Taxable benefits – must be convertible into money

- Finance Act 1997, s61

- Income and Corporation Taxes Act 1988, ss131(1), 154–165 and 198

7.4 Questions and suggested solutions

Note: you should also refer to the questions in Chapter 5 for those illustrating distinctions between Schedule D and Schedule E treatment.

QUESTION ONE

Adam is a doctor employed as a consultant by the NHS. His salary is £30,000 pa. He has received an offer of a job with a private health care provider called Newcare. Newcare have offered the following fringe benefits:

a) £10,000 to compensate Adam for loss of his status as NHS Consultant. Should Adam and Newcare decide to terminate his employment with Newcare at any point, no part of this sum is returnable;

b) The use of a Rover car, the purchase price of which will be £22,000, together with all servicing, repair, insurance and Road Fund Licence costs associated with it. The car is to be replaced every three years and will have a permanent car phone installed;

c) Full private medical cover for himself, his wife and children;

d) £5,000 pa towards the cost of childcare. Adam's wife works full-time as a dentist so Adam and she employ a full-time nanny at a cost of £12,000 pa;

e) The right to occupy 'Greenlanes', a large house near Newcare's main hospital, at a nominal annual rent of £3,000. The rateable value of 'Greenlanes' is £1,800.

Advise Adam of the income tax consequences of the above facts.

University of London LLB Examination
(for External Students) Revenue Law June 1997 Q1

General Comment

A common type of question on Schedule E requiring a practical demonstration of the basic charging principles and the types of income which fall within the schedule.

Skeleton Solution

Independent taxation of husband and wife – compensation or inducement payment: loss of status – benefits in kind – private use of car and car phone: ss157 and 157A – cash equivalents during years in use – medical insurance premiums and child care allowance – employment of nanny: liability for PAYE and NIC – no Schedule E deduction s198 for nanny's salary – value of accommodation: ss145 and 146.

Suggested Solution

Note: all references are to the Income and Corporation Taxes Act (ICTA) 1988 unless stated otherwise.

Adam and his wife will be taxed under Schedule E independently of each other, with their own personal allowance deduction of £4,535 under s257(1). Each is also entitled to their own bands of lower and basic rate tax as provided for in ss1 and 1A.

It is assumed that both Adam and his wife each earn in excess of £8,500 per annum and that they are therefore within the charge to tax on expenses and benefits in kind set out in ss153–164, in addition to those provisions in ss135–151. They will be taxed under Schedule E on the 'emoluments' from their respective employments as defined in s131, which includes all 'salaries, fees, wages perquisites and profits whatsoever'. Expenses payments made to an employee in their income category are taxed under s153 subject to a deduction for expenses which satisfy the tests of s198 and are treated as 'emoluments' for the purpose of s131. Additionally, the 'cash equivalent' of any benefit in kind provided to or for an employee or his family is treated as an emolument for s131 and subject to tax accordingly: s154(1).

Compensation payment

The extent of the charge to tax under Schedule E as provided for by s19 encompasses anything paid which represents an emolument which arises from the employment and is therefore a reward for the performance of the duties of the employment. As to whether a payment to Adam for loss of status as an NHS consultant falls into the category of emolument or not, one has to determine whether it is made as compensation for forfeiture of rights not connected with the employment or whether it is paid merely as an incentive to take up the employment. If the latter, it is likely to have the character of disguised remuneration for performing the duties of the employment and would therefore be taxable on the general charging principles outlined. It is not sufficient that it is connected with the employment as in *Hochstrasser v Mayes* (1959) 38 TC 673 it was held that the 'payment must be made in reference to the services the employee renders ... and it must be something in the nature of reward for services past, present or future'. In Adam's case he will most likely be able to rely on the decisions in *Jarrold v Boustead* [1964] 3 All ER 76 where payment for giving up the status of an amateur rugby player was held to be compensation for the permanent surrender of that status and was not taxable as an emolument arising from the services performed under the new employment. The only area of concern for Adam would be that his loss of status is not permanent nor irrevocable since he could presumably return to such a position in the future should he choose to do so – an option which was not open to the taxpayer in the case cited.

Use of car and car phone

The provision of a car and car phone which are available for the private use of the employee are taxable in accordance with the 'cash equivalent' for each (ss157–159A and Sch 6), provided the car is in fact used for private purposes and the cost relating to that private use is not fully reimbursed by the employee. Partial reimbursement will reduce the measure of the charge: s157(3)(a). The measure of the charge for the private use of a car which is less than four years old is set at 35 per cent of the price of the car, which for the first three years will amount to £7,700 and when renewed will be 35 per cent of the price of the new car. The scale charge is reduced by two-thirds if Adam's business mileage is at least 18,000 in a year, or by one-third of the business mileage is between 2,500 and 18,000: Sch 6 para 2. Adam is potentially liable for a further charge to tax if fuel is provided for his private use and is not reimbursed. The charge under s158 varies according to the engine size of the car.

Under s159A a flat rate cash equivalent of £200 applies on the provision of a car phone or mobile phone which is available for, and is actually used for, private purposes.

No other charge to tax arises in respect of the running costs of the car as these (other than the cost of a driver's services) are deemed to be included in the Sch 6 cash equivalent: s155(1).

Medical insurance cover

As outlined above, benefits provided for both an employee or his family are taxable. Adam will therefore be liable for a tax charge equivalent to the cost incurred by his employer in providing the benefits for himself, his wife and family. There are no specific provisions dealing with medical insurance cover and the benefit is taxable under the general provisions of s154 of an amount provided for in s156.

Childcare allowance

All expenses paid to or for an employee earning more than £8,500 per annum are taxable as emoluments by virtue of s153. The payment of £5,000 is therefore taxable and can only be reduced by any amount paid out by Adam which satisfies the tests of s198 as being paid out 'wholly, exclusively and necessarily' in the performance of the duties of the office or employment'. Expenses laid out to put one in a position to perform the duties but which do not arise in the actual performance of those duties cannot be deducted under s198. This principle has been tested extensively in the courts – notably in *Ricketts v Colquhoun* [1926] AC 1 and more recently in the related cases of *Fitzpatrick v IRC (No 2)* and *Smith v Abbott* [1994] STC 237.

Employment of nanny

Adam and his wife will be responsible as any other employer for dealing with the deduction and payment of PAYE and NIC attributable to their nanny's salary. On the principles outlined in the preceding paragraph, neither of them can claim a deduction against their own Schedule E liability for the cost of employing the nanny.

Provision of accommodation

All employees are within the charge to tax on the benefit arising from the provision of living accommodation by their employers: ss145 and 146. The charge under s145 is limited to the annual value of the accommodation, which by virtue of s837(2) is equivalent to the rateable value. However, as Adam pays rent in excess of this amount, no charge to tax will arise. If the cost of the house provided exceeds £75,000, any additional charge to tax arising under s146 may be reduced by the excess of £1,200 of the rent paid over the s145 charge.

QUESTION TWO

D is employed by Widgets plc as Managing Director and Chairman. He receives the following benefits under his contract of employment:

a) the use of a Rover car (market value at date of purchase £30,000), together with the services of a chauffeur for all business and social travel;

b) the use of a mobile telephone. Widgets plc pay the line rental costs and meet the cost of all business calls. D has to pay for his personal calls;

c) the use of a dining room at Widget's premises. Meals are provided in the dining room for senior staff only. Junior staff are provided with meal vouchers to a value of 15p per day per employee;

d) vouchers to a value of £1,000 redeemable at a leading department store in exchange for goods and services, but not for money.

Advise D of the likely INCOME TAX consequences of these facts.

University of London LLB Examination
(for External Students) Revenue Law June 1999 Q3

General Comment

This question explores the tax implications of benefits received through employment.

Skeleton Solution

Schedule E ICTA 1988: rule in *Tennant v Smith*; directors' Code, s154 – tax treatment of car: ss157, 155(1); Sch 6 – tax treatment of mobile phone – tax treatment of food provision: ss154, 155(5) – tax treatment of non-cash vouchers: s141.

Suggested Solution

Note: all references are to the Income and Corporation Tax Act (ICTA) 1988 unless stated otherwise.

The Schedule E charge to tax under s19 includes all income classed as emoluments by s131, ie salaries, wages, perquisites and profits whatsoever. Benefits in kind provided to or for an employee by reason of his employment are taxable perquisites by virtue of the combined provisions of the above sections and ss141–146 and 153–165.

Those benefits which can be converted into cash are chargeable on all employees under s19 on their market value. Excluded from the s19 charge are those benefits which cannot be converted into cash. Lord Halsbury said in the leading case in this area, *Tennant* v *Smith* [1892] AC 150, that something sought to be taxed 'is not income unless it can be turned into money'.

Those employees earning £8,500 and above and all directors are subject to further taxing provisions under ss153–165. Some of these benefits have fixed scales of charge, whereas others are subject to valuation, usually at market value. As a director of the company, D is automatically within the charge to tax on those benefits provided for in ss153–165 for the £8,500 per annum category of employee.

Provision of car and chauffeur

Since D is provided with a car for both business and private use he is liable for tax on the 'cash equivalent', which becomes part of his emoluments for Schedule E purposes. Private use is defined by s168(5)(f) as any use otherwise than for business travel. Business travel is also defined by s168(5)(c) as 'travelling which a person is necessarily obliged to do in the performance of his duties'. D will therefore avoid any charge to tax on the necessary business travel, but his benefit for private use is calculated on the basis of 15–35 per cent of the price of the car provided for him: Schedule 6, para 1. Likewise, D will be liable for the cost of the chauffeur to the extent that the car is driven for private use.

Provision of mobile telephone

Since April 1999 provision of mobile telephones have been treated as not providing a taxable benefit. Therefore, D will not be liable for any tax relating to the mobile phone.

Provision of meals

Section 155(5) excludes from charge under s154 meals provided by the employer in a canteen used by the staff generally. D is provided meals in a dining room for senior staff only, whereas junior staff are given meal vouchers. Therefore the provision of meals would not fall within the exception and would be a chargeable benefit to D.

Non-cash vouchers

Some non-cash convertible benefits are the subject of specific taxing provisions affecting all employees, and these include non-cash vouchers: s141. Section 89 FA 1994 amended ss141–144 ICTA 1988 to change the quantum of the charge under Schedule E to the amount represented by the expense incurred by the person at whose cost the voucher is supplied, and the charge is the total of the cost of supplying the voucher plus the money and the value of the goods or services for which it can be exchanged. Therefore, the entire £1,000 value of the vouchers will be chargeable to D.

QUESTION THREE

Elizabeth is employed as director of X Ltd at a salary of £50,000 per annum and is also provided with a package of benefits. She is permitted to have either the use of a car of up to 2,000cc in the price range of up to £12,000, or alternatively £2,000 per annum. She opts to have the car. There is a parking place available for her use at work. In addition Elizabeth is provided with free petrol for both private and business use and has the car serviced with a garage near her place of work. The bills for servicing the car are sent direct to X Ltd which pays them.

Elizabeth receives an expense allowance of £3,000 which she uses for entertaining clients of X Ltd and to pay her own hotel bills when she travels on behalf of the company.

Elizabeth employs a nanny to care for her two-year-old son. The salary of the nanny is £6,000 per annum, and X Ltd makes a payment to Elizabeth of £2,000 per annum for child care costs. The nanny receives free accommodation in Elizabeth's house. She also has all her meals provided at a cost to Elizabeth of £500 per annum. The nanny is permitted reasonable use of the telephone and has the use of a small five-year-old car.

Advise Elizabeth and the nanny of the income tax consequences of the above facts.

Adapted from University of London LLB Examination (for External Students) Revenue Law June 1992 Q1

General Comment

This question illustrates the principles of taxing employee and director benefits.

Skeleton Solution

Elizabeth a director: taxed on all benefits – car or salary: salary sacrifice: does *Heaton* v *Bell* apply? – provision of car: s157(1)(b) does not apply – type of car: tables in Schedule 6 apply – parking: parking place at work exempt: s155(1A) – petrol: scale in s158 applies – car bills: not taxed in addition to scale charge – expense allowance: taxed as income: s153(1) – entertainment expenses: no deduction: s577(1)(b) – hotel expenses: deductible if s198 satisfied – employed nanny: no deduction: s155A does not apply – nanny £6,000 pa: not within £8,500 regime for benefits – accommodation: in employer's house, not taxed – telephone: not a convertible benefit – car: only applies to £8,500 category of employee.

Suggested Solution

Note: all references are to the Income and Corporation Tax Act (ICTA) 1988 unless stated otherwise.

The Schedule E charge to tax under s19 includes all income classed as emoluments by s131, ie salaries, wages, perquisites and profits whatsoever. Benefits in kind provided to or for an employee or his family by reason of his employment are taxable perquisites by virtue of the combined provisions of the above sections and ss141–146 and ss153–165.

Those benefits which can be converted into cash are chargeable on all employees, under s19, on their market value or secondhand value and for other benefits, normally on the cost of providing the benefit. The case of *Wilkins v Rogerson* (1961) 39 TC 344 established the principle of secondhand value for convertible benefits.

Excluded from the s19 charge are those benefits which cannot be converted into cash. Lord Halsbury said in the leading case in this area, *Tennant v Smith* [1892] AC 150, that something sought to be taxed 'is not income unless it can be turned into money'. However some of the non-cash-convertible benefits are the subject of specific taxing provisions affecting all employees, and these cover:

a) non-cash vouchers: s141;

b) credit tokens/cards: s142;

c) credit vouchers: s143;

d) living accommodation: s145;

e) 'expensive' living accommodation: s146.

Those employees earning £8,500 and above and all directors are subject (s167) to further taxing provisions under ss153–165. Some of these benefits have fixed scales of charge, whereas others are subject to a valuation, usually at market value.

Director: Being a director of the company, Elizabeth is automatically within the charge to tax on those benefits provided for in ss153–165 for the £8,500 per annum category of employee.

Car or salary: Cars have a fixed scale of charge under s157 which applies if 'the benefit of the car is not ... chargeable to tax as the employee's income'. It is possible to argue that because of the decision in *Heaton v Bell* [1970] AC 728 the £2,000 salary foregone should be taxed as income and that the car benefit is capable of being converted into salary. If that is so, then the car scale benefit under s157 would be ignored and the salary and running expenses of the car would be taxed as income.

Provision of car: If the *Heaton v Bell* principle does not apply, the car scale benefit provisions of s157 would apply to tax the private benefit of the use of the car. The cash equivalent of the car is related purely to the carbon dioxide emission levels. Mileage does not affect the level of tax but type and size of engine will. The charges range between 15 and 35 per cent of the car's list price.

Parking place: The supply of a parking place at or near one's place of work is exempt from Schedule E taxation by s155(1A).

Free petrol: The car fuel table is based on the cylinder capacity (cc) of the car. For 2001–2002, the charge was £2,460 for cars up to 2,000 cc.

Car servicing: Section 155(1) relieves from tax any expenses connected with the running of the car, other than the cost of a driver's services. The scale charge provision under s157 is intended to be an all-inclusive charge for the supply and running of the car, and no extra benefit arises from the payment of the repair bills if s157 applies.

Expense allowance: The payment of an expense allowance is a taxable emolument under s153(1) and is included in Elizabeth's income for assessment purposes. She may claim a deduction for expenses wholly and exclusively and necessarily incurred in the performance of her duties as a director: s198.

Entertainment expenses: However, despite s198, Elizabeth may not claim an expenses deduction for business entertainment expenses incurred. This is precluded by s577(1)(b).

Hotel expenses: Elizabeth may claim a deduction for these expenses if they satisfy the rule in s198.

Employment of nanny: There is no tax deduction for the amount paid in employing a nanny, since this is to enable Elizabeth to work and is not in the course of her duties. Section 155A exempts the provision of nursery facilities provided by the employer at the place of work.

Nanny's salary: Elizabeth will be responsible for operating PAYE and National Insurance contribution deductions when paying her nanny and for paying over the deductions to the Collector of Taxes. The fact that her salary is below £8,500 means that she will not be taxable on any of the benefits arising under ss153–165.

Supply of accommodation: This would not be taxable because of s145(4)(b) as it is customary to provide accommodation for a nanny.

Supply of meals: This is not a convertible benefit which can be turned into cash and is not taxable on the nanny since no income has been foregone to enable her to receive this benefit. If there was any doubt, it may be possible to apply concession A74 to exempt the amount as being reasonable and as being supplied in a 'canteen' for employees generally.

Use of telephone: This again is a non-cash convertible benefit (*Tennant* v *Smith*), and no tax arises since the nanny's income is less than £8,500 inclusive of deemed benefits. Nor is it a bill of the employee which is being met by the employer since the contract is between the employer and the telephone company.

Use of car: The car scale benefit charge applies only to employees earning £8,500 or more. The nominal benefit under Schedule 6 for a car more than four years old is £1,460 and, if applicable, a petrol benefit of £500 which together with her salary is still not sufficient to bring her 'income' to £8,500.

QUESTION FOUR

Emma works for a United Kingdom company which owns several department stores in England. Her salary is £50,000 per annum. Although based in one of the stores, Emma's job entails visiting the other stores on a regular basis. The company provides her with the use of a car and pays the insurance for the car. She also gets free petrol for both business and private use. Emma has an annual allowance from the company of £500 which is to be used for entertaining clients of the company. The company provides free medical insurance for all their staff, free medical advice and hairdressing at the stores. All staff are entitled to purchase goods from the stores at a discount of 50 per cent.

Emma is permitted free use of the company's holiday home in the Lake District for herself and her family for two weeks a year.

In January 1996 Emma's father died and the company allowed her to take compassionate leave for a week and also gave her a sum of £100. The right to this is contained in Emma's contract with the company.

Advise Emma on the income tax implications of the above.

University of London LLB Examination
(for External Students) Revenue Law June 1996 Q2

General Comment

This question illustrates the principles of taxing employee salaries and benefits.

Skeleton Solution

Earnings in excess of £8,500: subject to expenses and benefits in kind legislation: ss153–168 ICTA 1988 – 'cash equivalent' is measure of taxable benefit: s154(1) – car benefit: 35 per cent of list price of car; Schedule 6 – benefit inclusive of running costs: s155 – petrol for private use: taxable amount per s158 table – entertainment expenses: excluded from s198 deduction by s577 – medical insurance and treatment: general application of cash equivalent principle – staff discounts: by concession wholesale price threshold – holiday home: marginal cost; ignore cost of ownership – compassionate leave payment – contractual right incurs liability.

Suggested Solution

Note: all references are to the Income and Corporation Taxes Act (ICTA) 1988 unless stated otherwise.

Emma is employed at a salary of £50,000 per annum, which will make her liable to tax at the higher rate of tax – 40 per cent. It also means that in addition to her liability for tax under the provisions of ss19 and 131, she is within the scope of the provisions relating to expenses and benefits for all employees as well as those specifically related to employees earning in excess of £8,500 per annum – under ss153–168. Although the measure of the benefit in each case is taken to be the 'cash equivalent' – s154(1) – there are varied rules for arriving at the cash equivalent in regard to specific benefits.

Provision of company car

Since Emma is provided with a car for both business and private use she is liable for tax on the 'cash equivalent', which becomes part of her emoluments for Schedule E purposes. Private use is defined by s168(5)(f) as any use otherwise than for business travel. Business travel is also defined by s168(5)(c) as 'travelling which a person is necessarily obliged to do in the performance of his duties'. Emma will therefore avoid any charge to tax on the necessary business travel, but her benefit for private use is calculated on the basis of 35 per cent of the price of the car provided for her: Sch 6, para 1.

Under s155(1), the taxable benefit is deemed to include all running costs of the car and therefore the payment of the insurance by the company does not give rise to an additional benefit. The provision of petrol for private consumption is taxed in accordance with s158, the amount of the benefit varying in accordance with the cc capacity of the car: s158.

Entertainment expenses

The receipt of a round-sum allowance for expenses is an emolument for Schedule E purposes and, for Emma to reduce the tax on that expense allowance, she would have to satisfy the rules of Schedule E relating to allowable expenses under s198. However, even if her expenses were incurred 'wholly exclusively and necessarily' in the performance of the duties of her employment, s577 specifically disallows business entertainment expenses as a deductible item for Schedule E purposes. Only if she were in receipt of a round-sum allowance for expenses generally would she be able to claim an allowance against the sum received for the other allowable items of expenditure.

Medical insurance and treatment

The provision of medical insurance cover by the company is not covered by any specific provision in the benefits-in-kind legislation. Any benefit is, therefore, subject to tax under s154 on the cost to the employer. Thus, Emma would be taxable on the amount paid by the company on her behalf.

On the other hand, the provision of free medical advice is unlikely to have a discernible cost attached to it in respect of each individual employee. If, for example, the facility is provided for all employees generally there would be no specific cost which could be taken to be in respect of an individual employee. On the basis of the decision in *Pepper v Hart* [1992] 3 WLR 1032, there is no marginal additional cost applicable to Emma's inclusion in the scheme. There would therefore be no cash equivalent for her to be taxed on. However, in the case of the hairdressing provision, since this would incur a specific cost that amount would be taxable as an emolument of her employment under s131.

Staff discounts

In contrast to the provision of free medical advice, there is always going to be a cost to the employer of Emma being able to purchase goods at a discounted price. Applying the decision in *Pepper* v *Hart*, the amount of the taxable benefit would again be the additional or marginal cost of providing the facility for employees. As a working rule, the Revenue's view is that a taxable benefit arises where the employee pays less than the wholesale price for the goods. The difference between that figure and the price paid is, according to the position set out by the Revenue in a press release following the decision in *Pepper* v *Hart*, the amount on which Emma would pay tax. Such a position could of course be challenged on appeal if it could be shown that a more accurate marginal cost basis for taxing the benefit could be established. This would more closely equate to the requirements of the law.

Holiday home

Again on the basis that the company is likely to incur a cost in either renting or providing a holiday home, Emma has a taxable benefit which under the general rules would be based either upon a proportion of the direct cost of renting the property for the two-week period or any cost of running it for that period. If the property is owned by the company then the rules of Schedule E are that the cost of the benefit in any year is the annual value of its use. When the asset is owned by the company, the actual cost of its acquisition is not taken into account, despite the fact that the employee does enjoy the benefit of that ownership: *IRC* v *Luke* (1963) 40 TC 630. This effectively ensures that only the marginal cost of in-house benefits becomes a taxable benefit. It is likely that in these circumstances a proportion of the gross rateable value would be taken into account.

Compassionate leave payment

Any sum received for which provision is made in the contract of employment, and for which no exemption arises under the provisions of ICTA 1988, ensures that the payment in question would be a taxable sum on account of it being derived directly from the employment.

QUESTION FIVE

For some years Anne has been employed by Sporting Ltd as the senior administrator of a health and sports club. Her current salary is £25,000 and she is also provided with subsidised health insurance.

Anne often works in the evenings which are the busiest time at the club. In order to help her purchase a house near the club complex the company made a loan available to Anne at a rate of interest of three per cent per annum. The cost of the house when Anne purchased it in 1990 was £90,000.

Anne is permitted to use the facilities of the club without payment. She swims in the pool regularly and also plays squash. Members of the club pay an annual subscription of £500 and in addition have to pay £2.50 per half hour for the use of a squash court

At Christmas, Sporting Ltd gave a lavish party for all the employees of the club. The cost to the club was £100 per head.

Occasionally Anne travels on business for the club using her own car. The company pays her for the cost of the petrol plus a standard mileage allowance for the use of the car.

Advise Anne on the taxation of her salary and the benefits.

University of London LLB Examination
(for External Students) Revenue Law June 1993 Q1

General Comment

This question illustrates the principles of taxing employee salaries and benefits.

Skeleton Solution

Higher-paid employee benefits – cash convertible benefits: *Tennant* v *Smith* – beneficial loan to employee: s160 ICTA 1988, official rate s178 FA 1989 – qualifying loan in excess of £30,000: s160(4), Sch 7 para 8 – health insurance: benefit in kind – use of employer's sporting facilities: s154 ICTA 1988; *Pepper* v *Hart*; s75 FA 1993/s197G ICTA 1988 – Christmas party expenditure: maximum exception £50 – car mileage allowance and reimbursement of expenses: *Pook* v *Owen*.

Suggested Solution

Anne receives a salary of £25,000 from her employers. This will be taxed under Schedule E using the PAYE system which will give effect to her personal allowances for the year as well as the lower and basic rates of tax. Any excess will be taxed at the higher rate of 40 per cent. If the basic rate band is exhausted, any taxable benefits in kind will be charged at the higher rate. The benefits may either be taxed during the course of the year to which they relate through reducing, by an amount equivalent to the taxable benefits, the amount of personal allowances made available under the PAYE system, or alternatively they may be taxed by the raising of an assessment under Schedule E after the end of the income tax year.

Because Anne's annual salary is in excess of £8,500 she will be liable to tax under Schedule E on all 'salaries, fees, wages, perquisites and profits whatsoever' as provided for in s131. Secondly, she will be liable, following the findings of *Tennant* v *Smith* [1892] AC 150, under ss141–146 on all benefits provided by her employer which are convertible into cash or which are legislated for in these sections, and thirdly also liable on the cash equivalent of all benefits which she receives and which are legislated for in ss153–165.

Loan at beneficial rate of interest

The amount of the benefit derived by an employee in respect of a loan made available by an employer at less than the 'official rate' of interest is liable to tax under the specific provisions of s160 Income and Corporation Tax Act (ICTA) 1988. This applies to loans made by the employer other than in fulfilment of a domestic, family or personal relationship.

The normal basis of the charge to tax is to tax the difference between the interest calculated at the 'official rate' (as determined under s178 Finance Act (FA) 1989) and the actual interest paid. However, since interest on loans for the purpose of acquiring an 'only or main residence' is eligible for tax relief under s353 ICTA 1988, there is no charge to tax on a beneficial loan falling within the scope of that section: ICTA 1988 Schedule 7, para 8 et seq. This relief applies to the first £30,000 of the loan. Anne's loan is for £90,000, and therefore one third of the interest is eligible for tax relief and is exempt from the s160 charge. The interest on £60,000 calculated at the official rate of interest applicable from time to time during the year is taxable as a benefit less a deduction for the three per cent interest paid.

Use of sports facilities

The provision of facilities for use by employees would, but for exemption under the FA 1993 legislation, be a taxable benefit under the charging provision of s154 ICTA 1988 for an employee earning in excess of £8,500 per annum. Therefore Anne would be liable to tax on the cost to her employer of providing the facility – the 'cash equivalent' as determined under s156. Based on the decision in *Pepper* v *Hart* [1992] 3 WLR 1032 the amount of that taxable benefit would be the additional or 'marginal' cost of providing that facility for each individual employee. The average cost based on the full cost being apportioned among the users was defeated in *Pepper* v *Hart* as the statutory basis. The charge made to others for using the facilities, in this case £500 per annum, similarly has no basis for a charge since it does not represent the cost incurred in providing the benefit.

Where, as in *Pepper* v *Hart*, a charge is made equivalent to that estimated cost, the charge to tax is reduced to nil. In the case of certain in-house facilities it is difficult to assess the amount, if at all, by which an employer's cost is increased by additional individual usage. The Finance Act 1993 in s75 provides a new section, s197G, in ICTA 1988 which will exempt most sporting facilities provided by employers from a charge to tax. This recognises the administrative problem of ascertaining what was accepted as being a small marginal cost for individual users of 'in-house' sports facilities provided by employers for the use of their employees in general. The legislation does not however give exemption where the facilities are open to the general public. One view of this provision would be that the facilities provided externally are exempt if private facilities are provided to employees of one or more employers, but the use of the same facilities, even by means of subscription or non-cash vouchers for public facilities, would not be exempted. Another possible interpretation is that facilities provided for employees of public sports centres are not exempt from the charge to tax, while the same facilities used by outside employees are within the exemption. However it would appear that Anne, as an employee of a public sports centre using those facilities which are used by 'members of the public generally', could be chargeable to tax on the cost of provision of that facility. However this would be squarely within the *Pepper* v *Hart* situation, and it was confirmed during the parliamentary debate on the new provision that employees of a local authority using its public facilities would come within the exemption.

Health insurance

There are no specific provisions regulating the charge to tax on the benefit derived from the provision of health insurance cover. Any benefit is therefore subject to tax, under s154 ICTA 1988, on the cost to the employer. The subsidy paid by the employer clearly equates to that cost, and Anne is chargeable to tax under Schedule E on that amount.

Christmas party

The provision of entertainment for staff is also caught by the provisions of s154. The cost of the taxable benefit would in that case be £100 per person. An extra-statutory concession (A70) published by the Inland Revenue exempts employees from any charge to tax where the cost per head does not exceed £50 and the function is an annual Christmas party open to the staff generally. However this is not a de minimis exemption, and where the entertainment cost per head exceeds £50 the full amount, in Anne's case £100, is taxable.

Car expenses

The reimbursement of travelling expenses was considered in *Pook* v *Owen* (1971) 45 TC 571, and the House of Lords ruled that the reimbursement was not an emolument of the employment. However, under s153 ICTA 1988 expenses paid to employees earning more than £8,500 are regarded as emoluments, but under ICTA 1988 a deduction can be made from Anne's taxable income for the actual proportion of car-running expenses which can be attributed to being incurred by her in the performance of her duties.

Chapter 8

The Foreign Element – Schedule D and Schedule E

8.1   Introduction

8.2   Key points

8.3   Key cases and statutes

8.4   Questions and suggested solutions

8.1 Introduction

In general, an individual closely connected with the UK will pay tax in the UK on his worldwide income – an individual only vaguely connected with the UK will pay UK tax only on income arising in the UK.

Four connecting factors are used to determine liability to UK tax:

a) domicile;

b) residence;

c) ordinary residence;

d) company residence.

Domicile

Generally where a person is born or the place in which the individual intends to settle permanently.

A person's domicile is not affected by having the right to vote in the United Kingdom, through being registered as an overseas voter on the electoral roll. Non-domiciled individuals are generally assessed on a remittance basis in respect of foreign income: ss65(4) and 192 ICTA 1988.

Residence

a) No statutory definition but see Inland Revenue booklet IR 20.

b) An individual is resident if he either:

i) spends six months (183 days) or more in the UK in a year of assessment: s336(1) ICTA 1988; or

ii) spends habitual and substantial periods in UK over several years of assessment: ie an average of three months or more for four consecutive years.

c) There are no provisions in the Income Tax Acts for residence to be determined other than on a full income tax year basis. However the part-year position is covered by an extra statutory concession A11 – revised 29 January 1996. The concession allows for separate periods where an individual comes to the United Kingdom to take up permanent residence or to stay for a period of at least two years. Similarly, the concession applies to split the tax year if the individual leaves the United Kingdom, having been resident here, for the purpose of taking up permanent residence abroad.

The effect of the concession is to treat a person as not resident and not ordinarily resident in the UK from the day of departure until the day prior to their return. Any tax liability which is determined by residence is applied separately by reference to the residence status of each part of any split tax year.

See *Dawson* v *IRC* [1989] STC 473 – residence of a trust. The position is now clarified in s11 FA 1989.

Ordinary residence

a) No statutory definition but somewhat narrower than residence. Normally the place to which, when absent, the taxpayer intends to return: see Inland Revenue booklet IR20.

b) *IRC* v *Lysaght* [1928] AC 234: Viscount Sumner: 'I think the converse ... is extra-ordinary and that part of a man's life adopted voluntarily and for settled purposes, is not extra-ordinary.'

Company residence

Companies have no domicile, only residence: see: s66(1) FA 1988 and *De Beers Consolidated Mines Ltd* v *Howe* [1906] AC 455. For company residence see Chapter 15.

8.2 Key points

Schedule D, Cases I and II

a) Residents

Section 18(3) ICTA 1988: a UK resident is taxed on all profits from a trade, profession or vocation carried on in the UK even if some part of the same business is carried on overseas

b) Non-residents

Liable to UK tax on profits from a business carried on in the UK.

i) *Erichsen* v *Last* (1881) 4 TC 422 distinguished a trade within UK and trading with the UK.

ii) Sections 126–129 and Schedule 23 FA 1995: agents in the UK or 'UK representatives' (eg branch or agency) may be liable for tax due from a non-resident.

iii) UK members of a partnership are collectively deemed to be the UK representative of a non-resident member: s126(2) and (7) FA 1995.

iv) Exclusion for investment managers and brokers: s127 FA 1995.

Schedule D, Cases IV and V

a) Case IV

Taxes income from securities outside the UK. Income from Foreign State securities are taxed under Schedule D Case III (pre-1996–97 these were taxed under Schedule C which is now repealed).

b) 'Securities'

i) Not stocks and shares.

ii) Includes secured debts, loans, debentures etc: *Williams* v *Singer* [1921] 1 AC 41.

c) Case V

Taxes income from 'possessions' outside the UK, including rents from foreign properties. Although income from such properties is taxed under Case V of Schedule D, the profits and losses are calculated in the same manner as those for a Schedule A rental business: see Chapter 4. For years 1995–96 to 1997–98 transitional arrangements under s65A keep the profits or losses from overseas properties separate from those of UK properties, so that the two may not be set off against each other. See Chapter 4 for losses from such an 'overseas property business' post-1998.

A UK paying agent passing on foreign dividends to a UK resident will need to deduct and account for tax under the paying agent rules of s18(3B)–(3E) ICTA 1988 (formerly s123).

Case V includes income from shares and foreign pensions. Income from foreign employment is assessed under Schedule E.

The basis of computation – Schedule D

a) Cases I and II

The usual rules apply to all profits and gains whether or not remitted to the UK.

b) Cases IV and V

Section 65(1) ICTA 1988: actual year basis – taxes on full amount whether or not remitted to the UK, except:

i) Section 65(2) ICTA 1988: if the income is from a foreign pension a 10 per cent deduction is allowed. (*Note*: although pensions are Case V income, foreign employment income is Schedule E.)

ii) Section 65(5) ICTA 1988: non-domiciled taxpayers are taxed only on sums remitted to the UK – see table below.

iii) The principle to be applied in respect of foreign income assessable under Schedule D Cases IV and V is that the arising basis – s65(1) – applies if a person is resident AND ordinarily resident AND domiciled in the UK. The remittance basis – s65(5) – applies to a person with any other status. The basis for both is the actual amount arising or remitted in the year of assessment.

iv) Section 65A ICTA 1988 applies to income chargeable under Case V from land and property outside the UK. Schedule A computation principles are applied to compute the income – s65A(2).

TYPE OF INCOME	INVESTMENT INCOME	FOREIGN PENSIONS	FOREIGN TRADES
Taxpayer resident, ordinarily resident, and domiciled UK	Full amount arising	Amount arising minus 10 per cent	Full amount arising
Taxpayer resident, ordinarily resident but not domiciled in UK	Remittance basis	Remittance basis	Remittance basis
Taxpayer resident, not ordinarily resident but domiciled in UK	Remittance basis	Remittance basis	Remittance basis
Taxpayer resident but not ordinarily resident and not domiciled in UK	Remittance basis	Remittance basis	Remittance basis

Schedule E

The foreign aspect of Schedule E is dealt with in a combination of ss19, 192 and 193 ICTA 1988.

Section 19

a) Case I applies the arising basis to world-wide earnings where the employee is both resident and ordinarily resident; it excludes (s192) the 'foreign emoluments' of non-domiciled employees with no UK duties but gives relief (s193) for long-term (at least 365 days') employment overseas in other cases.

b) Case II applies the arising basis to the UK duties of non-residents or at least not ordinarily resident residents (ie to NRs or NOR/Rs), again with s192 treatment of non-domiciled persons.

c) Case III applies the remittance basis to any non-domiciled resident.

Section 192

Subsection 2 exempts from Case I (and the arising basis) treatment the emoluments of a non-domiciled person employed wholly abroad by a non-resident employer.

Section 193

Provided for 100 per cent relief from UK tax, in conjunction with Schedule 12, for the emoluments arising from long-term 'qualifying' periods of employment abroad, irrespective of the residence status for the year of assessment. Except for seafarers, s63 Finance Act 1998 put an end to this 'foreign earnings deduction' with effect from 17 March 1998 which applied without satisfying the normal non-resident rule of being absent for at least a complete income tax year. The effect of the withdrawal is that the departing person may be treated as non-resident from the date of departure only if the absence will include at least one complete income tax year and the concession of splitting the tax year will apply.

8.3 Key cases and statutes

- *Erichsen* v *Last* (1881) 4 TC 422
  Non-residents – liability to tax – trade within UK

- *IRC* v *Lysaught* [1928] AC 234
  Ordinary residence – abode adopted voluntarily and for settled purposes

- Finance Act 1988, s66(1)

- Income and Corporation Taxes Act 1988, ss19, 65, 192–193 and 336(1)

8.4 Questions and suggested solutions

QUESTION ONE

Paddington is employed as a sales executive by Bears Ltd, a UK company, at a basic salary of £15,000 pa plus commission. In 1991–92, Paddington spent 175 days in Peru on business for Bears Ltd. Bears Ltd also paid for flights for his wife and children to visit him in Peru. Paddington paid for their accommodation in Peru. In March 1992, Paddington received £1,000 from a Brazilian firm to thank him for giving them business from Bears Ltd.

Discuss the income tax implications of the above and what difference if any would it make if Paddington were a sole trader.

Written by the Author

General Comment

This question explores the taxation implications of foreign employment.

Skeleton Solution

Foreign employment – resident and ordinarily resident in the UK – Schedule E, Case I liability – provision for tax-free visit by family: s194(2) ICTA 1988 – third party payment: whether for services or personal; *Moorhouse* v *Dooland*; *Calvert* v *Wainwright* – if sole trader, Schedule D; no corresponding provision for family visit – liability on world-wide profits.

Suggested Solution

Assuming that P is resident, ordinarily resident and domiciled in the UK, he will be chargeable to income tax on his salary, commission and any other earnings from B Ltd under Schedule E Case I: s19 ICTA 1988. His emoluments under s19 should also include any travelling expenses reimbursed to him by his employers: s153 ICTA 1988.

His residence in the UK in 1991–92 would be determined by the fact that he spent more than 183 days in the year in the UK (IR20).

If, however, P was resident but not ordinarily resident within the meaning given by Viscount Sumner in *IRC* v *Lysaght* [1928] AC 234 then any part of his emoluments related to duties performed in Peru would be taxable.

His emoluments for UK duties would still be charged under Schedule E, Case I. Special provision is also made in respect of the expense reimbursed to P by B Ltd of bringing his wife and children over to Peru for a visit. Section 194(2) ICTA 1988 provides that where an employee works abroad for a continuous period of at least 60 days, and his employer reimburses him the expense of his spouse and children under the age of 18 in travelling to visit him, then although that reimbursement must be brought into charge as an emolument under s153 ICTA 1988, an equivalent amount may be allowed by way of deduction: effectively, therefore, the reimbursement is not a chargeable emolument.

As far as the payment of £1,000 is concerned, such payment will be brought into charge to tax under Schedule E, if, from the standpoint of the recipient, they can be seen as a reward for services past, present or future: *Moorhouse* v *Dooland* (1955) 36 TC 1. It was stressed in *Calvert* v *Wainwright* (1947) 27 TC 475, however, that if the payment was in fact made by reason of the recipient's personal qualities, then it would not be taxable. The payment received by P is on the borderline but would most likely be seen as a reward for services and therefore be treated as an emolument.

If, however, P was resident but not ordinarily resident in the UK in 1991–92 then such payment would escape tax unless it was remitted to the UK.

If P was a sole trader, he would be taxable under Schedule D Case I and charged to tax under s18 ICTA 1988 on his annual profits and gains.

As a resident and ordinary resident, the s18 charge would cover his worldwide profits and gains but as a resident, but not ordinary resident then any profits and gains arising in Peru would only be caught by s18 if remitted to the UK.

The travelling expenses of bringing his wife and children to Peru for a visit would not be an allowable deduction from profits. Under s74(1)(a) ICTA 1988, P's own travelling expenses would only be a deductible expense if incurred wholly and exclusively for the purposes of the trade. Thus, if P had gone to Peru for a combined holiday and business trip, none of his travelling expenses would be allowed.

As far as the payment of £1,000 is concerned, the same reasoning as in *Calvert* v *Wainwright* must apply. If the payment was in recognition of P's personal qualities it would not be taxable; if made in return for services provided it will be a trading receipt. Although if P was not ordinarily resident albeit resident in the UK, then s18 would only apply on a remittance basis.

QUESTION TWO

Consider the rules determining residence for individuals and companies. Are these rules satisfactory?

University of London LLB Examination
(for External Students) Revenue Law June 1992 Q3

General Comment

An essay-type question which requires thorough knowledge of the residence rules.

Skeleton Solution

Individuals

Current tests for residence of individuals: no statutory definition – Inland Revenue code (IR20) – case law: *Levene v IRC, Lloyd v Sulley, Cooper v Cadwalader, Reed v Clark* – the 183 days' test and the income tax year – ordinary residence: no statutory definition – Inland Revenue consultative document – continuing difficulties: planning for avoidance, uncertainty.

Companies

Basis for assessment to corporation tax – current test for residence: incorporation, central management and control – case law tests: *De Beers, Bullock v Unit Construction Company* – Inland Revenue Statement of Practice 1990 – continuing problems: parent/subsidiary, double taxation agreements.

Suggested Solution

Note: all references are to the Income and Corporation Taxes Act (ICTA) 1988 unless stated otherwise.

Residence of individuals

Residence of individuals in the United Kingdom is not based on citizenship or nationality but largely on a code drawn up by the Inland Revenue following a number of court cases. There is no statutory definition of residence and, together with the allied concept of ordinary residence, its meaning has evolved from the various decisions of the courts and the Commissioners. The courts have largely regarded the question of residence as being one of fact and therefore one on which the Commissioners have the final say in appeal cases.

The provisions of s336 deal with the exclusion from Schedule D and Schedule E liability for a temporary resident who is here 'not with the intention of establishing his residence there' and introduce the concept of a six months' presence being required before the provisions are ineffective.

The code drawn up by the Inland Revenue upon which much of the practice in the matter of residence and ordinary residence is based, is published in a booklet known as 'IR20'. It is said that the code includes the principles of the cases which were decided in favour of the Inland Revenue but ignores those which favoured the taxpayer.

Residence was considered as the 'place of usual abode' in *Levene v IRC* [1928] AC 217 which is based on the ordinary dictionary definition. One of the other leading cases *Lloyd v Sulley* (1884) 2 TC 37 established the rule of a house available to the taxpayer in the UK being sufficient to imply residence unless there was a total absence from the UK throughout the income tax year.

Regular visits over a series of tax years can give rise to residence as in *Cooper v*

Cadwalader (1904) 5 TC 101 where visits of two months in each of three years were held to be sufficient to establish residence here.

A later case of *Reed* v *Clark* [1985] STC 323 held that residence was not lost for the purposes of liability under s334 if absence abroad was for the purpose of occasional residence abroad, having been previously ordinarily resident here.

Under the code of practice, for a person to be resident his presence in the UK must normally be for 183 days in the tax year, unless accommodation is 'available', when one visit will cause residence to arise. The accommodation may be bought or rented but property owned which is not available because it is let will not imply residence.

Residence, once determined, applies strictly for a complete tax year although in practice the Inland Revenue will divide the year under extra-statutory concession A11 for the purpose of establishing income or gains liable to tax in the year of arrival in or departure from the UK.

Ordinary residence is broadly equal to habitual residence so that it is acquired by being in the UK year after year. It is therefore possible for tax purposes to be ordinarily resident in the UK without being resident for the particular year and vice versa.

Residence and ordinary residence are the fundamental requirements for determining prima facie liability to income tax under Schedules D and E (ss18 and 19) and to capital gains tax (s2 of the Taxation of Chargeable Gains Act (TCGA) 1992). Residents are subject to tax on their worldwide income if they are also ordinarily resident and domiciled, whereas those who are non-resident, not ordinarily resident and non-domiciled are generally taxed only on UK source income.

An Inland Revenue consultative document on 'residence in the United Kingdom' (July 1988) acknowledged the 'complex set of rules attempting to codify ancient case law and sketchy statutes'. Due to the increased complexity of taxpayers' affairs and the generally greater mobility of taxpayers and capital the rules are not as relevant as when they were formulated or when the principal cases were decided. The current rules allow for tax-free disposal of capital gains and avoidance of tax on income during periods of absence from the UK.

The rules also lead to major delays in ascertaining certainty of liability to tax since those coming to the UK will be given provisional rulings on their tax status for up to three years if the permanence of their stay cannot be predicted at the outset. Rulings are also given on a provisional basis on a person leaving the UK for other than permanent employment abroad. This complexity is compounded by the question of a single visit bringing liability to UK tax while a number of visits which do not involve presence at midnight on any day are ignored.

In many instances, therefore, the rules for the residence of individuals are unsatisfactory since they lack simplicity, consistency and certainty in their application to a variety of circumstances.

Company residence

'Residence' is the basis of the charge to UK corporation tax on companies' income and gains: ss6 and 11 ICTA 1988 and s2 TCGA 1992. With effect from 15 March 1988 the UK expanded its catchment area for companies regarded as resident in the UK. Until that date companies were regarded as resident here if their central management and control was situated in the UK. From that date, companies which are incorporated in the UK are automatically resident here as are those which satisfied the previous criteria of central management and control, which still remains as a test.

Companies which were incorporated in the UK but non-resident at the above date will become UK resident on 15 March 1993 unless they were carrying on business at 15 March 1988 and emigrated pursuant to a Treasury consent to do so. Other companies incorporated in the UK which emigrate in pursuance of a Treasury consent and which carry on business afterwards, will not become resident on the basis of UK incorporation.

The central management and control test was determined by *De Beers Consolidated Mines* v *Howe* [1906] AC 455 on the basis that 'A company resides, for the purposes of income tax, where its real business is carried on … and the real business is carried on where the central management and control actually abides.' This was supported by subsequent decisions and in particular by *Bullock* v *Unit Construction Company* (1959) 38 TC 712 which described the *De Beers* test 'as precise and unequivocal as a positive statutory injunction' [and] as constituting the test of residence'.

Central management and control has been distinguished in the cases from day to day control and from shareholders' control. In the final analysis it is where the highest policy decisions are made, sometimes evidenced by where the board of directors meet.

The Inland Revenue published a Statement of Practice SP 1/90 on 9 January 1990 setting out how it will apply the central management and control test. In essence it will try to:

a)   ascertain whether the directors in fact exercise central management and control;

b)   determine where they exercise it, being not necessarily where they meet; and

c)   ascertain if the directors do not, then who does, exercise central management and control and where.

There are continuing difficulties which are acknowledged in the Revenue's statement of practice. The first concerns to what extent a parent controls a subsidiary if they operate in different territories. In that case if the parent merely acts as one board member would, it will not be taken to control it. If, however, the subsidiary merely rubber stamps the decisions of the parent then it will regard the subsidiary as resident where the parent is.

The second major difficulty is in the area of applying double taxation treaties where the treaty partner operates a different 'residence' test from that under which a company is being held to be resident in the UK. Both will seek to tax and regard will need to be paid in each treaty case to what is known as the 'tie-breaker' clause to determine where the company's residence lies.

The Revenue also continues to acknowledge that 'The case law test ... is not always easy to apply'.

QUESTION THREE

Jane is employed by Taps Ltd, a company which designs, installs and maintains fitted kitchens and bathrooms. Jane is one of the company's designers. She visits clients in their homes, discusses their plans and then draws up a design and costings. She does this in a studio in her own home and travels to the company's offices only occasionally for meetings. Most of her dealings with the company are by email and fax. Jane uses her own car to travel to clients' houses and is reimbursed her travelling expenses by the company at 42p per mile.

Jane subscribes to several design journals to keep abreast of current trends and to certain on-line technical drawing services which she accesses whilst drawing up her designs. She is entitled, every five years, to have a free fitted bathroom or kitchen from discontinued lines, either for herself or her family. She has recently taken advantage of this to have a new kitchen fitted for her grandmother. Jane has also been appointed by Modern Bathrooms magazine for five years as one of the judges for their annual design award. This involves her looking through all the entries for the award, which are sent to her home, and attending several expenses paid meetings in London.

Advise Jane as to her liability to income tax on these facts.

University of London LLB Examination
(for External Students) Revenue Law June 2002 Q1

General Comment

This question explores the tax implications of benefits received through employment.

Skeleton Solution

Schedule E ICTA 1988: rule in *Tennant* v *Smith* – tax treatment of travel expenses – deductible expenses – 'cash equivalent' is measurement of taxable benefit.

Suggested Solution

Note: all references are to the Income and Corporation Tax Act (ICTA) 1988 unless stated otherwise.

Assuming Jane receives a salary of over £8,500, she will be liable to tax under Schedule E on all 'salaries, fees, wages, perquisites and profits whatsoever' as provided for in s131. Benefits in kind provided to or for an employee by reason of his employment are taxable perquisites by virtue of the combined provisions of the above sections and ss141–146 and 153–165.

Those benefits which can be converted into cash are chargeable on all employees under s19 on their market value. Excluded from the s19 charge are those benefits which cannot be converted into cash. Lord Halsury said in the leading case in this area, *Tennant v Smith* [1892] AC 150, that something sought to be taxed 'is not income unless it can be turned into money'.

Travelling expenses

The reimbursement of travelling expenses was considered in *Pook v Owen* (1971) 45 TC 571, and the House of Lords ruled that the reimbursement was not an emolument of the employment. However, under s153 ICTA 1988 expenses paid to employees earning more than £8,500 are regarded as emoluments, but under ICTA 1988 a deduction can be made from Anne's taxable income for the actual proportion of travel expenses which can be attributed to being incurred by her in the performance of her duties.

Magazine subscriptions

Expenses incurred wholly, exclusively and necessarily in performance of the duties of employment are deductible under Schedule E. In *Smith v Abbott* and *Fitzpatrick v IRC* [1994] STC 237, groups of journalists were denied a deduction for the cost of newspapers purchased and read in connection with their employment. The House of Lords ruled that the expenses were incurred to enable the journalists to perform the duties of their employment better and were not incurred in the actual performance of those duties. It would be likely that Jane's subscriptions to the design journals would be seen in the same light and, therefore, not deductible.

Free fitted bathroom or kitchen

Benefits provided for both an employee and his family are taxable. Jane will therefore be liable for a tax charge equivalent to the cost incurred by Taps Ltd in providing the new kitchen for her grandmother.

Expenses incidental to appointment as judge

The payment of expenses is a taxable emolument under s153(1) and is included in Jane's income for assessment purposes. She may claim a deduction for expenses wholly and exclusively and necessarily incurred in the performance of her duties as a judge.

Chapter 9

Taxation of Income of Partnerships

9.1   **Introduction**

9.2   **Key points**

9.3   **Key case and statutes**

9.1 Introduction

Section 1 of the Partnership Act 1890 defines a partnership as 'the relation which subsists between persons carrying on business in common with a view to profit'.

9.2 Key points

Assessment

A partnership in England is not a separate legal entity but a collection of individuals. Section 111 ICTA 1988 computes the liability jointly but by reference to each member's personal tax position. Liability is placed on the partnership so that each partner is liable not only for his own share but jointly for the entire sum.

Self-assessment

a) Composite partnership tax return required, to include each partner's share of income and gains: ss12AA and 12AB TMA 1970.

b) Individual partners to submit own tax return inclusive of share of partnership income: s8(1B) TMA 1970.

c) Individual partners return to include self-assessment of their liability, inclusive of the partnership income and gains: s9(1) TMA 1970.

Profits and losses

Profits and losses are allocated for tax purposes according to the sharing ratio which prevails for the accounting year on which the income or loss is based.

a) Partners' salaries and interest on capital put into the partnership are not a deduction from profits but are a distribution of profit. Taxable profits are allocated first by reference to salaries and interest and the balance by reference to profit sharing ratios.

b) Rents paid to partners for use of premises are however deductible – the property is not partnership property.

c) Partners' personal expenses are not deductible: see *MacKinlay* v *Arthur Young McClelland Moores* [1990] STC 898.

d) Losses arising to individual partners from the allocation in (a) – ie, if these amounts exceed taxable profits – are not claimable unless the partnership itself has made a taxable loss. Differing types of loss claims may be made (ss380 and 385) by individual partners.

e) Profits allocated to a company member of a partnership are charged to corporation tax: ss114–116.

f) Limited partnerships – rules to restrict allowable losses to capital invested – ss117 and 118: *Reed* v *Young* [1986] 1 WLR 649; [1986] STC 285.

Change of partners

a) Change gives rise to a cessation and new business: s113 only in so far as the new or retiring partners are concerned.

b) Where a partnership ceases, each partner is assessed on his share of profits in the final year, based on the profits from the end of the accounting period which formed the basis of assessment for the year preceding the final year, up to the date of cessation – eg a partnership whose accounts year ends annually on 31 August will be assessed for 2000–01 on profits for the year ended 31 August 2000. If it ceases on 30 September 2001, the taxable profits for each partner for 2001–02 will be those for the period from 1 September 2000 to 30 September 2001. If the partnership continues but a partner retires on 30 September 2001, he will be taxed for 2001–02 on the same 13-month period mentioned above, whereas continuing partners will be taxed on their share of profits for the year ended 31 August 2000.

c) New partners joining a partnership are taxed as if they commenced a new business at that date.

See Chapter 8 regarding assessment of income from foreign partnership.

Capital gains

Capital gains of partnerships are dealt with in Chapter 18.

Limited liability partnerships

A limited liability partnership (LLP) is designed to build onto the flexible nature of partnership activity some of the limitation of liability normally associated with registered companies, where limitation by shares or guarantee is the norm. The LLP arose out of the Limited Liability Partnership Act 2000, operative from 6 April 2001. For liability purposes, the members a LLP are only liable to the extent of their capital contribution. However, like a traditional partnership, the management of the LLP is left to the members. In term of tax consequences, the normal fiscal transparency will continue to apply, despite the corporate legal nature of the LLP.

9.3 Key case and statutes

* *Stekel* v *Ellice* [1973] 1 WLR 191
  Partnership taxation – computation of profits – partners' salaries

* Finance Act 1994, ss184–189

* Finance Act 1995, s117

* Income and Corporation Taxes Act 1988, s112

* Limited Liability Partnership Act 2000

Chapter 10

Schedule D Case VI

10.1   Introduction

10.2   Key points

10.3   Key cases and statute

10.1 Introduction

Schedule D Case VI taxes profits not falling within any other schedule. It is sometimes referred to as the catch-all schedule and is used to tax certain types of receipts (post-cessation receipts of a business – ss103 and 104 ICTA 1988) as well as being the vehicle whereby some of the anti-avoidance sections in the legislation are put into effect. For example the tax benefit of a transaction in securities (s703(3) ICTA 1988), transfers of assets abroad (ss739(4)–776(3)) and the capital profit derived from what were previously termed 'artificial transactions in land' under s776(3) ICTA 1988 are turned into taxable amounts by deeming the relevant amount to fall within Case VI. Similarly, the settlement anti-avoidance provisions of ss660A–660G dictate that any resulting charge on the settlor (under s660C) will be under Schedule D Case VI. Also taxed under Case VI – the 'catching up' charge on the change to 'true and fair view' accounting, discussed at Chapter 5.

See Chapter 4 on Schedule A for FA 1995 changes to the tax in income from property, which will now take furnished letting and lease premiums into Schedule A which was previously Case VI income.

10.2 Key points

One of the main points is that Schedule D Case VI is used to tax a receipt which might otherwise arise as a Schedule D Case I profit but for the steps taken etc to try to avoid its being taxable. Where it becomes subject to the anti-avoidance sections, being within Case VI means that it loses its trading income characteristics and accordingly, for example, the ability to absorb loss relief.

Scope of the charge: s18(3) ICTA 1988

Section 18(3) charges tax 'in respect of any annual profits or gains not falling within any other case of Schedule D and not charged by virtue of Schedule A or E'.

In addition certain types of income fall under Case VI by means of specific statutory provisions, eg post-cessation receipts – ss103(1) and 104(1) ICTA 1988 – and the 'catching up' charge on the change to 'true and fair view' accounting, discussed at Chapter 5: Sch 6, para 2(2)(b) FA 1998.

Income not taxable under Case VI

a) Capital receipts (ie Case VI taxes only 'income' but some anti-avoidance sections – eg s776(3)(a) treats capital as being income and taxes it under Case VI.

b) Profits resembling trading profits: *Jones* v *Leeming* [1930] AC 415.

'Annual'

There is no requirement of recurrency. 'Annual' means in a particular year of assessment. See *Hobbs* v *Hussey* [1942] 1 KB 491.

Furnished lettings and furnished holiday lettings

Section 15(1) ICTA 1988: previously taxed under Case VI – now wholly within Schedule A – including furnished holiday lettings: s503(1)(a).

Assessment, losses and capital allowances

a) Current year basis.

b) Losses under Case VI may be set off against other Case VI profits only, in the same or future years.

10.3 Key cases and statute

- *Hobbs* v *Hussey* [1942] 1 KB 491
  Schedule D Case VI – annual profits – no requirement of recurrency

- *Jones* v *Leeming* [1930] AC 415
  Scope of the charge – isolated transaction of sale

- Income and Corporation Taxes Act 1988, ss18 and 392

Chapter 11

Schedule D Case III

11.1 **Introduction**

11.2 **Key points**

11.3 **Key cases and statutes**

11.4 **Questions and suggested solutions**

11.1 Introduction

The charge to income tax under Schedule D Case III is imposed by s18(3) ICTA 1988 and relates to tax in respect of 'any interest of money ... or an annuity or other annual payment [and] all discounts [and] income from securities ... out of the public revenue of the United Kingdom or Northern Ireland.' With effect from 6 April 1996 Schedule C (public revenue securities) was abolished and income previously charged under that Schedule became chargeable under Schedule D Case III.

Corporation tax – 'loan relationships'

For corporation tax purposes in regard to accounting periods ending after 31 March 1996, s18(3) is redefined to include 'profits and gains arising from loan relationships'. The effect of the new provisions, brought in by Finance Act 1996, are that both capital and revenue profits from corporate and government securities are charged as income for corporation tax purposes. Those entered into for trading purposes give rise to Case I receipts, others give rise to Case III income. In addition, where this income might previously have been assessed under Case V because of a foreign source, it too becomes subject to the new 'loan relationships', regime under Schedule D Case I or III – see Chapter 15.

The enactment of s347A ICTA 1988 led to significant changes of the tax treatment of covenants made after 15 March 1988 within the Schedule. It means that certain payments – mainly concerning deeds of covenant and maintenance payments – may not be considered as a charge on the income of the payer nor form part of the payee's income and that no deduction may be made by the payer.

Where a covenant has been made before 15 March 1988, ie an obligation existed prior to this date (see s36(3) FA 1988), then the 'old' rules apply, ie the above presumptions do not apply. Covenanted payments to charity were taken out of the Case III net and dealt with under Gift Aid as a result of the FA 2000.

The main means of collection of tax on Schedule D Case III income is by deduction at source on payment – includes bank and building society deposit account interest – ss4, 348 and 349 ICTA 1988. The rate of deduction is set at basic rate by s4(1) for annuities and annual payments – s1A(2)(a)(i) but lower rate for interest and other savings income – s4(1A) and s1A(2)(a).

11.2 Key points

Interest

Bennett v *Oyster* (1930) 15 TC 374: 'payment by time for the use of money'. It is presumed that there is a capital sum owed, per Megarry J in *Re Euro Hotel (Belgravia) Ltd* [1975] 3 All ER 1075: 'Interest is, in general terms, the return or consideration or compensation for the use or retention by one person of a sum of money belonging to ... or owed to another.' It presupposes the existence of a debt. Another leading case is *Chevron Petroleum (UK) Ltd* v *BP Petroleum Development Ltd* [1981] STC 689, in which a payment made to adjust the ratios in which each of these two companies had contributed to the cost of oil field developments included an 'interest factor' to adjust for the fact that one had effectively borne part of the contribution due by the other and therefore to whom the sum was due. The interest factor element of the payment was adjudged to be interest.

The four tests to be satisfied from these three leading cases are:

a) Is the payment calculated by reference to a sum of money?

b) Is that sum of money due from one person to another?

c) Is the payment calculated by reference to a period for which the sum in (b) is outstanding?

d) Does it represent 'payment by time for the use of money' or 'compensation for delay in payment'?

Annuity

Foley v *Fletcher and Rose* (1858) 28 LJ Ex 100, per Watson B: 'An annuity means when an income is purchased with a sum of money and the capital ... has ceased to exist.'

Annual payments

There is no definition in the legislation, but Jenkins LJ in *IRC* v *Whitworth Park Coal Co* [1958] 2 All ER 91, at 102, stated six criteria:

a) they must be construed ejusdem generis with annuities and interest;

b) there must be a legal obligation to pay the sum: *Stedeford* v *Beloe* [1932] AC 388;

c) they must be capable of recurrence: *Moss Empires* v *IRC* [1937] AC 785;

d) they must be income (as opposed to capital) in the hands of the payee:

   i) payment by instalments: *Foley* v *Fletcher and Rose* (1858) 3 H & N 769 and *IRC* v *Hogarth* (1940) 23 TC 79;

   ii) income transactions: *IRC* v *Church Commissioners for England* [1976] 2 All ER 1037;

   iii) dissection into capital and income: *Secretary of State in Council of India* v *Scoble* [1903] AC 299 and *Vestey* v *IRC* [1961] 3 All ER 976;

e) they must be pure profit income in the hands of payee, ie should not be able to make any deductions from the income before it is taxed:

   i) income of payee: *Campbell* v *IRC* [1968] 3 All ER 588;

   ii) receipts of trade or profession: *Howe* v *IRC* [1919] 2 KB 336;

   iii) counter stipulations by the payer: *IRC* v *National Book League* [1957] 2 All ER 644;

f) income must not be charged under Schedule A.

Discounts

Ditchfield v *Sharp* [1983] STC 590 provides an indication of modern meaning of 'discount'. It refers to the dictionary meaning as 'the deduction made from the amount of a bill of exchange … by one who gives value for it before it is due'. For corporation tax purposes, discounts are taxed under the 'loan relationships' provisions of FA 1996: ss80–105 and Schedules 8–15.

Compare differences between a discount and a premium: see *Lomax* v *Peter Dixon Ltd* 25 TC 353. Where a commercial rate of interest has been applied to the loan it will indicate a premium; if not, then a discount.

Basis of assessment: s64

For income falling under Schedule D Case III, the basis of assessment is made on the income of the current year of assessment. Under s1A ICTA 1988, all Case III income (and income – collectively called 'savings income' is charged to the lower rate (as opposed to the basic rate) of income tax, unless the taxpayer is liable to tax at the higher rate. The lower rate applies to individuals, personal representatives of deceased persons and trustees of life interest trusts and the withholding of tax at source from such income is confined to tax at the lower rate: s4(1A) ICTA 1988.

Deduction at source

Section 348 applies the deduction at source principle to Case III amounts other than interest where the payments are made out of profits or gains brought into charge to income tax. The recipient must permit the deduction. Payments to which ss119 or 120 apply (relating to rents for mines and quarries and electric wayleaves) are subject to this mechanism.

Section 349 applies the deduction at source principle where non-interest Case III income is paid out of profits which have not been subject to income tax. It also applies the deduction to certain payments of annual interest.

Under both sections, the rate of tax deducted at source is the lower rate of tax: see also s4(1A) ICTA 1988.

Section 348

Section 348 allows the payer to retain the tax deducted if the payment is made 'wholly out of profits or gains brought into charge to income tax' – ie the payer has already accounted for the tax to which the payment relates.

Section 349

Section 349(1) applies a deduction at source mechanism to payments other than interest payable wholly or partly from income which is not subjected to tax, and s350 assesses the payer for the tax withheld.

Section 349(2) provides the means of deducting tax from annual interest payments made by (a) a company, (b) a partnership which has a corporate member, (c) any person to a non-resident – with exceptions for payments to and from banks in the ordinary course of their UK business.

For the distinction between s348 and s349 see *IRC* v *Whitworth Park Coal Co* [1961] AC 31; (1959) 38 TC 531.

Annual interest and short interest

'Annual interest' means interest on an obligation which is intended to mature in a year or more. Anything else is 'short interest'.

Section 350

After payment has been made the payer must inform the Inland Revenue who will then assess him to basic or lower rate tax: see s350(1A) ICTA 1988. The payee receives a net payment and Form IR 185 to account for the tax paid.

Failure to deduct

Sections 348 and 349: failure by the payer to deduct confers no penalty under s348. Although s350 refers to collection from the payer, the payee may be assessed: *Grosvenor Place Estates* v *Roberts* [1961] 1 All ER 341; (1960) 39 TC 433.

There is no right of later recovery by the payer – the words 'shall on making the payment deduct' were plain: *Tenbry Investments Ltd* v *Peugeot Talbot Motor Co Ltd* [1992] STC 791

TMA 1970, s106(2)

'... every agreement for payment of interest ... or other annual payment in full without allowing for any deduction shall be void.'

It is not therefore possible to ignore ss348 and 349, since s106(2) TMA 1970 operates to void this clause in an agreement.

Title to income

See *Peracha* v *Miley* [1989] STC 512, where interest on an account held by a bank as security against company borrowings was held to belong to the individual taxpayer and assessable on him.

11.3 Key cases and statute

- *Bennett* v *Oyster* (1930) 15 TC 374
  Schedule D Case III – definition of interest

- *Chevron Petroleum (UK) Ltd* v *BP Petroleum Development Ltd* [1981] STC 689
  Schedule D Case III – definition of interest

- *Ditchfield* v *Sharp* [1983] STC 590
  Schedule D Case III – taxation of discounts

- *Euro Hotel (Belgravia) Ltd, Re* [1975] 3 All ER 1075
  Schedule D Case III – definition of interest

- *IRC* v *Whitworth Park Coal Co* [1958] 2 All ER 91
  Schedule D Case III – annual payments

- Income and Corporation Taxes Act 1988, ss1A, 4(1A), 18(3), 347A–347B and 348–349

11.4 Question and suggested solution

a) What is meant by 'other annual payments' within s18(3) ICTA 1988?

b) What types of interest are taxable under Schedule D Case III?

Written by the Author

General Comment

This question analyses the term 'other annual payments' within s18(3) ICTA 1988.

Skeleton Solution

Annual payments: *IRC v Whitworth Park Coal Co Ltd* criteria – meaning of 'annual': *Moss Empires Ltd* v *IRC* – pure income profit: *Howe* v *IRC* – excludes capital payments and payments subject to pre-tax deductions.

Suggested Solution

a) There is no statutory definition of 'other annual payments': s18(3) ICTA 1988. The courts have, however, through a series of decisions, given us certain characteristics which are required for a payment to be an 'other annual payment'.

   In *IRC v Whitworth Park Coal Co Ltd* [1958] 2 All ER 91 it was held that the payment must be ejusdem generis with 'interest' and 'annuities', as if s18 reads 'any interest ... annuity or similar such payment'.

   Furthermore, the payment should have been made under a legally binding obligation such as a deed of covenant or court order. A voluntary payment will not fulfil the definition. The legal obligation may, however, arise through a contract under seal so that no consideration is necessary.

   'Annual' in this sense means only that the payment must be capable of recurrence: *Moss Empires Ltd* v *IRC* [1937] AC 785. It is irrelevant that the liability to pay gives no indication of the amount of the payment to be made.

   The payment must be pure income profit in the hands of the payee: *Howe* v *IRC* [1919] 2 KB 336. Thus a capital payment will not satisfy s18 and neither will any payment subject to any deductions before tax is calculated.

   If the payment is made in return for goods or services it will not be an annual payment and this rule has been applied to elaborate schemes for the payment of school fees by deed of covenant in return for education: *Campbell* v *IRC* [1970] AC 77.

   Where the payment is made to a charity, the presence of a counter-stipulation need not deprive the payment of the quality of pure profit income.

b) Examples of interest taxable under Schedule D Case III include:

   i) Interest from ordinary and investment accounts with the National Savings Bank. However, per s325 ICTA 1988 the first £70 of any such interest received in any one year of assessment is tax free.

   ii) Interest on a loan (except for company trading purposes loans: see Chapter 15 regarding 'loan relationships').

   iii) Income received from government stocks is usually received after deduction of lower rate tax and following the abolition of Schedule C by FA 1996, is taxable under Schedule D Case III. There may, nevertheless, be a tax credit given or extra tax to pay depending on the highest marginal rate of the recipient.

   iv) Short and annual interest.

Chapter 12

Trust Income

12.1   Introduction

12.2   Key points

12.3   Key cases and statutes

12.4   Questions and suggested solutions

12.1 Introduction

Two groups of people may fall liable to tax on trust income:

a) Trustees receiving income of the trust.

b) Beneficiaries receiving income from trustees, ie from the trust.

12.2 Key points

Taxation of trustees

a) No specific statutory provision renders trustees liable to income tax in their capacity as trustees.

b) Sections 15 and 18 ICTA 1988 charge tax on 'the persons receiving or entitled to the income' (Schedules A and D).

c) TMA 1970 contains specific provisions relating to trustees, eg ss72 and 73.

d) For when trustees are liable in general see Viscount Cave in *Williams* v *Singer* [1921] 1 AC 41; *Reid's Trustees* v *IRC* (1929) 14 TC 512; *Dawson* v *IRC* [1989] 2 WLR 858; [1989] STC 473.

Note: the effects of *Dawson* were countered by FA 1989 s110 so that a trust with at least one UK trustee is liable to income tax on UK income providing the settlor was resident, ordinarily resident or domiciled in the UK when the funds were settled or, in the case of a will trust, at the time of his death.

The scope of the charge on trustees

'Trustees' liable to tax are not 'individuals', so that:

a) they are not entitled to personal allowances;

b) trustees of life interest trusts pay only basic rate tax: s1(2) ICTA 1988 and *IRC v Countess of Longford* [1928] AC 252. They do however pay tax on 'savings income' at only the lower rate of tax: s1A ICTA 1988. Trustees of discretionary trusts are liable to additional rate tax (the combined tax rate is now referred to – see s686(1A) ICTA 1988 – as 'the rate applicable to trusts') under s686 ICTA 1988. The rate is currently 34 per cent. From 6 April 1999 the rate applicable to dividend income is also set by s686(1A)(a) at 25 per cent (the 'Schedule F trust rate') for life interest trusts and 34 per cent for discretionary trusts.

Taxation of beneficiaries

Note: trust income paid to a beneficiary will already have suffered tax at either the lower rate or the special trust rate of tax. The ultimate liability depends on the beneficiary's own marginal rate of tax.

a) Beneficiary with a vested right to income: see *Baker v Archer-Shee* [1927] AC 844.

   Any sums received by the trustees for the purpose of paying income to the beneficiaries will be treated as the income in the hands of the beneficiaries.

   Any tax already paid by the trustees on such sums will be seen as paid on behalf of the beneficiaries: *IRC v Hamilton-Russell's Executors* [1943] 1 All ER 474.

   This is true even if the trustees do not actually pay the beneficiaries.

b) Where a beneficiary has a vested interest in income which is contingent or at the discretion of the trustee, the beneficiary cannot be liable to income tax until actual receipt of the income.

c) Maintenance, advancement and protection trusts

   Read s31 Trustee Act 1925. There are four income tax consequences for infant beneficiaries under s31:

   i) Only an infant beneficiary with a vested and absolute interest in personalty can be liable to higher rate tax on undistributed trust income.

   ii) An infant with only a vested interest is not liable to income tax on undistributed income: see *Stanley v IRC* [1944] 1 KB 255.

   iii) Where an infant with no vested interest in capital, receives income, he is liable to income tax.

   iv) An infant who satisfies a contingency requiring him to reach any age over 18 and obtains a vested interest in income will thereafter be liable to income tax whether or not he actually receives the income: *IRC v Hamilton-Russell's Executors*.

Taxation of settlors

a) The settlor of a trust who retains an interest in the trust property or income, will be taxed on the income arising from it: s660A(1).

b) A settlor retains an interest if the property or any income from it is capable of being applied for the benefit of the settlor or the settlor's spouse: s660A(2).

c) Circumstances in which the settlor's interest is excluded from s660A(1) include accumulation and maintenance trusts, marriage settlements and where the settlor's benefit or interest arises from bankruptcy: s660A(4)–(9).

Sections 686 and 687 ICTA 1988

Section 686 charges additional rate tax (the combined tax rate is now referred to – see ICTA 1988 s686(1A) – as 'the rate applicable to trusts') on trustees of certain discretionary trusts. The rate is currently 34 per cent. From 6 April 1999 the rate applicable to dividend income is also set by s686(1A)(a) at 25 per cent (the 'Schedule F trust rate') for life interest trusts and 34 per cent for discretionary trusts.

Section 687 ensures that distributions of trust income which have already borne income tax and additional rate tax are not subject to double taxation. However as explained in Chapter 3, the tax credit on dividends paid on or after 6 April 1999 is not repayable. From that date a trustee may not deduct dividend tax credits when accounting for tax at 34 per cent under ss686–687. The net result is to reduce the trust income available for distribution through the requirement to account for tax, and the income of the beneficiary therefore includes only repayable tax credits – at 34 per cent.

Payments out of capital treated as income

Some capital payments from a trust may be seen as income in the hands of the beneficiary: see *Brodie's Will Trustees* v *IRC* (1933) 17 TC 432, per Finlay J; *Stevenson* v *Wishart* [1987] STC 266; *Cunard's Trustees* v *IRC* [1946] 1 All ER 159.

Income tax and the administration of an estate

Personal representatives

Personal representatives are liable to income tax on any income arising during the administration of an estate (*note*: no additional rate applies). Schedule 18 para 2 FA 1995 amended s695 ICTA 1988 in respect of administrations completed after 5 April 1995 – determining the year of assessment of the relevant income. *Note*: for capital gains made on or after 6 April 1998, personal representatives are liable for the increased rate of tax – the 'rate applicable to trusts' under s686 ICTA 1988: s4(1AA) TCGA 1992, inserted by s120 FA 1998.

Beneficiaries under a will

See ss695–702 ICTA 1988: *Commissioner of Stamp Duties (Queensland)* v *Livingston* [1965] AC 694.

Legacies and annuities

a) Interest may be payable to the legatee of a general legacy and any interest so paid is treated as Schedule D, Case III income of the legatee: see *Dewar* v *IRC* [1935] 2 KB 351.

b) Interest due to the legatee of a specific legacy will be treated as income of the legatee from the date of death unless the will provides otherwise.

c) Annuities will be seen as income of the annuitant from the date of death.

12.3 Key cases and statutes

*   *Baker* v *Archer-Shee* [1927] AC 844 (HL)
    Trust income – taxation of beneficiaries

*   *Dawson* v *IRC* [1989] 2 WLR 858
    Trust income – taxation of trustees – liability to income tax

*   *IRC* v *Countess of Longford* [1928] AC 252
    Trust income – scope of charge on trustees – life interest trusts

*   *IRC* v *Hamilton-Russell's Executors* [1943] 1 All ER 474
    Trust income – taxation of beneficiaries

*   *Reid's Trustees* v *IRC* (1929) 14 TC 512
    Trust income – taxation of trustees – liability to income tax

*   *Stanley* v *IRC* [1944] 1 KB 255
    Trust income – taxation of beneficiaries – maintenance, advancement and protection trusts

*   *Williams* v *Singer* [1921] 1 AC 41
    Trust income – taxation of trustees – liability to income tax

*   Income and Corporation Taxes Act 1988, ss686(1A) and 660A–660G

*   Taxes Management Act 1970, ss72–73

*   Trustee Act 1925, s31

12.4 Questions and suggested solutions

QUESTION ONE

In 1997 Edna transferred £100,000 and some profitable farm land to Fiona and Gerald as trustees on trust for sale for Edna's children, Harold and Imogen, equally. On 6 April 2002 Harold was 14 and Imogen was 19. In 2002–2003 the income arising from the farm land for income tax purposes was £15,000 and the income arising by way of bank deposit interest from the fund of money was £7,500. During the year Fiona and Gerald paid Harold's school fees of £2,500 but accumulated the remainder of the income. Advise Edna, Fiona and Gerald, who seek your opinion on the income tax implications of these facts.

Would your advice be different if the settlement had been made by Joan, Edna's mother?

Adapted fromUniversity of London LLB Examination
(for External Students) Revenue Law June 1984 Q3

General Comment

This question illustrates the principles of taxing income arising from a trust.

Skeleton Solution

Settlements on children: s670 ICTA 1988 – element of bounty required: *IRC v Plummer; Thomas v Marshall* – accumulation and maintenance settlement: ss660A–660B ICTA 1988 – trustees' income tax liability; persons receiving or entitled to the income; s21 – beneficiary's entitlement to tax credit – s686 ICTA 1988 regime not applicable to interest in possession trusts: *Stanley v IRC* – application of s660B if settlement by non-parent.

Suggested Solution

Section 660G ICTA 1988 defines a 'settlement', for the purposes of the anti-avoidance provisions relating to trusts created for the benefit of the settlor's infant children, as including 'any disposition, trust, covenant, agreement, arrangement, or transfer of assets'.

This extraordinarily wide definition appears only to be limited by the principle in *IRC v Plummer* [1980] AC 896 that it does not apply to any transaction which does not involve an 'element of bounty'. Thus, as *Thomas v Marshall* [1953] AC 543 showed, the simple act of opening a post office account in the name of your infant child creates a settlement ('a transfer of assets') within s670. So, too, here the transfer of the £100,000 and the conveyance of the farmland trustees in trust for Edna's children absolutely, creates a settlement within that section.

Thereafter, by general trust law, half the income will belong to Imogen absolutely and the other half will be accumulated in trust for Harold on attaining 18 – it is only the fact that Harold cannot give a good receipt which prevents him obtaining the income immediately. Clearly, therefore, this will be an irrevocable accumulation trust within ss660A(5) ICTA 1988: Edna cannot in any way ever hope to enjoy the benefit of the property again. Section 660B states that where, by virtue of any settlement not falling within the general provisions of s660A and during the life of the settlor, income is paid to or for the benefit of a child of the settlor, the income, if the child is unmarried and under the age of 18, is treated as for all the purposes of the Taxes Acts, as the income of the settlor and not as the income of any other person. That is to say, it is treated as Edna's and as Harold's.

The mechanics of taxation for 2002–03 will, thus, be as follows:

a) The £15,000 income from the farmland will, presumably be rental income chargeable to tax under Schedule A. The income will be assessed on a current year basis (s22(2) ICTA 1988) and will be assessed on the trustees as the persons receiving or entitled to the profits and gains: s21. Being trustees, they will be liable to tax at the basic rate only: trustees are not an 'individual' and higher rate tax is only imposed, by s1(2) ICTA 1988, on the total income of an individual. If liable under Schedule D Case I, they will by now be liable on a preceding year basis under s60(1) ICTA 1988 on the profits arising in the accounting period ending in the preceding year of assessment. Again, they would only be liable at the basic rate.

b) They will receive bank interest for 2002–03 gross under s349(2) ICTA 1988 and will be charged under Schedule D Case III. Under s64 ICTA 1988 income tax under Schedule D Case III, is computed on the full amount of the income arising in the preceding year of assessment, so tax will actually be payable by the trustees on the £7,500 in 2003–04, once more at the basic rate alone. *Note*: Interest is paid now net of tax and the basis of assessment has changed to current year basis after 1996–97 and the tax rate on 'savings income' is restricted to the lower rate.

Technically, the trustees are in breach of trust in not distributing to Imogen her half share of £11,250 (or perhaps, the net sum corresponding to the gross sum of £1,250, since they will be entitled sufficient income to discharge their own tax liability), unless Imogen has expressly consented to the retention. Imogen will, in any event, be taxable on the income as if she had received it: *IRC v Hamilton Russell's Executors* [1943] 1 All ER 474. She will be chargeable under the appropriate Schedules – Schedule D Case I or Schedule A and Schedule D Case III – but this time, as an individual, she will bring the gross sum into the total income and, as an individual, will possibly be liable to tax at the higher rates. The tax paid by the trustees will be credited against her own liability and she will be able to reduce the amount of the £11,250 by any unused personal allowance she may have. If this results in a total tax liability below that paid by the trustees, she will be able to make a repayment claim for the excess.

As far as Harold's half share is concerned, the only reason why he too is not entitled both to the income and his part of the trust capital is because, being an infant, he cannot give a good receipt for it. Section 686 ICTA 1988 does not, therefore, apply because the income is Harold's before being distributed, since he has a vested and absolute interest in it: *Stanley* v *IRC* [1944] 1 KB 255. When the trustees pay out £2,500 on his behalf in school fees, this will be paid out of taxed income and must, therefore, be grossed up at the basic rate. The sum so found must then be treated as Edna's income under s663 ICTA 1988. The undistributed remainder will be subject to income tax at Harold's tax rates, enabling the Revenue to assess the trustees at the higher rates of tax if Harold has any other income but requiring them to give them credit for any part of Harold's personal allowances which may not otherwise have been exhausted; his vested and absolute interest results in the income being treated as Harold's, even though not distributed. Section 660B ICTA 1988 will not apply to this income, though, since there will have been no application of it, as required by the section.

The difference which would flow from the settlor being Joan would be the exclusion of s660B ICTA 1988: all income to which Harold was entitled, whether distributed or not, would simply be treated as his and would be charged at his tax rates.

QUESTION TWO

With reference to decided cases, show how beneficiaries of a trust are subject to income tax on trust income.

Written by the Author

General Comment

This question explores the tax liability of trust beneficiaries on trust income.

Skeleton Solution

Beneficiary's liability for income tax: interest in possession, accumulation, discretionary trusts – distribution under discretion – arising basis for life tenant: *IRC* v *Hamilton-Russell's Executors* – annuitant: *Woodhouse* v *IRC* – direct and indirect distributions to beneficiaries: *IRC* v *Miller*, *IRC* v *Wemyss* – distributions on other circumstances: *Brodie's Will Trustees* v *IRC*, *Lindsay & Hostin* v *IRC* – whether distributions of income nature: *Stevenson* v *Wishart*.

Suggested Solution

Taxation of trust income for beneficiaries

A beneficiary under a trust will include the following amounts as part of his total income for income tax purposes:

a) trust income in which he has a vested interest, whether or not it is paid to him or accumulated in the trust;

b) amounts of an income nature applied under the terms of the trust for his benefit;

c) amounts of an income nature paid at the discretion of the trustees to or for his benefit.

The amounts thus treated as income will be grossed up at the basic rate, or, where appropriate, the basic and additional rates and taxes on the beneficiary as part of his income for the year of assessment concerned. The beneficiary's personal allowances may be available and the income may be liable to the higher rates. A tax credit for tax deducted by the trustees as evidenced by a form R185E will be available. Note that composite rate tax passed on by the trustees cannot lead to a repayment for the beneficiary.

It is possible for payments out of capital to be treated as payments of income where the beneficiary uses the receipt to pay on-going 'income' expenses.

A beneficiary who is a life tenant will be entitled to the income of the trust as it arises, regardless of whether it is actually paid out or accumulated and he will be subject to income tax on this entitlement: *IRC v Hamilton-Russell's Executors* [1943] 1 All ER 474. However, if the beneficiary has a right only to an annuity and not to the actual income or a part of the income of the trust, he will only be assessed if the annuity is paid: *Woodhouse v IRC* (1936) 20 TC 673.

Amounts paid at the discretion of the trustees to, or for the benefit of, a beneficiary are subject to income tax on the beneficiary as part of his income for the year of assessment when they are paid. This also applies where a beneficiary's right to income is vested but the trustees have an overriding power to divest him of it.

If a beneficiary is entitled to have amounts of trust income paid for his benefit those amounts paid form part of his income: *IRC v Miller* [1930] AC 222. This applies where the income is paid in accordance with his instructions instead of being paid direct to him unless he has disposed of his right to the income: *IRC v Wemyss* (1924) 8 TC 551.

Payments to a beneficiary will be treated as income, not necessarily because they were made out of trust income but because they take on the nature of income in the beneficiary's hands. Thus payments out of capital will be taxed on the beneficiary as income if:

a) the trustees were directed under a trust deed to make up a deficiency of trust income payments to a beneficiary out of trust capital: *Brodie's Will Trustees v IRC* (1933) 17 TC 432; or

b) the trustees exercise a discretion to make regular payments out of capital to augment a beneficiary's income: *Lindsay and Hostin v IRC* (1933) 18 TC 43.

Payments out of capital which are thereby treated as annual payments will be income of the beneficiary under Schedule D, Case III. It will be received net of tax (basic and, if appropriate, additional rate) and grossed up as income in the normal way. The trustees will have to account for basic rate tax on the payment and may be assessed under s687 ICTA 1988 to cover any deficit resulting on the 'tax pool' of credits used to cover R185 payments.

Exceptions to the income nature will apply as follows:

a) If the recipient is also entitled to the capital he will not be taxed to income as it is paid to him. For example, a beneficiary who becomes absolutely entitled to the trust capital at age 30 might be given part of the capital at an earlier age perhaps to become accustomed to managing part of the capital before receiving all of it.

b) In *Stevenson* v *Wishart* [1987] STC 266 large regular payments out of a trust for an elderly beneficiary's nursing home fees were treated as capital, contrary to the Revenue's assertions, despite the fact that the beneficiary was a potential beneficiary of the trust income. All the trust income had been distributed to other beneficiaries. The courts seemed to have based their decision on the fact that the trustees could appoint capital to her and did so.

c) The Revenue prefer 'income' to 'capital' if income tax on the beneficiary and, where necessary, the trustees, exceeds the inheritance tax chargeable on the trust. Thus small payments of capital which would be covered by the recipient's unusued personal allowances will not usually be deemed to be income.

d) Where income to which a beneficiary has a vested right is accumulated, the income is taxed on the beneficiary. However, where the beneficiary has only a contingent right to the income, any income accumulated becomes capital. When the accumulated income is eventually paid out it has taken on the nature of capital and the beneficiary is not chargeable to income tax thereon: *IRC* v *Blackwell Minor's Trustee* [1926] 1 KB 389.

QUESTION THREE

a) Samuel transferred assets valued at £300,000 in April 1999 to trustees to hold upon trust to invest in such investments as the trustees should think fit and thereafter to hold the income and capital upon discretionary trusts in favour of a wide class of objects including his children, grandchildren and several charities.

In 2001–02 the trustees received a substantial income from the trust assets and made the following payments in exercise of their discretion:

i) £10,000 to one of the trust charities

ii) £10,000 to Samuel's grandson who is aged 22 and just starting up his own business

iii) £10,000 to Samuel's daughter who already has a large income but who has an extravagant lifestyle.

Advise on the income tax consequences of these facts.

b) Susan transferred assets valued at £300,000 in April 1999 to trustees to hold on trust for such of her grandchildren as should attain the age of 21, remainder to the National Trust, a charity. In April 1999 she had two grandsons who were aged 11 and 13.

In 2001–02 the trustees used some of the trust income to pay the expensive private school fees of the two grandsons and they accumulated the rest.

Advise on the income tax consequences of the above facts.

Adapted from University of London LLB Examination
(for External Students) Revenue Law June 1992 Q5

General Comment

This question focuses on the tax implications of income arising from discretionary trusts and accumulation and maintenance trusts.

Skeleton Solution

a) Income tax effective for settlor, when 'income' of beneficiary – discretionary trust regime: additional rate of tax – addition to other income, additional tax on beneficiary or repayment using personal allowances or losses – higher rate tax liability.

b) Nature of accumulation and maintenance trust: rate of tax on income – when 'income' of the beneficiaries – repayment of tax for beneficiaries on distribution – taking accumulated income as capital – after attainment of majority.

Suggested Solution

a) The setting up of the discretionary trust will be effective for income tax purposes and will relieve Samuel from income tax liability on the income from the assets transferred into trust.

The trustees become liable for payment of income tax arising on the income, not only at the basic rate of tax but at an additional rate of 10 per cent levied on discretionary trusts.

Where income is paid to a beneficiary the payment is regarded as one paid net of the total income tax levied on the trustees – it is 'grossed up' for this purpose and the grossed up figure represents the taxable income of the beneficiary.

The beneficiary in receipt of income from a discretionary trust will be liable to income tax at his own appropriate rate of tax but will be able to claim a credit for the income tax and additional rate tax paid on the income by the trustees. If the beneficiary is liable to tax at less than the rate of tax paid, repayment of tax will arise. On the other hand if the beneficiary's rate of tax is greater than 35 per cent an additional payment of tax will be due from him.

The trustees will, on distributing the income, furnish the beneficiary with a certificate showing the 'grossed up' income and the total tax paid. The beneficiary will use this certificate to obtain credit or repayment for the tax paid.

i) *Payment of income to charity*

The charity will have received grossed up income on which tax at 35 per cent will have been paid. As the charity is a body which is exempt from income tax on its income it will be able to claim full repayment of the 35 per cent tax paid on the income by the trustees.

ii) *Payment to grandson*

The grandson is about to commence in business and presumably this will generate income for him. If he does make profits, the rate of tax due on those profits will be ascertained and the grossed up amount of the trust income will be added to the figure. Subject to a deduction for personal allowances and any other deductions to which he is entitled a rate of tax on the total income will be arrived at. If there is liability beyond the 35 per cent rate of tax paid on the trust income there will be an upward adjustment, or if there is only liability at basic rate on at least part of the trust income some repayment of tax will be due and will be credited against the overall tax bill.

If the business is not profitable in the early years the losses may be used to effect some repayment of tax paid on the trust income.

The full 35 per cent is available for repayment.

iii) *Payment to daughter*

If Samuel's daughter were a minor and unmarried then the settlement would be ineffective and there would be no transfer of income from Samuel's income to reduce his liability.

As it appears that the daughter is probably not a minor, the settlement is effective and the income is treated as hers for all income tax purposes. On her existing large income it is likely that a tax rate of 40 per cent applies, so she will have to pay an additional 5 per cent tax on the grossed up amount of trust income.

b) Susan has set up an accumulation and maintenance trust for the benefit of her grandchildren during their life to age 21. The trust income in this period will belong to the trustees and will be counted neither as Susan's income nor as income of the beneficiaries as it arises.

The trust is essentially a discretionary trust with power to accumulate income and to make payments for the maintenance, education etc of the beneficiaries. Only when such payments are made does the income become that of the beneficiaries.

Tax is paid on the trust income in the normal way applicable to discretionary trusts, ie it is taxed at 35 per cent and when released for the benefit of beneficiaries will have a credit for this full amount of tax attached to it. The corresponding 'income' of the beneficiaries is the grossed up equivalent of the amount paid, ie £65 payment represents income of £100 taxed at 35 per cent.

When the beneficiaries benefit from payments made on their behalf, the appropriate income is theirs for the purpose of claiming tax repayment on their personal allowances and basic rate band up to the grossed up equivalent of the income.

Income which is not released for the maintenance or education of the beneficiaries is allowed to be accumulated within the trust until they reach their majorities, in this case at age 21. The accumulated income is not an income payment to the beneficiary, but the accumulations are taken tax-free as capital. There is no recovery of the 35 per cent tax borne on the accumulation of income.

When the first grandson reaches his majority the income arising to his share after that date is no longer discretionary but is his by right. There will be no 10 per cent surcharge or 'additional rate' liability imposed on his share of the income. He will also take the accumulated income as capital, as outlined above, and the process will be repeated on the second grandson reaching his majority.

Thereafter the trust is no longer a discretionary one, and income arising will belong to the National Trust, which as a tax-exempt charity will be able to claim repayment of the basic rate tax paid by deduction from the income received by the trustees, or paid by the trustees on assessment by the Inland Revenue.

It is possible to elect to mandate the income direct to the beneficiary charity so that the trustees are not the recipients of income and so avoid any need for assessment.

Chapter 13

Settlements – Anti-Avoidance

13.1 **Introduction**

13.2 **Key points**

13.3 **Key cases and statute**

13.4 **Questions and suggested solutions**

13.1 Introduction

For many years higher rate taxpayers have attempted to alienate part of their income to a connected person such as a spouse or child to lessen their tax liability. This was usually carried out by means of a settlement or covenant. The present statutory anti-avoidance provisions are to be found in Part XV ICTA 1988, ss660A–694. Generally, the effect of these provisions is to make such covenants and settlements ineffective as tax planning and tax-saving tools and to treat trust income as income of the settlor where the settlor retains an interest in the trust property or income. References are to ICTA 1988 unless otherwise indicated.

Replacement of former anti-avoidance provisions of ss660 et seq

With effect from the year 1995–96 the anti-avoidance provisions relating to settlements, which had been gradually added but not necessarily co-ordinated over the years, were replaced with fewer sections providing substantially the same effect. The repealed provisions were those of ss660–676 and 683–685. The new provisions are ss660A–660G. The main change of any substance is that while the existing provisions excluded certain settlements which existed when they were introduced, the new provisions apply to all settlements whenever created and they extend the general definition of settlement to include transfer of assets. This latter item was in the past confined to settlements on children.

The new sections were introduced by Sch 17 FA 1995 and are constructed to set out the provisions relating to (s660A) settlements where the settlor has retained an interest, (660B) payments to unmarried minor children of the settlor – where not already caught by s660A, (s660C) the mode of assessing the settlor, (s660D) adjustments between settlor and trustees, (s660E) settlements with more than one settlor, (s660F) information powers and (s660G) the definition of settlement and settlor.

Sections 677 and 678 of ICTA 1988 remain in place and for all purposes of interpreting the meaning of undistributed income throughout the new provisions, s682 remains in force.

The changes in the tax treatment of covenants now contained in s347A (see Chapter 11) cancels the need for further anti-avoidance provisions and for this reason ss660 and 661 were repealed.

13.2 Key points

Part XV has three basic aims

a) To prevent income in a settlement only bearing basic rate tax. This is now ineffective due to the 'additional rate' of tax imposed on trust income under s686.

b) To prevent income alienation within the family between higher rate and those paying tax at a lesser or nil rate.

c) To prevent short-term tax planning whereby the taxpayer's income may be lessened while still retaining at least an interest in the assets giving rise to the income.

Section 660G

Settlement has a wide meaning and includes any disposition, trust, covenant, agreement or transfer of assets: see *Thomas* v *Marshall* [1953] AC 543; *IRC* v *Plummer* [1980] AC 896; *Chinn* v *Collins* [1981] AC 583.

Following *Moodie* v *IRC, Sotnick* v *IRC* [1993] STC 188, the decision in *Plummer* was held by the House of Lords to be inconsistent with the 'new approach' to anti-avoidance and self-cancelling annuity schemes were no longer therefore effective settlements.

The essence of the provisions, as rewritten in ss660A–660G, is to tax the settlor on income of any settlement in which the settlor or the settlor's spouse has retained an interest: s660A. A settlor retains an interest if the property or any income from it is capable of being applied for the benefit of the settlor or the settlor's spouse: s660A(2). Section 660A is supplemented by the provisions relating to their unmarried minor children even when no interest has been retained: s660B.

The principal exceptions from s660A are to be found in s660A(4)–(9):

a) an outright gift between spouses;

b) irrevocable allocation of pension rights between spouses under a relevant statutory scheme;

c) settlements on former spouses on separation or divorce;

d) partnership annuities under bona fide commercial arrangements;

e) settlements consisting of annual payments to a charity;

f) most accumulation and maintenance settlements.

Settlor is defined as 'any person by whom the settlement was made ... [either] directly or indirectly ... if he has provided or undertaken to provide funds ... for the purpose of the settlement', or has made with any other person a reciprocal arrangement for that person to make or enter into the settlement': see *IRC* v *Mills* [1975] AC 38.

Deeds of covenant

The previous ss660–662 contained provisions relating to deeds of covenant, including both covenants to charities and 'dispositions for short periods'. The latter had become redundant since only covenants in favour of charities remained tax deductible and created an effective transfer of income from payer to beneficiary. The provisions were repealed by FA 1995 and amendments to ss347A and 347B provide the continuity for the provisions on covenants in favour of charities. Essentially these must be capable of lasting for a minimum of three years and must not be capable of being terminated earlier without the consent of the recipient.

Sections 660B: covenants and settlements on children

This section supplements the revised settlement provisions in maintaining the treatment of income as that of the settlor even where the settlor has not retained any benefit in the settlement.

Each child has its own personal allowance and its income is not aggregated with that of the parent. Section 660B prevents abuse of this position by deeming the income to remain as that of the parent where the child is under 18 years of age or unmarried. Payments under deed of covenant between individuals are no longer effective in transferring income from one to the other following the introduction of s347A in 1988, under which no deduction of tax at source is made.

13.3 Key cases and statute

- *Moodie* v *IRC*; *Sotnick* v *RC* [1993] STC 188
  Settlements – anti-avoidance – s660G ICTA 1988

- *Young* v *Pearce*; *Young* v *Scrutton* [1996] STC 743
  Settlements – anti-avoidance – s660A ICTA 1988

- Income and Corporation Taxes Act 1988, ss660A–694

13.4 Questions and suggested solutions

QUESTION ONE

Ermintrude has a son Dougal, aged 16, who is a member of the Herb Garden Fund, a registered charity. The Fund is appealing for donations and Ermintrude is prepared to give them £2,000 per year for a maximum of five years.

Advise Ermintrude as to the most tax-efficient way of doing so.

Written by the Author

General Comment

This question illustrates how deeds of covenant can be used as a tax-efficient means of donating money to charities.

Skeleton Solution

Deed of covenant – withholding tax on payment – deduction from total income – ICTA 1988 s348 – charity exemption s505 – time limit for charitable covenants.

Suggested Solution

Ermintrude should realise that it will be possible for her to provide the charity with £2,000 without reducing her own after-tax income by such a large sum. This can be achieved by Ermintrude entering into a deed of covenant under seal to pay the charity £2,000 per annum commencing on the 1 April 1987 and payable on the same day in each of the next succeeding four years.

By this method, the charity will receive income liable to tax, prima facie, under Schedule D Case III. Provided, though, that it applies that income for charitable purposes only its income from this source will be exempted from income tax by s505 ICTA 1988. Since Ermintrude is 'quite wealthy' it may safely be assumed that she is in receipt of a substantial taxable income out of which the payment will be made. In these circumstances s348 ICTA 1988 will apply, and Ermintrude will be able to deduct a sum equal to basic rate tax from the payment before she hands the residue over to the charity: s348(1)(b). That sum she can retain for herself. This deduction the payee is obliged to allow by s348(1)(c) on receiving the rest as being a full discharge of the payer's obligation to pay £2,000. The sum deducted is, in turn, by s348(1)(d) treated as basic rate income tax paid by the charity which, not being liable to tax on the payment, can make a repayment claim on the Revenue.

Next, Ermintrude will be able to deduct the full £2,000 from her total income, in accordance with s835 ICTA 1988. Finally, having obtained both a total income deduction and having retained the sum under s348(1)(b), she will have received a greater tax saving than she would have been liable to pay tax – so that matters are adjusted by s3 ICTA 1988 imposing an additional charge to tax on Ermintrude at the basic rate on the amount of the covenanted income.

It should be noted that none of the anti-avoidance provisions contained in Part XV ICTA 1988 will apply here. In this case, s660A will apply since the payments to be made by Ermintrude are covenanted payments to charity and are payable for a period capable of exceeding three years – in fact being payable over a period of four years and one day: see s347A(7). Similarly, s347A excludes covenanted payments to charity from the effect of s347A(1) provided that the charity has not incurred any non-qualifying expenditure, as defined by ss505 and 506 ICTA 1988.

As far as other possible taxes are concerned.

a) No CGT can be payable, since the disposal by Ermintrude is of sterling only (which is not an asset for CGT).

b) Whilst the covenant will remove some money from Ermintrude's estate for inheritance tax, the transfers by which this will be done will be exempt as being normal expenditure out of income under s21 IHTA 1984, as:

    i) normal expenditure of Ermintrude's;

    ii) made out of her income, taking one year with another; and

    iii) leaving her with sufficient income to maintain her usual standard of living.

QUESTION TWO

Colin, who is a higher rate taxpayer, made the following dispositions during the year of assessment 2001–02:

a) He executed a deed whereby he covenanted to pay to the University of London annually on 1 May each year for seven years such a sum as will, after deduction of income tax at the basic rate for the time being in force, leave £750.

b) He settled £50,000 on trust for his children contingently upon attaining the age of 25. He has two sons, one aged 18 the other 11. The trustees used most of the income this year to pay the school fees of the two boys and they accumulated the remainder.

c) He transferred shares worth £100,000 to his wife. The shares produce an annual income of £10,000.

Advise Colin of the income tax consequences of these transactions.

Adapted from University of London LLB Examination
(for External Students) Revenue Law June 1990 Q2

General Comment

This question explores the implications of anti-avoidance provisions of Part XV of ICTA 1988.

Skeleton Solution

a) Deed of covenant – effective charge on income – charity recipient – not affected by s347A(2)(b) ICTA 1988 – gross equivalent.

b) Settlement on children – one adult one minor – anti-avoidance provisions of ss660 et seq – settlor retaining an interest – exception for accumulation and maintenance settlements – beneficiary's right to income – *Williams* v *Singer, Baker* v *Archer-Shee* – settlor's unearned income – *Ang* v *Parrish* – accumulation and maintenance – income tax provisions ss660A et seq.

c) Inter-spouse transfers – post independent taxation – recipient's own income.

Suggested Solution

a) In executing the covenant Colin has created a charge on his income. The sum covenanted to the University of London, assuming that the University is a charity for tax purposes, is intended:

i) to form the Schedule D Case III income of London University; and

ii) to be a deduction for Colin.

If the payment is a 'covenanted payment to charity' it will escape the new treatment of charges on income introduced by s36 FA 1988: see s347A ICTA 1988, especially s347A(2)(b). A covenanted payment to charity is defined in s347A(7) ICTA 1988 as 'a payment made under a covenant otherwise than for consideration in money or money's worth in favour of a body of persons or trust established for charitable purposes only whereby the ... annual payments ... become payable for a period which may exceed three years'. The payments under the covenant executed by Colin appear to satisfy this definition.

The sum expressed to be payable to London University is such amount as after deduction of tax at the basic rate leaves £750. The £750 is therefore a net sum. Since basic rate tax is currently 25 per cent the gross figure which the £750 represents is £1,000. On making the payment of £1,000 Colin in effect deducts basic rate tax. The mechanism whereby this deduction occurs will be that contained in s348 ICTA 1988, since Colin as a higher-rate taxpayer will be making the payments wholly out of profits or gains brought into charge to income tax. The effect of s348 is as follows:

i) Colin is charged to BRT without deducting the £1,000. He will therefore suffer the £250 BRT in respect of that sum.

ii) When Colin pays the £1,000 to the charity he may recoup the £250 tax he has suffered giving the charity merely £750 and a tax credit for the £250. Colin is under no obligation to make this deduction. The charity must, however, permit the deduction to be made, and the sum of £250 retained (in effect) by Colin is deemed BRT paid by the charity.

Colin's liability to HRT is unaffected by s348. Since the sum is a covenanted payment to charity, Colin may deduct it as a charge on income in computing his HRT liability. Neither s660 nor s683 will apply to return the £1,000 to his income for all IT purposes or even excess liability purposes.

The charity (London University) may, of course, reclaim the income tax deducted from the £1,000.

b) Colin has created a settlement for his two children, one of whom is 18 and the other 11. The settlement requires to be looked at as two entities, each reflecting the presumptive share of each son.

The first question to which regard must be had is the application of the anti-avoidance provisions in Part XV of ICTA 1988. With regard to the elder son's presumptive share, no problem seems to arise since on the facts s660A cannot apply. Nor do the strict provisions relating to settlements on a settlor's infant children apply since the elder child is no longer an infant. Section 660B is therefore excluded. Nor on the facts do ss677–678 apply. Section 660A however may present a difficulty. This applies to settlements where the settlor retains an interest; where it applies all the undistributed income is attributed to the settlor for all income tax purposes without right of reimbursement against the trustees. However a settlor is entitled exceptionally to create a settlement on a beneficiary contingently on the attaining by the beneficiary of an age not exceeding 25 years. This is an exception (in s660A(4)) to the general rule in s660A(1). Such is the case here. Therefore the settlement escapes s660A.

It could be argued that Colin has not absolutely divested himself of the settled property since he could take the property via a resulting trust were his children both to die before 25. The section does not apply if inter alia the only circumstance in which the settlor may take is the death under 25 or some lower age of a person who would have obtained a vested interest on attaining that age.

The anti-avoidance provisions therefore do not apply.

With regard to the elder child's half share of the income, the income tax position will be as follows. Section 31 of the Trustee Act 1925 gives the child a vested interest in the income, even though the settlement as such does not. The income will be taxed on the trustees at basic rate, if they receive it: *Williams* v *Singer* [1921] 1 AC 41. The trustees will not be liable to ART since the income does not fall within either s686 or s687 ICTA 1988. If the income is paid directly to the beneficiary, the trustees will not suffer IT liability; instead the beneficiary will be directly assessed. If the trustees receive the income and pay income tax on it the income tax paid by them will be credited to the beneficiary when they pay the trust income on to him. The income received by him will be DIII income, since the rule in *Baker* v *Archer-Shee* [1927] AC 844 has no application on these facts. To the extent that the beneficiary is not liable to income tax he may reclaim the sums paid by the trustees.

With regard to the presumptive half share of the infant child, s660B will apply, causing some considerable problems for the settlor. Under s660B any sums paid under a settlement to the infant child of a settlor are deemed to be the settlor's income for all income tax purposes. The income thus 'returned' to the settlor for IT purposes is unearned: *Ang* v *Parrish* [1980] STC 341. This is subject to an exception: s660B(1) does not apply if the settlement is an irrevocable accumulation trust of capital: s660B(2). As long as income is accumulated under such a trust s660B(1) does not apply. Where, however, any sums (whether capital or income) are paid out of such a settlement they are deemed to be the income of the infant to the extent of the cumulative total of accumulations. Thus to the extent that the income is expended to meet the school fees of the 11-year-old, s660B(1) applies to it and attributes it back to Colin for all IT purposes. To the extent that the income is accumulated it will be deemed paid to the infant and will therefore again fall within s660B(1). If however the settlement falls within the exception in s660A(5) (the facts are insufficient to draw a firm conclusion) then the anti-avoidance provisions will not apply during accumulation.

To the extent that s660A and s347A(1) do not apply the income will be taxed on the trustees at basic rate: s1(2) ICTA 1988. Since the settlement is subject to s31 Trustee Act 1925, so that the trustees are obliged to accumulate such income as is not paid out, then the trust falls within s686 ICTA 1988 and ART is payable (at 10 per cent) in addition to BRT. If, conversely, the settlor suffers BRT and HRT in respect of income falling within s660A or s660B he may claim a reimbursement of the tax suffered from the trustees.

c) When Colin transfers the shares to his wife she thus has investment income of £10,000. As the income arises after 6 April 1990, the new rules for taxation of married couples apply.

Chapter 14

Matrimonial Taxation

14.1   Introduction

14.2   Key points

14.3   Key case and statutes

14.4   Questions and suggested solutions

14.1 Introduction

Marriage and the breakdown of marriage will affect the tax position of both parties.

14.2 Key points

Method of taxation pre 6 April 1990

Prior to the reforms of 1988–90, which introduced independent taxation of married couples, the income of married couples living together was, with certain exceptions, treated and assessed as the husband's income irrespective of its source. Since the reforms married couples are treated as two single individuals with their own allowances and basic rate bands of tax.

Method of taxation post 6 April 1990

Income tax – married couples living together

Assessment and personal allowances

a)   From 6 April 1990 each spouse is taxed separately with own personal allowance: s257(1).

b)   Age-related married couple's allowance – s257A – can be claimed as to half by wife from 1993–94 – s257BA (introduced by Sch 5 of F(No 2)A 1992) – or apportioned by election under s257BB. From 1995–96, relief for the amount of the married couples' allowance is given only at 15 per cent under s256(2), reduced to 10 per cent from 6 April 1999 – s27(1)(a) FA 1998 amending s256(2).

Jointly held property

Income from jointly held property accrues to each in equal shares, subject to actual ownership ratio: ss282A and 282B.

Capital gains treatment of married couples

Under independent taxation each party has his or her own annual exemption. There is no set-off of losses between the parties and losses after 6 April 1990 may only be carried forward against the future gains of the loss-making spouse. Disposals between husband and wife continue to give rise to no gain/no loss position, with the acquiring spouse taking over the original acquisition cost for future disposal: s58 TCGA 1992.

Income tax – separated couples and maintenance payments

Section 282 ICTA 1988 couple living together unless separated by court order or separation likely to be permanent.

Section 257F ICTA 1988 allows husband still to obtain benefit of the married couple's allowance where separated but not divorced, in transition from old to new system. Apart from this the new system does not alter the position of separated couples.

If husband and wife cease living together, they are treated as separate persons for income tax purposes from the date of separation: ss257(1) and 282(1) ICTA 1988.

Maintenance payments

a) See s36(3) FA 1988 for separation agreements made pre 15 March 1988.

   Note: s660A ICTA 1988 will not apply here. From 1989–90 maintenance payments are paid gross and are not a charge on the income of the payer. Reliefs for pre 15 March 1988 agreements were withdrawn on 5 April 2000.

b) For agreements involving (at least one) older spouse, made post 15 March 1988, qualifying maintenance payments within s347B ICTA 1988 allow a reduction in tax for the payer of 10 per cent of the actual maintenance paid up to a ceiling of £2,070 maintenance: s257A(5A).

Capital gains and married couples

Section 58 TCGA 1992: inter-spousal disposals will be treated as no gain/no loss transactions, ie roll-over relief is given.

Capital gains and separations

Section 286: the husband and wife are connected persons until the decree absolute, see *Aspden* v *Hildesley* [1982] STC 206 and s17 TCGA 1992.

The effect of this is that, after divorce, transactions between them are regarded as being for an arm's length price between independent persons, but between separation and divorce the Revenue can, under s17 TCGA 1992, substitute market value for whatever consideration, if any, passes between them, subject to a concession for the disposal of the matrimonial home as part of the separation/divorce agreement.

Disposal of matrimonial home to former spouse

See Inland Revenue Concession D6.

Inheritance tax – married couples

See ss11 and 18 IHTA 1984.

14.3 Key case and statutes

- *Aspden* v *Hildesley* [1982] STC 206
  Matrimonial taxation – capital gains – separations

- Income and Corporation Taxes Act 1988, ss257A, 282A and 282B

- Taxation of Chargeable Gains Act 1992, s58

14.4 Questions and suggested solutions

QUESTION ONE

Discuss, and consider the consequences of, the special legislative treatment afforded to spouses for the purposes of income tax, capital gains tax and inheritance tax.

University of London LLB Examination
(for External Students) Revenue Law June 1996 Q8

General Comment

This question explores the treatment of spouses under the various tax laws.

Skeleton Solution

Income tax: personal allowance and married couples allowance: ss257, 257A, 257BA and 257BB ICTA 1988; individual lower rate bands of tax; implications of separation or divorce; periodic payments non-taxable, no allowance to payer – capital gains tax: CGT; two sets of annual exemptions: s3 TCGA 1992; exemption for inter spouse transfers: s58 TCGA 1992; effects of separation and divorce on CGT spouse exemption – inheritance tax: inheritance tax exemption for transfers between married couples and on separation or divorce: ss11, 11(6) and 18 IHTA 1984; need for planning in regard to timing of transfers on separation and divorce.

Suggested Solution

INCOME TAX

Personal allowances

Since 1990 each spouse has been taxed separately, each being entitled under s257(1)

Income and Corporation Taxes Act (ICTA) 1988 to a single person's personal allowance. There is also an age-related married couples allowance under s257A, which initially can be claimed by the husband, but which can be transferred to the wife under the rules in s257BA if the allowance remains unused by him. The allowance may also be apportioned as agreed by the parties. One anomaly would appear to remain that while s257BA allows a wife the entitlement to one-half of the allowance, it is only when her husband's use of the allowance is nil that under s257BB she is entitled to the full allowance. In circumstances where the husband has the use of at least part of the allowance, no provision would appear to be made for a wife to have an entitlement to the remainder, except upon a joint election to that effect. The married person's allowance is not given by reduction of taxable income but by a reduction of tax due on their respective incomes calculated at 15 per cent of the allowance.

Being taxed as separate individuals entitles each spouse to their own lower and basic rate bands of tax. It also creates the opportunity for transfer of income producing assets between them, with the result that the recipient's rate of tax is applied to the income. This does create a tax planning opportunity but only where there is an unconditional disposal of the relevant property. As will be seen below, such transfers do not incur any liability for either CGT or IHT and therefore may proceed without tax penalty.

Separation or divorce

The special situation of spouses ceases to operate for income tax purposes when there is a separation which, having regard to the circumstances at the time, appears likely to be permanent. When a couple cease to live together in circumstances which are likely to be permanent, the tax effects in respect of personal allowances are:

a) As regards the husband, the entitlement to the full amount of the married couple's allowance remains for the whole year of separation.

b) As regards the wife, she will be entitled to share the married couple's allowance as to half by right or greater if agreed between the parties.

Both continue to claim their normal personal allowance as before.

Any annual sums which a spouse covenants to pay direct to his children will not be deductible for income tax purposes. They will also represent non-taxable income in their hands and will not therefore be chargeable to tax under Schedule D Case III as annual payments.

CAPITAL GAINS TAX

Section 58 TCGA 1992 provides for transfers between spouses to take place without giving rise to either a gain or a loss. The transferor is therefore treated as disposing of the asset at its original acquisition price or value, and the recipient is treated as receiving the asset at that same price or value.

A capital gains tax charge arises only when an onward transfer to a non spouse takes place and this would include the gain accrued during the first spouse's period of ownership.

Any capital gains realised by a married person are charged at the individual's own rate of tax. In addition, each person has an annual exemption which can be set against the gains before any charge to tax arises. This means that for 1995–96 spouses could in appropriate circumstances make £12,000 of chargeable gains tax free, if the assets were either jointly held or held in separate names.

Separation and divorce

As with income tax, the ending of a marriage or indeed a permanent separation has consequences in that the arrangements for flexibility of income, allowances and transfers of assets within the family unit are no longer operative.

In dealing with transfers and other arrangements on separation and divorce regard must be taken as to when s58 applies and when, due to the breakdown of the marriage, the parties are no longer regarded as spouses for the purpose of applying that section. Section 58 applies only to couples while married and while living together, and therefore on permanent separation any disposals of assets will not be on a no gain/no loss basis, but will be made at their current market value.

Section 286 TCGA 1992 regards the couple as 'connected persons' up until the time when the decree absolute is obtained. For capital gains tax purposes transactions until that point are not treated as made on an arm's length basis so that market value is substituted under s17 TCGA 1992 for any or no consideration given for the transfer.

If spouses on separation were proposing to transfer property other than the matrimonial home after separating, this would mean that the transferor for CGT purposes will be treated as selling it for its market value and a capital gain may therefore accrue subject to reduction for indexation allowance during ownership. Likewise, and subject to indexation allowance, the transferee will be liable for CGT on any further appreciation in the value of the assets since acquisition date on a future sale.

If the transfer were delayed until after the divorce the transferor would be treated as disposing of the assets for what is actually received in return – eg, if assets were exchanged. In due course on a sale of the assets the gain will be calculated on the appreciation in value since acquiring them. Depending on the respective actual values of the assets exchanged in such a redistribution of property, the relevant CGT position can be adversely affected.

INHERITANCE TAX

Inheritance tax is chargeable on transfers of capital and arises when that transfer is a 'transfer of value' as defined by the inheritance tax legislation. Under s1 of the Inheritance Tax Act (IHTA) 1984 'tax shall be charged on the value transferred by a chargeable transfer'. Section 2 defines a chargeable transfer as one which is not an exempt transfer. Section 3 defines a 'transfer of value' as a disposition made by a person as a result of which the value of his estate immediately after the disposition is less than it would be but for the disposition.

Transfers between married couples are not transfers of value by virtue of the special provisions of s11 IHTA 1984 if the transfers are for the maintenance of the other party. Section 11(6) further provides that 'marriage' includes a former marriage if the disposition or transfer is made on the occasion of the dissolution or annulment of the marriage. It follows that almost all maintenance orders and agreements are outside the scope of inheritance tax, even though they reduce one party's estate.

In addition, s18 IHTA 1984 provides for general exemption to be accorded to any transfer of value between spouses where property becomes comprised in the other spouse's estate. This covers transfers other than for the maintenance of the other party. This provision, however, extends only to transfers between spouses and there is no extension to former spouses similar to the s11 provisions for maintenance transfers. Therefore, once a divorce has taken place transfers of value are chargeable to tax in the normal way. It would be vital, therefore, to ensure that the disposals which are contemplated take place before a decree absolute.

There may be some measure of reliance to be placed on a statement by the Capital Taxes Office of the Inland Revenue that on a divorce it will normally accept that s10 IHTA 1984 will apply to exempt any transfers of value on the basis that they are not intended to confer gratuitous benefit on any person. However, it must be doubtful to what extent this non-statutory ruling can be relied on with certainty for transfers made after a divorce.

Therefore, it would seem that if whatever arrangements are proposed should be carried out before the decree absolute any potential inheritance tax liability will be eliminated.

QUESTION TWO

Harry and Sally have been married for many years and have two children aged 16 and 14. Harry owns a very profitable business which gives him a high income. Sally has no earned income but receives £750 pa from a trust created under the will of her grandfather.

Last year Harry entered into a covenant with the National Trust which is a registered charity. He covenanted to pay on 29 September each year for six years such a sum as will after deduction of income tax at the basic rate for the time being in force leave £150.

Sally has recently left Harry and is considering divorce. Harry has offered to pay her £8,000 pa as maintenance for herself and £2,000 pa for each of the children. He is also willing to transfer a sum of capital to trustees to provide for the education of the two children.

Explain to Harry and Sally the income tax consequences of the above facts.

University of London LLB Examination
(for External Students) Revenue Law June 1991 Q1

General Comment

This question illustrates the principles of the independent taxation rules.

Skeleton Solution

Harry and Sally: independent taxation rules: personal allowances – Harry: tax on profits of business: Schedule D, Case 1 – Sally: trust income: paid under deduction of tax – National Trust: charitable covenant: s347A ICTA 1988; s671 ICTA 1988 – breakdown of marriage: revert to single status – maintenance under separation agreement: s347B ICTA 1988 – education of children: accumulation and maintenance settlement.

Suggested Solution

Under the independent taxation rules which came into force on 6 April 1990, Harry and Sally will be taxed independently, each on his or her own income, and each has to take responsibility for his or her own tax affairs.

Both Harry and Sally will be entitled to a personal allowance of £4,535: s257(1) Income and Corporation Taxes Act (ICTA) 1988.

Harry will have to pay income tax under Schedule D Case I on the profits that he receives from his business.

The £750 which Sally gets from the trust each year will already have borne tax at the basic rate, either because it was income paid under deduction of tax, or because the trustees paid basic rate tax under the appropriate Schedule or Case. Therefore that payment of tax will be deemed to satisfy Sally's basic rate liability on the amount of the unearned income. Because this is Sally's only source of income for the year and it does not exceed her personal allowance (ie the tax paid), she will be able to reclaim the tax paid by the trustees, ie £250.

Harry covenants to pay to the National Trust a sum of £150 after deduction of basic rate income tax for six years. This would qualify as a charitable covenant. Section 347A ICTA 1988 provides:

> 'Subject to subs(2) below any income which by virtue or in consequence of any disposition made directly or indirectly by any person (other than a disposition made for valuable and sufficient consideration), is payable to or for the benefit of any person for a period which cannot exceed six years shall be deemed ... to be the income of the person, if living, by whom the disposition was made ...'

However, so long as the covenant is drafted so as to be capable of lasting for more than three years as required by s347A, the sum paid will be a charge on the income of the payer, will be paid subject to deduction of basic rate income tax under s348, and will be taxed as the income of the charity, which may therefore reclaim the basic rate tax deducted at source.

When Sally left Harry, the parties revert to single status. For income tax purposes, marriage ends when the parties separate under circumstances indicating that the separation is long term. This separation seems to have some degree of permanence.

The new system of independent taxation does not alter the tax treatment of separated couples because they were already taxed as separate individuals.

If Harry is maintaining Sally under a separation agreement or court order then the sums payable thereunder will no longer be deductible in computing his liability and neither will the payment constitute D III income in Sally's hands.

If the payments are 'qualifying maintenance payments' within s347B ICTA 1988 then the payer is entitled to a relief equal to the size of the payment or the size of the married couple's allowance, whichever is less.

A payment is a qualifying maintenance payment if it:

a) is made under a UK court order or a separation agreement governed by the law of a part of the UK; and

b) is made by one of the parties to a marriage (including a dissolved or annulled marriage) either

   i) to or for the benefit of the other party and for the maintenance of the other party; or

   ii) to the other party for the maintenance by the other party of any child of the family; and

c) is done at a time when:

   i) the two parties are not a married couple living together; and

   ii) the party to whom or for whose benefit the payment is made has not remarried; and

d) is not a payment otherwise available for relief or caught by the anti-avoidance provisions.

Thus, as with payments entitling the payee of maintenance under an existing obligation to an additional relief, payments directly to children do not attract favourable tax treatment in s347B(1) ICTA 1988.

Harry is also willing to transfer a sum of capital to provide for the education of the two children. For income tax purposes the settlement is treated as an accumulation and maintenance settlement and the trustees would be subject to basic and additional rate tax (ie 34 per cent) on any income accumulated. However, as it is a settlement concerning parent and infant children, one must also look at the provisions of both ss660A and 660B. If Harry sets up an irrevocable capital settlement within s660A(4)(d) ICTA 1988 then the accumulated income will not be treated as Harry's income. However, when the trustees make payments to the two children for their educational fees, then the payment out of the funds will be treated as Harry's income up to the amount that is accumulated (s660B(3) ICTA 1988), with Harry receiving a tax credit for the tax that the trustees have paid in respect of the income that they subsequently distributed: s677 ICTA 1988. If Harry has set up a revocable capital settlement then all the income of the settlement, whether accumulated or paid for the purposes of the children's education, will be deemed to be Harry's income, and Harry will be taxed accordingly: s660B ICTA 1988.

Chapter 15

Corporation Tax

15.1   Introduction

15.2   Key points

15.3   Key cases and statutes

15.4   Question and suggested solution

15.1 Introduction

Companies pay 'corporation tax' on income and capital gains. A company for tax purposes is defined in s832(1) ICTA 1988 and discussed in *Conservative and Unionist Central Office* v *Burrell* [1980] 3 All ER 42.

Section 11 ICTA 1988: generally, only UK resident companies and UK branches or agencies of non-UK resident companies will pay corporation tax (see s11(2) ICTA 1988 and s10 TCGA 1992). Non-resident companies pay income tax.

Section 208 ICTA 1988: dividends and other distributions paid by UK companies are exempt from corporation tax to avoid double taxation.

15.2 Key points

The charge to corporation tax

Section 9 ICTA 1988: income is calculated as per usual under the schedular system and aggregated with any capital gains to give total profits.

Section 12(1) ICTA 1988: tax is charged on a current year basis on the profits of each accounting period apportioned according to the financial year (not year of assessment) in question.

The financial year is from 1 April to 31 March. Financial year 2004 begins 1 April 2004.

Corporation tax is payable nine months after the end of the accounting year to which it relates or 30 days after the assessment is raised, whichever is the later. Companies do not currently self-assess, although they have a 'pay and file' system (see below).

Corporation tax rates

Corporation tax is generally paid at one standard rate which may vary from one financial year to the next, eg for financial year 1998 it was 31 per cent and for financial year 1999 at 30 per cent.

Section 13 ICTA: small companies, ie with profits not exceeding £300,000 (s13 ICTA 1988), pay a lower rate of corporation tax, which for the financial year 2003 was 19 per cent.

Companies whose profits are between £300,000 and £1,500,000 (s13 ICTA 1988) receive tapering relief which reduces the rate of tax accordingly between the full rate and the small companies rate.

For the purpose of determining whether small companies' rate applies, profits include dividends and other 'distributions' of UK resident companies, although under s208 ICTA 1988 these are not chargeable to corporation tax.

Prior to the abolition of Advance Corporation Tax (ACT) in respect of company dividends and distributions on or after 6 April 1999, a dividend etc plus its tax credit was referred to as 'franked investment income' under s238 ICTA 1988. From 6 April 1999 the concept of 'franked investment income' and its uses ceased to exist.

Anti-avoidance provisions in s13(4) and (5) ICTA 1988 prevent large companies dividing into smaller companies in order to claim the small companies rate.

Computation of income

In general the income chargeable to corporation tax is arrived at by applying the normal rules for each schedule – for example the deductible expenditure rules for Case I income: s74 ICTA 1988. There are, however, additional rules for the charging and for deductibility of interest, discounts and other profits, gains or losses arising from what are termed 'loan relationships'. This covers receipts or payments arising from a company's financing arrangements, in any form other than share capital (see below).

'Loan relationships' – companies' interest, discount etc receipts and payments

Prior to changes introduced by ss80–105 and Schs 8–15 Finance Act 1996, companies could only obtain a deduction for yearly or annual interest under the form of a charge on income. Such interest payments were not deductible in computing the profits of the company. In respect of interest payments falling after 31 March 1996, such interest payments are no longer regarded as 'charges on income'. A completely new regime under the term 'loan relationships', was introduced. Section 337A excludes interest from charges on income or from any other deduction except as provided for under the new loan relationship regime.

The new regime provides a framework for the tax treatment, both as regards the creditor and the debtor, of all payments or receipts of interest, discounts, premiums etc and profits or losses (whether capital or revenue) arising in respect of debt obligations of companies. The essence of the new regime is to tax as income all profit whether arising by receipt of interest or any increase in value of the loan and to allow as a deduction for corporation tax purposes all interest payments, expenses or losses associated with each loan relationship, whether such interest, expense or loss arises on capital or revenue account. The deduction under the new system will be taken as a deduction in calculating the profits of the company and not, as was previously the case under s338, as a charge on income (see below).

Charges on income

These must be ultimately borne by the company and be for valuable and sufficient consideration. Under s401(1) charges on income incurred before the trade, profession or vocation are commenced are treated as incurred on the first day of trading. This basis applies to those set up after 5 April 1995 – prior to which such expenditure was treated as a loss of the year of commencement on which the usual trading loss reliefs could be claimed.

Special rules exist for companies: ss338–340 and s249 ICTA 1988. See *Ball v National & Grindlay's Bank* [1973] Ch 127; *British Insulated & Helsby Cables Ltd v Atherton* [1926] AC 205; *Heather v PE Consulting Ltd* [1973] Ch 189; *E Bott Ltd v Price* [1987] STC 100; *MacNiven (Inspector of Taxes) v Westmoreland Investments Ltd* [2001] 2 WLR 377.

Losses

Trading losses can be set-off against income or gains of the same accounting period or carried forward against profits of the same trade in future periods: see *Scorer v Olin Energy Systems Ltd* [1985] STC 218 and *Rolls Royce Motors Ltd v Bamford* [1976] STC 162. Losses incurred in an accounting period ending on or after 2 July 1997, may only be carried back for one year: s39(9)–(12) F(No 2)A 1997. Between 31 March 1991 and this date, the carry back period was three years, setting off the loss against the most recent year's profits first. Case VI losses are isolated for relief against Case VI profits only: ss393–396.

Capital losses can only be set-off against current or future chargeable gains (except re losses on unquoted trading company shares: s573 ICTA 1988). Also see s397, farming and market gardening losses.

See Chapter 4 for the treatment of 'Schedule A business' and 'overseas property business' losses.

See *Beauchamp v FW Woolworth plc* [1989] STC 510 – loss on foreign currency loan not allowed on grounds that it arose on a capital and not revenue account transaction.

Sections 343 and 344 ICTA 1988: special rules for company reconstructions maintaining the same ownership.

See also s75 ICTA 1988 re management expenses of investment companies.

Sections 402–413 ICTA 1988: group relief is available where a group company makes a loss provided that s402(3) ICTA 1988 is satisfied. The decision in *Sainsbury plc v O'Connor* [1991] STC 318, on the meaning of 'arrangements' for the purpose of ss410 and 413 re change of control of a company, gave rise to changes to Sch 18 ICTA 1988, introduced by FA 1992, which focus on the true economic ownership of a company. See *Steele v EVC International BV* [1996] STC 785 regarding the meaning of 'connected persons' in determining 'control'. This gave rise to an amendment to s410 ICTA 1988, inserted by s68 FA 1997.

Similarly relief is also available to consortia: see *ICI v Colmer* [1996] STC 352, where the House of Lords decided that companies had to be UK resident for the purpose of the holding company definition in s413(3) and referred the question of whether this produced conflict with European law to the European Court of Justice, whose findings are reported at [1998] STC 874. The European Court held that there was a conflict only where the subsidiaries were based in the European Community.

Pay and file system

The pay and file provisions which applied for accounting periods ending on or after 1 October 1993 contained in the Taxes Management Act 1970 (inserted by ss82–90 and Sch 6 Finance Act (No 2) 1987) cease to apply to accounting periods ending on or after 1 July 1999 and are replaced by 'self-assessment' for companies: see below.

Self-assessment

a) Introduced for companies for accounting periods ending or after 1 July 1999: Schs 18 and 19 FA 1998.

b) Corporation Tax Return and self-assessment form is due 12 months after the end of the accounting period: para 14 Sch 18 FA 1998.

c) Companies within the full rate of corporation tax are subject to payment of corporation tax by instalments, phased in gradually by increasing the percentage of the quarterly instalments each year over a four-year period from 1999.

d) The self-assessment return form must include claims for group relief and capital allowances, which must be specific and quantified: paras 66–77 and 78–83 Sch 18 FA 1998 respectively

e) All liabilities to tax must be included and self-assessed: para 1 Sch 18.

f) Liability for tax under s419 ICTA 1988 on loans to company participators and tax due under s747 ICTA 1988 on profits of controlled foreign companies are to be included: see Sch 17 FA 1998.

g) Companies' inter-group company transactions must be returned on the basis that prices charged or interest rates applicable have been measured as they would have been if the transactions were carried out with unconnected parties – see 'transfer pricing' provisions in Sch 16 FA 1998.

Prior to this the onus was on the Inland Revenue to enquire and establish controlled foreign company and transfer pricing profits.

15.3 Key cases and statutes

- *Ball* v *National and Grindlay's Bank* (1971) 47 TC 287 (CA)
  Corporation tax – charges on income – payments

- *Conservative and Unionist Central Office* v *Burrell* [1980] 3 All ER 42
  Corporation tax – definition of company for tax purposes

- *Imperial Chemical Industries plc* v *Colmer (Inspector of Taxes)* [1998] STC 874
  Corporation tax – losses – consortium relief

- *Steele* v *EVC International BV* [1996] STC 785
  The meaning of 'connected persons' in determining 'control' – gave rise to the s68 FA 1997 amendment to s410 referred to above in section 16.2

- Finance Act 1998, Schs 18 –19

- Income and Corporation Taxes Act 1988, ss11 and 208

15.4 Question and suggested solution

Discuss the concept and significance of residence for companies.

University of London LLB Examination
(for External Students) Revenue Law June 1991 Q3(a)

General Comment

This question explores when companies are liable to UK tax.

Skeleton Solution

Liability of company to UK tax: ss8(1) and 11 ICTA 1988 – central management and control test – now s66 FA 1988: residence of company.

Suggested Solution

The Income and Corporation Taxes Act (ICTA) 1988 s8(1) provides that a UK resident company is liable to corporation tax on all its profits wherever arising. A foreign situs company is only liable to UK corporation tax if it trades in the UK through a branch or agency: s11 ICTA 1988.

Companies have traditionally been treated as resident in the UK if their central management and control was situated in the UK. This is a question of fact, not of law.

The law went through a dramatic change on 15 March 1985. Until that time the only test used was the common law test of 'central management and control'. That test has been partly replaced by what is now s66 Finance Act (FA) 1988 which provides that a company incorporated in the UK will be resident in the UK. There are two exceptions:

a) a company is allowed to move its residence with Treasury permission;

b) companies which were in existence when the law was changed and were managed abroad were given five years either to wind up, get Treasury permission, or accept residential status. The five-year period ended in March 1993.

All other companies formed in the UK are resident. As regards companies incorporated elsewhere, the old common law test still applies, ie you have to look to see where the 'central management and control' is.

The 'central management and control' test was first laid down in *De Beers Consolidated Mines* v *Howe* [1906] AC 455. Lord Loreburn stated:

> '… it is easy to ascertain where an individual resides, but when the enquiry relates to a company, which in a natural sense does not reside anywhere, some artificial test must be applied. A company cannot eat or sleep, but it can keep house and do business. We ought, therefore, to see where it really keeps house and does business. An individual may be of foreign nationality, and yet reside in the UK. So may a company. The decision of Kelly CB and Huddleston B in *Calcutta Jute Mills* v *Nicholson* (1876) 1 TC 83 and *Cesena Sulphur Company* v *Nicholson* (1876) 1 TC 88 involved the principle that a company resides for the purposes of income tax where its real business is carried on. Those decisions have been acted upon ever since. I regard that as a general rule, and the real business is carried on where the "central management and control actually abides".'

Chapter 16

Dividends and Distributions of Companies

16.1 Introduction

16.2 Key points

16.3 Key statutes

16.4 Question and suggested solution

16.1 Introduction

The system of taxing company dividends and other distributions underwent a fundamental change as from 6 April 1993 and again with effect from 6 April 1999. For pre-1993 dividends, tax accounted for under the Advance Corporation Tax (ACT) system satisfied the recipient's basic rate tax liability. After 1993, the rate of ACT accounted for by the company was reduced and the recipient receives a lesser credit. On dividends between 6 April 1993 and 5 April 1999 the individual recipient is no longer liable to basic rate tax on dividend income but to lower rate only. On dividends from 6 April 1999, companies no longer pay ACT and instead of the lower rate of tax, basic rate taxpayers are liable to tax at only 10 per cent – now called the 'Schedule F ordinary rate': s1B ICTA 1988. The 10 per cent liability is however satisfied by a tax credit (despite the abolition of an ACT payment by the company). The credit is ⅑th of the dividend, so that a dividend of £90, has a credit of £10, satisfying tax at 10 per cent on £90 + £10, being the amount which has to be brought into account under s20(1),(2) ICTA 1988. Those liable to higher rates continue to have to pay the full difference in rates. From 6 April 1999, higher rate taxpayers are liable for tax on dividends at the 'Schedule F upper rate' of 32.5 per cent: s1B ICTA 1988. Special rates apply to trust recipients: see Chapter 12.

16.2 Key points

Dividends and distributions

a) For distributions prior to 6 April 1999, companies pay ACT: s209 et seq ICTA 1988.

b) ACT payment credited to recipient as tax credit to meet liability: s231 ICTA 1988.

c) Individual recipients liable to lower rate of tax followed, with effect from 6 April

1999, by 10 per cent 'Schedule F ordinary rate' in line with reduction and subsequent abolition of ACT: s1B ICTA 1988. Tax credit of ⅑th sufficient to meet first 10 per cent liability of all non-corporate recipients.

d) Higher rate taxpayers liable at 'Schedule F upper rate' of 32.5 per cent from 6 April 1999, meeting additional 22.5 per cent tax after tax credit as above: s1B ICTA 1988.

e) Company and pension fund recipients barred form claiming repayment of tax credit through set-off of losses from 2 July 1997 – s242 ICTA 1988 abolished – s20(5) and Sch 8 F(No 2)A 1997 – see s231A ICTA 1988 and para 6 Sch 4 F(No 2)A 1997.

f) Company recipients of dividends no longer treat them as 'franked investment income' (FII). The abolition of ACT from 6 April 1999 means that the FII concept loses its significance: see para 11 Sch 3 FA 1998.

g) Surplus ACT will not accumulate beyond 5 April 1999. Existing surplus ACT may be set off against future corporation tax within the same limitations which existed prior to 6 April 1999 – see below. New 'shadow ACT' scheme introduced.

'Distributions'

Defined in ss209–211 ICTA 1988 eg dividends and redeemable share capital (ie redeemable for cash) but not distributions on winding up. Note special rules for combined bonus shares and repayments of share capital: ss210 and 211. Any matter treated as a distribution is not deductible against the profits for corporation tax purposes. Important implications for items disallowed in this manner: s208(1) ICTA 1988.

'Qualifying distributions'

a) Pre-6 April 1999

Defined in s14(2) ICTA 1988.

i) Only qualifying distributions will give rise to liability for ACT.

ii) The distribution plus ACT (ie the gross amount) is called a 'franked payment'.

iii) 'Franked investment income' is a franked payment received by a company: s238 ICTA 1988.

iv) Section 13 ICTA 1988: ACT is payable within 14 days of the end of the quarter in which the distribution is made.

b) Post-6 April 1999

i) No liability at time of distribution – ACT abolished – s31 FA 1998.

ii) Distributions are not 'franked payments' – para 11 Sch 3 FA 1998 – but liability to income tax is calculated on dividend plus tax credit – s20(1) ICTA 1988.

iii) In the hands of a company, no longer treated as 'franked investment income' – para 11 Sch 3 FA 1998.

ACT set off

a) Pre-6 April 1999

Section 239 ICTA 1988: any ACT already paid may be set off against mainstream corporation tax (MCT), provided that the ACT currently does not exceed 20 per cent of the company's total taxable profits for the financial year in question. 'Taxable profits' for these purposes relate only to UK source profits. ACT is not recoverable against mainstream corporation tax on foreign source profits but see para (j) below for reclaim of ACT on qualifying 'foreign income dividends' (FIDs) paid out of foreign source profits.

b) Post-6 April 1999

The abolition of ACT means there is no ACT for the current period to set-off against mainstream corporation tax. Set-off of surplus ACT in existence at 6 April 1999 is dealt with below.

Surplus ACT: s239(3) and (4) ICTA 1988

a) Pre-6 April 1999

Any ACT that cannot be set off under s239 may be rolled back against the previous six years, taking the latest year first, and any still unrelieved may be carried forward.

b) Post-6 April 1999

i) From this date no further ACT will accumulate but unused ACT will continue to be set off under what is called the 'shadow ACT' scheme introduced by s32 FA 1998.

ii) Full administrative details are included in the Corporation Tax (Treatment of Unrelieved Surplus ACT) Regulations 1999 (SI 1999/358) published on 16 February 1999. Broadly speaking, the same restrictions are to be imposed on the maximum amounts which can be set off each year – if it would have been deductible under the old system – s239(1) ICTA 1988 – it will continue to be set-off in the future until it is used up, but only if there is a gap between the maximum 20 per cent of corporation tax profits of the accounting period and a notional amount of ACT (the 'shadow ACT') which would have been payable on the distributions in the (post-April 1999) accounting period. Then the surplus ACT can be allowed to fill that gap to reduce the corporation tax payable. Shadow ACT does not reduce the corporation tax payable – it is merely inserted for the purpose of calculating whether relief for the surplus ACT can be allowed.

Example

A company has accumulated surplus ACT of £60,000 at 6 April 2002. Its profits for the next following accounting period amount to £60,000 and it pays a dividend of £25,000. The ACT position is as follows:

Maximum set-off for year ending April 2003: 20% x £60,000 = £12,000

Shadow ACT: 25% x £25,000 = £6,250. Gap for set-off of surplus ACT £12,000 – £6,250= £5,750.

Corporation tax liability reduction = £5,750.

Surplus ACT carried forward £60,000 – £5,750 = £54,250.

'Franked investment income' (FII)

a) Pre-6 April 1999

Section 231(2) ICTA 1988: companies exempt from corporation tax may reclaim tax already paid on FII received.

Ordinary companies can use FII to offset ACT payable to the Inland Revenue: s241 ICTA 1988. See also Chapter 15. Foreign income dividends (see para (j) below) in the hands of companies are not franked investment income for corporation tax purposes: s246E.

b) Post-6 April 1999

i) Exempt companies lost the right to repayment of tax credits from 6 April 1999: s30(4) F(No 2)A 1997.

ii) All companies lost the right to recover the tax credit on their franked investment income through the use of losses – s242 ICTA 1988 – with effect from 2 July 1997: s20(5) F(No 2)A 1997.

iii) Pension funds lost the right to repayment of tax credits on dividends with effect from 2 July 1997: s231A ICTA 1988.

iv) Foreign income dividends scheme under ss245A et seq ICTA 1988 ceased to apply on the abolition of ACT: s36 F(No 2)A 1997.

Surplus FII

a) Pre-2 July 1997

If FII exceeds ACT payable in a given accounting year, relief is given under s242 ICTA 1988 against other unrelieved deductible items:

i) trading losses;

ii) charges on income;

iii) ss75 or 76 ICTA 1988: management expenses;

iv) certain capital allowances;

v) s573(2) ICTA 1988: capital losses.

Any further excess may be carried forward.

b) Post-2 July 1997

All companies lost right to recover the tax credit on their franked investment income through the use of losses – s242 ICTA 1988 – with effect from 2 July 1997: s20(5) F(No 2)A 1997.

Groups and consortia: special rules

a) Pre-6 April 1999

See ss247 and 248 ICTA 1988. Such dividends may be paid free of ACT.

b) Post-6 April 1999

The provisions cease to be required following the general abolition of ACT and were repealed: paras 19–20 Sch 3 FA 1998.

Stock dividends

Companies may distribute shares as dividends instead of cash dividends. These do not attract liability for ACT. Recipient is treated as receiving tax credit for lower rate tax up to 5 April 1999, when the credit is reduced to meet liability at the new Schedule F ordinary rate of 10 per cent: s1B ICTA 1988 and see s249.

Foreign income dividends (FIDs)

a) Pre-6 April 1999

Dividends paid out of foreign income may be treated as 'foreign income dividends' (FIDs): s246A. Payment of ACT is not dispensed with but may be reclaimed by the company. There is no tax credit available to the recipient: s246C. An individual who receives such a dividend is, however, treated as receiving a tax credit equivalent to the lower rate of tax (s246D), so that his liability other than to higher rate tax is satisfied.

Foreign income dividends in the hands of companies are not franked investment income for corporation tax purposes: s246E.

b) Post-6 April 1999

The foreign income dividends scheme provisions under ss245A et seq ICTA 1988 were repealed with effect from 6 April 1999, coinciding with the abolition of ACT – announced by s36 F(No 2)A 1997.

International holding companies (IHCs)

a) Pre-6 April 1999

This is an extension of the FIDs scheme set out above under which there is no initial payment of ACT on payment of dividends by those companies which satisfy the eligibility test of international holding companies (IHCs). The main tests are satisfied if the company (IHC) is wholly owned by a foreign company, or by a foreign company whose shares are listed on the UK Stock Exchange, or is 80 per cent owned with a 5 per cent minimum interest held by each non-resident non-company shareholder or by foreign held companies IHCs will be able to receive and redistribute profits from foreign subsidiaries without any UK domestic tax. The provisions are contained in ss246S–246Y ICTA 1988.

b) Post-6 April 1999

The international holding company provisions under ss245A et seq ICTA 1988 were repealed with effect from 6 April 1999, coinciding with the abolition of ACT – announced by s36 and Sch 6 F(No 2)A 1997.

16.3 Key statutes

- Finance (No 2) Act 1997

- Finance Act 1998

16.4 Question and suggested solution

SuperCo plc is a UK registered company. In the accounting period to the end of December 1996 it made profits of over £10 million. During the accounting period SuperCo made the following dividend payments to its shareholders:

a) £50,000 to a registered charity, the Clapham Dogs' Home;

b) £50,000 to Bertram, a higher rate taxpayer resident in the UK;

c) £2,000 to Claudia, a taxpayer resident in the UK whose only other income is £1,500 pa;

d) £150,000 to DangerCo, a UK registered company; and

e) £10,000 to the trustees of the Evergreen Trust, a private discretionary settlement.

Advise the parties on the income tax and corporation tax consequences of the above facts.

University of London LLB Examination
(for External Students) Revenue Law June 1997 Q3

General Comment

The payment of a dividend by a company brings a liability for advance corporation tax. The tax is regarded as meeting the lower rate liability of the recipient individual shareholder, providing the shareholder is resident in the United Kingdom. In appropriate circumstances the tax is repayable to non-liable persons. Corporate shareholders and non-residents are treated differently.

Skeleton Solution

Tax credit to shareholder if a resident individual: s231 – s20(1); taxable amount = dividend plus tax credit – company's set-off of ACT against mainstream corporation tax: s239 – charity exemption: s505(1)(c)(iii) – liability for basic rate taxpayers met by tax credit; liability confined to lower rate by s1A – liability for higher rate taxpayers; additional 20 per cent of gross amount under s20(1) – tax credit repayable if not liable to tax – resident companies not liable for corporation tax on UK dividends received: s208 – franked investment income of company; set-off of claims under s241 or s242.

Suggested Solution

Note: all references are to the Income and Corporation Taxes Act (ICTA) 1988 unless stated otherwise.

Company's corporation tax

SuperCo plc will be required to account for advance corporation tax (ACT) on payment of the company's dividend. The rate of ACT is equal to one-quarter of the amount of the dividend declared and is payable 14 days after the end of the quarter in which the dividend is paid. The ACT is available as a tax credit to any UK resident shareholder under s231 ICTA 1988.

On the other hand, SuperCo plc will also be able to treat the ACT as part of its liability to mainstream corporation tax (MCT) charged on the company's profits for the year ended 31 December 1996. The amount of ACT available for set off in this manner is limited under s239 to ensure that the company cannot set off an amount greater currently than a rate of 20 per cent on the chargeable profits and gains for the period in which the distribution or dividend is made. Any excess is relieved by carry back against the previous six years' profits, or can be carried forward against corporation tax liability in future accounting periods: s239(3) and (4).

Shareholders' tax liability

As noted above, the receipt by a UK resident individual of a dividend from a UK company entitles the shareholder to a tax credit corresponding to the proportionate amount of the ACT paid on the dividend. Section 231(1) also excludes a company from the tax credit, although UK resident companies are in fact not chargeable to corporation tax in respect of dividends received from other UK companies.

a) The payment of a dividend to a registered charity will result in the reclaim of the tax credit applicable to the dividend. Charities enjoy exemption from UK tax on most income, and provision for exempting dividends can be found in s505(1)(c)(iii). Under s231 a tax credit equivalent to the amount of advance corporation tax paid on the dividend is available to the recipient to set off against its tax liability and to be repaid if the tax liability is less than the tax credit. In view of the charity's exemption from tax, the tax credit amounting to 25% x £50,000 = £12,500 will be repaid to it on the making of a claim to that effect.

b) Bertram, being a UK resident individual, will be entitled to a tax credit equivalent to 25 per cent of the net dividend received. These combined figures of dividend and tax credit are added under s20(1) to produce the amount on which liability to UK tax is charged. The effect of this is to give a tax credit to the individual which corresponds, at present rates, to 20 per cent of the gross amount chargeable. (A dividend of £80 would carry a tax credit of £20, with £100 being chargeable to tax at the taxpayer's effective rate of UK tax.) Bertram is liable to tax at 40 per cent and, in view of this, he will have a further payment of tax due from him in respect of his dividend, amounting to an additional 20 per cent of the gross taxable amount. For income tax purposes, therefore, he is treated as having received a gross dividend of £62,500, being the net dividend of £50,000 plus the tax credit of 25 per cent – £12,500 – as dictated by s20(1). His tax liability on this gross dividend amounts to £62,500 x 40% = £25,000 less the tax credit of £12,500, leaving a further payment due by Bertram of £12,500.

c) Claudia has an income of only £1,500 per annum plus the dividend of £2,500 which, added together to the tax credit (£2,000 x 25% = £500) on the dividend, makes a gross taxable dividend of £2,500. Her total income is therefore £4,000 and her current rate of tax is nil since her personal allowance of £4,045 exceeds her income. In these circumstances she has received taxable income to which a tax credit of 20 per cent of the gross taxable amount is attached. The tax credit is available for repayment to her and in her circumstances she will be able to reclaim the full amount of the tax credit – ie £500.

d) The UK incorporated DangerCo has no liability for tax on dividends received from other UK companies under s208. The dividend does, however, enter into the computation of the company's profits for the purpose, for example, of calculating whether the company is liable to tax at the small companies rate of tax or at the standard rate. The amount taken into account is the net dividend plus the tax credit – £150,000 + £37,500 = £187,500. The receipt of the dividend and tax credit is regarded as 'franked investment income' and the tax credit may be utilised to discharge liability of DangerCo to account for tax on any dividends or 'qualifying distributions' which it may make: s241. If the gross dividend received exceeds the equivalent gross of any dividend paid by DangerCo, the balance is treated as 'surplus franked investment income'. If the company has losses, it may be able to claim repayment of the tax credit on this surplus franked investment income under s242, which remains unrelieved after the set-off against its own liability.

e) In the hands of the trustees of the discretionary Evergreen Trust the income is, as in the other examples above, regarded as a gross amount made up of the dividend plus the tax credit – £10,000 + £2,500 = £12,500. The trustees are taxable on this income at a special rate provided for in s686 – the 'rate applicable to trusts'. Currently the rate of tax for this purpose is 34 per cent and the tax liability therefore amounts to £12,500 x 34% = £4,250. However, as the dividend carries a tax credit of £2,500 the trustees will deduct this from their liability, leaving an additional payment due in the sum of £1,750. When the income is distributed to beneficiaries it is regarded as having suffered tax at 34 per cent and any excess over the beneficiary's own rate of tax will be repayable. Alternatively, if the beneficiary is liable at the higher rate there will be an additional liability of 6 per cent on the gross amount. If, therefore, a payment of £6,600 were made to a beneficiary, this would be treated as income of £10,000 on which tax of £3,400 had been paid.

Chapter 17

Close Companies

17.1   Introduction

17.2   Key points

17.3   Key case and statutes

17.4   Question and suggested solution

17.1 Introduction

A company which is controlled by a small number of people has greater freedom to operate for the personal benefit of its shareholders than publicly owned companies have. A special tax regime was introduced to ensure adequate taxation of the accrued earnings of the owners of close companies, whether or not the company profits were taken out in the form of dividends or earnings or left to accumulate. With the gradual reduction of personal tax rates to approximate with the level of tax on company profits, the tax benefit of retaining company profits in such companies has largely disappeared, and with it much of the special regime.

17.2 Key points

Close companies

Defined in s414 ICTA 1988 as a UK resident company controlled by up to five people or by its directors – not close if more than 35 per cent owned by the public: s415.

Special rules exist in respect of close companies which aim to:

a) extend 'distributions' to include certain payments in kind;

b) treat other transactions as 'distributions'.

c) deny small companies' rate of corporation tax to 'close investment holding companies': ss13 and 13A.

Statutory definitions required

a) 'participator': s417 ICTA 1988;

b) 'associate': s417(3) ICTA 1988;

c) 'director': s417(5) ICTA 1988;

d) 'loan creditor': s417(7) ICTA 1988;

e) 'control': s416 ICTA 1988;

f) 'distributions': s418 ICTA 1988 extends the definition under s209 ICTA 1988;

g) 'loan': s419(2) ICTA 1988.

Special rules for close companies

a) Loans to a participator:

   i) Where the participator is an INDIVIDUAL these are treated as distributions liable to tax at a rate equivalent to ACT (but is not treated as ACT): s419 ICTA 1988.

   Since ACT is abolished from 6 April 1999, the provisions now specify payment of an amount equal to 25 per cent of the relevant amount: para 24 Sch 3 FA 1998.

   ii) Loan includes incurring a debt to the close company.

   iii) Full-time employees without at least 5 per cent interest are exempt up to £15,000: s420(2).

   iv) Prior to FA 1996, repayment of the loan before assessment was still subject to interest: see *Earlspring Properties Ltd* v *Guest* [1993] STC 473. The method of accounting for tax on loans to the participators of close companies was changed by s173 Finance Act 1996. Tax was previously due within 14 days of the end of the accounting period in which the loan was made; now tax is due nine months after the end of the period. No tax is payable if the loan has been repaid by the time the tax becomes due for payment.

   v) Self-assessment provisions for companies require that tax under s419 is accounted for in the relevant tax return – para 1 Sch 18 FA 1998, in common with the normal corporation tax liability.

b) Deemed distributions

   Expenditure incurred on behalf of participators is treated as distributions of profit and prior to 6 April 1999 was subject to ACT in the same way as normal 'qualifying distributions' – s418 ICTA 1988 – not activated if the participator is also subject to the benefit in kind provisions of s154. From 6 April 1999, although ACT no longer applies to such distributions, they are not deductible in computing the company profits: s208 ICTA 1988.

c) Transfer of assets at an undervalue: s125 TCGA 1992

   i) Aimed at ensuring that a company under close control does not distribute assets advantageously to its shareholders. Where assets are transferred out of a close company in a transaction which is not 'at arm's length', the acquisition cost of the shares held by each of the shareholders is reduced in proportion to the value taken out of the company's assets as a result of the transaction. The amount is apportioned to each shareholder and deducted from the acquisition cost when the shares are ultimately disposed of.

ii) By concession the rule is not applied if the participator or his associate is treated as receiving an income distribution under s209(2)(b) or (4) ICTA 1988 or a capital distribution under s122 TCGA 1992 or the transferee is assessed under Schedule E as an employee on the difference between the amount paid and the value of the asset transferred.

Close investment holding companies

Under s13A close investment holding companies are disentitled from the small companies' rate of corporation tax.

This does not apply to trading companies, holding companies or property companies letting to unconnected persons.

See s231(3A)–(3D) ICTA 1988 for anti-avoidance provisions designed to avoid uneven distribution to lower rate taxpayers.

Gains of non-resident 'close companies': s13 TCGA 1992

Although a non-resident company is beyond the scope of the foregoing close company provisions, provision is made in s13 TCGA 1992 for assessing the participators (as defined in s417 ICTA 1988) on capital gains of companies which, except for being non-resident, would be close companies. The individual must be UK domiciled and either resident or ordinarily resident. No assessment is made if the participator has less than a 5 per cent interest in the company. Prior to FA 1996 changes, only shareholders (rather than participators) were within the charge to tax.

Gains apportioned under these provisions are not eligible for reduction by taper relief (discussed in Chapter 18): see s13(10A) TCGA 1992.

17.3 Key case and statutes

- *Joint* v *Bracken Developments Ltd* [1994] STC 300
  Close companies – loans to participators – charge to tax

- Income and Corporation Taxes Act 1988, ss13A and 414–417

- Taxation of Chargeable Gains Act 1992, s125

17.4 Question and suggested solution

What is a close company? Why is it important to know whether a company is a close company?

University of London LLB Examination
(for External Students) Revenue Law June 1990 Q1

General Comment

This question explores the tax implication for close companies.

Skeleton Solution

Close company – opportunity for reduction of personal tax rate of shareholders – apportionment of income to shareholders under old rules for close companies (pre-FA 1989 s103) – new regime limited to Close Investment Holding Companies (CIHC) – small companies' rate of corporation tax not available – ICTA 1988 s13A – loans to participators – liability for quasi ACT.

Suggested Solution

When income tax was at high marginal rates but corporation tax was at lower rates and CGT at the old 'fixed' rate of 30 per cent it would have been possible to have avoided income tax using a company as follows.

Suppose T is a taxpayer paying income tax at, say, 98 per cent on £100,000 worth of Schedule F income (ie dividends from shares in UK companies). Clearly, if the £100,000 Schedule F income is all in the top band of his income his tax bill will be £98,000 and his net income £2,000. It would be sensible for T to transfer his shares to an (investment) company which would receive the dividends and pay instead only corporation tax on that income. As long as CT is lower than the taxpayer's marginal rate a saving in tax would result. In order to get his hands on the income, however, the taxpayer could sell the shares in the investment company (which would have risen in value as a result of the dividends stored in the investment company). This sale would normally be treated as a disposal of an asset (the shares) in the usual way and would only attract capital gains tax at 30 per cent, not income tax at 98 per cent. Quite a saving would result by turning income into capital in this way. In order to counter this avoidance the close companies provisions were introduced. These provisions have been greatly amended recently by s103 FA 1989 to accommodate the substantial disappearance of the opportunities for tax saving resulting from the harmonisation of income tax rates, corporation tax rates and CGT rates; now that the rates are the same (in effect) no saving will result merely from turning income into capital.

The old close company rules

The principal objects of the old rules were twofold: to deem income hoarded in a close company to its shareholders (this was called 'apportionment') and to treat certain transactions (eg the provision of certain benefits in kind) as if they were a distribution (ie Schedule F income) from the company. This statutory apportionment or deeming ensured that the shareholders of a close company paid income tax on the investment income of the company as if they had received the income. Thus the tax saving was avoided.

Crucial to this system was the definition of 'close company'. A 'close company' was, prior to the amendments of FA 1989, a company either (i) under the control of five or fewer 'participators'; or (ii) under the control of the directors; or (iii) more than half of whose income would, were it deemed, ie apportioned to participators who were directors, go to five or fewer directors. 'Control' meant, according to the old rule, control over the company's affairs. Examples of situations in which, say, five people had control of a company would be where they owned:

a) the greater part of the share capital (or the issued share capital); or

b) the greater part of the voting power of the company.

These harsh and complex rules applied, immediately before the FA 1989, to non-trading companies only (so that trading companies could be as close as they liked without the apportionment rules applying) and only to UK resident companies (so that non-resident companies also escaped the apportionment of income). Where income was apportioned the income tax was recoverable from the company itself.

The new rules: FA 1989

Under the new rules statutory apportionment of the income of non-trading, UK resident close companies is abolished. However the close companies provisions are retained, though amended, as the basis for a new creature, the close investment holding company. Where the company qualifies as a CIHC, s105 FA 1989 provides that it shall not enjoy the benefits of the small companies' rate of corporation tax: see s13 FA 1988.

A close company is deemed to be CIHC unless it complies with s13A FA 1988 (introduced by FA 1989). A company complies with s13A if it exists either:

a) to carry on a trade(s) on a commercial basis; or

b) to carry on investments in land intended to be let to persons other than connected persons; or

c) in order to hold certain clauses of investment or coordinate the activities of two or more companies of that sort; or

d) to coordinate the activities of companies falling in (a) or (b) above.

Since a company cannot be a CIHC without being a close company it remains important to know the meaning of 'close company' even though apportionment has been abolished. Under the new rules a company is close if:

a) it is resident in the UK;

b) it has five or more participants or (however many) participants who are directors who possess or are entitled to acquire rights which would entitle them to more than half the asset on a winding-up (disregarding any rights anyone may have as a loan creditor).

A person is a participator (see s417 FA 1988) if he possesses or is entitled to acquire share capital or voting rights in the company or is a loan creditor or is entitled to participate in distributions (or could acquire a right to do so) or is able to secure that the income or assets of the company are applied for his benefit.

Chapter 18

Capital Gains Tax: General

18.1   Introduction

18.2   Key points

18.3   Key cases and statute

18.4   Questions and suggested solutions

18.1 Introduction

Capital Gains Tax (CGT) is a tax on capital not income. The distinctions between capital and income must therefore first be discerned. The criteria for this have been discussed in Chapter 5 of this book. The principal Act is the Taxation of Chargeable Gains Act 1992 (TCGA 1992) to which reference will be made in this chapter unless otherwise indicated.

18.2 Key points

The charging provision: s1(1) TCGA 1992

Tax shall be charged in respect of capital gains accruing to a person on the disposal of assets.

Note:

a) Losses are computed in the same manner as gains: s16.

b) Computations: s15 et seq.

c) Animal exemption: under s3, the first £6,800 of chargeable gains is excluded (£3,400 for trustees). An exemption of £6,800 is available to personal representatives for year of death and subsequent two years' disposals: s3(7) TCGA 1992. Trustees of trusts for the disabled receive the same exemption as individuals: para 1(1) Sch 1 TCGA 1992.

d) Individuals pay tax on their gains at their marginal rate of income tax – ie 20, 23 or 40 per cent.

e) Companies pay corporation tax on gains at either the small companies rate or the full corporation tax rate: see Chapter 15.

f) For disposals on or after 6 April 1998, the rate of capital gains tax chargeable on all trustees and representatives of deceased persons is the 34 per cent 'rate applicable to trusts' under s686 ICTA 1988: see 4(1AA) TCGA 1992. Prior to that date this rate applied only to trustees of discretionary and accumulation settlements.

The basic premise of the Act is to charge to tax the profits realised on the sale of a capital asset. There must be a chargeable person, chargeable asset, chargeable gain and chargeable disposal for the tax to be charged. If any of these elements are missing then no CGT will be payable.

Persons

a) The legislation refers to 'person' rather than individual. This definition will therefore include other legal personalities. Corporations do not pay capital gains tax but pay corporation tax. However the CGT element of corporation tax is still computed in the same manner as for 'persons' but note, no annual exempt amount is allowed.

b) Residence is a necessary element of the charge. Liability will include any person 'in a year of assessment during any part of which he is resident in the UK or during which he is ordinarily resident in the UK': s2(1) TCGA 1992.

Temporary non-residents

For departures on or after 17 March 1998, new provisions – the capital gains tax charge on 'temporary non-residents' apply: s10A TCGA 1992, introduced by s127 FA 1998. This provides for a charge to capital gains tax on disposals made in the year of departure from the United Kingdom. In addition, tax is chargeable on gains made on the disposal of assets held at the date of departure, if the period between the date of departure from and return to the United Kingdom does not include five complete tax years. Assets acquired during the period of absence are not chargeable under these provisions: s10A(3)(a).

The new rules do not apply to persons unless they were resident or ordinarily resident in the United Kingdom for at least part of four of the seven tax years preceding their departure: s10A(1)(d).

c) Extra-statutory concession D2 restricts charge to tax on gains made from date of UK arrival.

d) Sections 10–13 deal with foreign traders disposing of assets within the UK and foreign domicile assets and the assessment of individual shareholders of non-resident companies for the gains made by companies which would be treated as close companies if they were UK resident (see Chapter 17). There is no taper relief – s2A TCGA 1992 – for gains apportioned under s13.

e) See *R v IRC, ex parte Fulford-Dobson* [1987] STC 344 – a failed attempt to utilise the concession D2 (see above), by gift from wife to husband and subsequent sale after he became non-resident. Concessions will not be applied where tax avoidance is attempted. The 'temporary non-residents' charge under s10A – discussed above effectively limits post-departure moves of this kind.

f) Married couples are taxed separately on their capital gains and each has their own annual exemption figure. The revised rules for identification of shares (see below) do not prevent inter-spouse 'bed and breakfast' operations to increase the base cost.

Assets

Section 21(1): assets are not defined but include options, debts and incorporeal property generally, currency other than sterling and property created by the person disposing of it.

Note: first transfer of a debt is not usually brought to charge.

Almost all forms of properties whether corporeal or incorporeal are brought into charge: see *O'Brien* v *Benson's Hosiery (Holdings) Ltd* [1979] STC 735; *Zim Properties* v *Procter* [1985] STC 90.

The courts favour the approach that if an asset can be turned to capital account and by doing so can realise a gain, then it is probably a chargeable asset. In *Zim Properties*, the 'right to sue' was held to be an asset in itself, and with no corresponding acquisition cost might have led to taxing the full receipt as gain: see the Inland Revenue concession referred to in question 5 following under *Assets for capital gains*.

Disposal of an asset

A disposal of an asset is the 'trigger-point' to the charge to CGT. Disposal involves an alienation of title or some permanent dissociation of your entitlement to enjoy the asset. Section 21(2): disposal of an asset will also include disposal of a part and part disposal of an asset. Loans of assets will not generally constitute a disposal. Some transactions will be considered a deemed disposal (see *Zim Properties*). A disposal of an asset may also give rise to an allowable loss: s16. If there is no 'disposal' or the legislation directs that a transaction will not be treated as a disposal, there is no liability to CGT – see in particular the 'shares for shares etc' exchange transactions to facilitate reorganisations and take-overs: s127 TCGA 1992 and ss126–138 generally.

a) Part disposal

   Section 21: '… there is a part disposal where an interest or right in or over the asset is created by the disposal'. See also s42 regarding computation.

b) Section 22 provides also that disposal shall occur where a capital sum is received although no disposition of title has occurred. These situations are usually in the nature of compensation for damage, destruction or surrendering of rights: see *Kirby* v *Thorn EMI* [1987] STC 621 and *Marren* v *Ingles* [1980] STC 500.

c) Value shifting

Sections 29–34 are anti-avoidance provisions to ensure that paper transfers designed not to attract the CGT charge are considered deemed disposals.

d) Section 28: timing of a disposal

You should look first at the contractual alienation of title in the contract. In most cases this will be easy to discern and provide the timing for CGT purposes to trigger the charge. If the contract is contingent or conditional then the charge is usually triggered by the satisfaction of the condition or contingency: see *Eastham* v *Leigh London and Provincial Properties* [1971] Ch 871.

Computation

Sections 15 et seq

a) The tax payable is calculated by using the formulae below for individuals. Companies have no annual exempt amount.

   i) Disposal price – acquisition price = gross gain.

   ii) Gross gain – allowable expenditure + annual exempt amount (for individuals) + any unusued transferable losses.

   iii) Net gain – (indexation allowance) = net chargeable gain (two parallel calculations required to rebase March 1982 or original cost in most cases).

   iv) Gain is charged at top marginal rate of income tax (after gain has been added to income) = tax payable. Companies' gains are part of profits charged to corporation tax.

   Note: Indexation allowance – ss53–57 TCGA 1992 provides relief for inflation. It continues for companies but for others it ceased at April 1998 – ss125 and 141 FA 1998, being replaced by taper relief under s2A TCGA 1992 – see below. Indexation allowance will still apply to disposals of assets held at 5 April 1998, but the amount of allowance will be limited to the April 1998 level: s122 FA 1998.

b) Part disposal follows the above formulae, but initially the value of the part is obtained by the fraction in s42.

   Part disposals are apportioned by the fraction:

   $$\frac{A}{A + B}$$

   where A is the value of the consideration for the disposal and B is the market value of the part undisposed of.

c) Rebasing cost: the legislation allows rebasing of the acquisition cost of the asset to

March 1982 by FA 1988. It was presumed that the substitution of the market value of that asset held before that date would be more advantageous than using the indexed acquisition value of the time of previous disposal to the owner. In practice two calculations are made, and the taxpayer will be permitted to use the calculation which is most advantageous to himself. These calculations are complex and therefore only an understanding of the mechanics of these procedures need be shown in the examinations.

d) Indexation losses: where indexation allowance (see (a) above) results in a deduction which converts a gain into a loss, that loss is now excluded from relief by restricting the amount of indexation deduction to an amount which reduces the gain to nil. No indexation deduction is added to transactions already producing a loss (FA 1994 amending ss53–56 TCGA 1992).

e) Taper relief: s2A and Sch A1 TCGA 1992. Introduced from April 1998 and applies for income tax purposes only for disposals by individuals, personal representatives and trustees.

The effect of the relief is to reduce the chargeable gain according to the length of time the asset has been held. The reduction is greater for business assets, which is the reason why retirement relief – see retirement relief section below – for disposals of businesses or business assets will no longer be required after taper relief reaches an effective level for existing businesses.

Taper relief is then added as set out below. Losses are deducted from gains before the application of taper relief: s2A(1) TCGA 1992 inserted by s121(1) FA 1998.

Business assets

Taper relief for business assets applies – paras 3–9 Sch A1 TCGA 1992 – to:

i) an asset used for the purposes of a trade carried on by an individual (either alone or in partnership) or by a qualifying company of the individual (defined in (iii) below);

ii) an asset held for the purposes of an office or employment to which the individual is required to devote substantially the whole of his time; or

iii) shares in a qualifying company – ie a trading company or the holding company of a trading group: where an individual holds at least 5 per cent of the voting rights and is a full time working director or employee; or where an individual holds at least 25 per cent of the voting rights.

Where the asset is held by trustees or personal representatives, the interests of the individual referred to above are to be read as those of the trustees or the personal representatives of the deceased.

The relief for business assets is 7.5 per cent per annum for each complete tax year after 5 April 1998 for which the asset has been held: s2A(3)(a) TCGA 1992.

Assets acquired before 17 March 1998 qualify for a bonus year of relief. For example, an asset purchased on 1 January 1998 and disposed of on 1 August 2001 for a gain of £10,000 will be treated as having been held for four complete tax years – ie 1998–99 to 2000–01 plus a bonus year. Taper relief of 4 x 7.5% = 30% x £10,000 = £3,000 will be deducted from the gain.

Note that there is no proportional relief for the period from 6 April 2001 to 1 August 2001. Indexation relief from January 1998 to April 1998 will apply.

Assets used partly for business and partly for non-business use will have their relief apportioned according to their use during the last ten years of ownership – paras 2 and 21 Sch A1 TCGA 1992 – or for the period from 6 April 1998 to the date of disposal if that is shorter. Therefore any non-business use prior to 5 April 1998 is ignored. If the asset in the example above had been used for non-business purposes during the final tax year, there will be three years of taper relief at the business asset rate and one year at the non-business rate.

Non-business assets

The principles for determining business assets are as set out above. Any asset not meeting these conditions are therefore non-business assets, for which the annual rate of taper relief for each complete tax year falling after 5 April 1998 is 5 per cent but unlike the relief for business assets, it does not start to apply until the third complete tax year: s2A(3)(b) TCGA 1992. The maximum relief therefore over a ten-year period is therefore 8 x 5% = 40%. There is no addition of a bonus year for assets held at 17 March 1998.

Wasting assets

These are assets with a predictable life of less than 50 years (s38), eg plant and machinery. Allowable expenditure is restricted to a straight line basis over the predictable life of the asset.

Market value: ss17, 18, 29, 30, 286

The TCGA 1992 presumes gains to be calculated on the basis that all transactions have been made at commercial values and are 'bargains at arm's length'. The Act will therefore substitute market value in certain circumstances to prevent distortion of the gain calculation.

Section 17 shall '... be deemed to be for a consideration equal to the market value of the asset'. For valuation see s272. The Act also presumes that some family arrangements are not at market value because they are made between 'connected persons': ss18 and 286.

Mansworth v *Jelley* [2003] STC 53: an employee was granted options to acquire shares in his employer's parent company. He exercised the options to sell the shares. The Court of Appeal upheld the Revenue's CGT assessments on the basis that the base value of the shares was the sum of the price paid for the shares on the exercise of the options and the market value of the options when originally granted.

Transactions to and from trading stock: s161

Where an asset exists as trading stock and is removed as a capital item, or vice versa, market value of the asset will be substituted.

Special rules for identification of securities

Sections 104–114 TCGA 1992, as amended by FA 1998.

Calculation of the chargeable gain on the disposal of shares requires identification of the allowable expenditure attributable to the shares, after any indexation, losses, or taper relief from the disposal proceeds. This in turn requires the identification of the shares disposed of. Where a person acquires the same class of shares in the same company in the same capacity on more than one occasion, the means of calculating the allowable expenditure will vary depending on whether the person making the disposal as an individual (or trust) or a company.

a) Individual shareholders (and trusts)

For shares acquired before 6 April 1998 the calculation of the allowable expenditure is by reference to a 'pool' of shares rather than on each share individually. From 6 April 1998 pooling has been abolished for individuals and trusts (but not for companies). As a result where shares are directly held by individuals, they will need to account for shares acquired before 6 April 1998 on the basis of the pooling rules: s104(2)(aa). For shares acquired after that date, the allowable expenditure for the disposal must be calculated by reference to each share individually (save where there is a rights or bonus issue made in respect of shares that were acquired before 6 April 1998).

Disposals made after 5 April 1998 are to be identified in the following order:

i) acquisitions and disposals of shares of the same class by the same company on the same day are identified with each other (s105(1));

ii) with acquisitions within 30 days following the disposal on a first in first out (FIFO) basis (s106A(5));

iii) with previous acquisitions after 5 April 1998 on a last in first out (LIFO) basis (s106A(6));

iv) with the section 104 pool (s106A(8));

v) with the pre-6 April 1982 pool (the 1982 pool) (s106A(8));

vi) with acquisitions before 6 April 1965 (para 4(3) Sch 2 TCGA).

The s104 pool is for securities held on 5 April 1998 but not before 6 April 1982 and the 1982 pool is for securities held at 5 April 1982 but not before 6 April 1965. The s104 pool is to be treated as acquired when the first shares were acquired in the s104 holding and at 31 March 1982 for a 1982 holding.

Shares identified with a pool

If the shares are matched with a 'pool' of shares it will be necessary to calculate the average base cost of the shares disposed of by reference to the pool and then apply indexation, losses and then taper relief to those shares.

b) Gains made by companies

If a company holds shares these continue to be subject to 'pooling rules' and indexation relief (even after 6 April 1998 since there is no taper relief provision for companies). The pooling rules for corporation tax (which will apply to offshore companies) also have identification rules matching acquisitions with disposals.

Identification rules

The following is a list of the order of priority in which shares being disposed of by a company should be identified:

i) Acquisitions and disposals of shares of the same class by the same company on the same day are identified with each other: s105(1).

ii) If a company holds not less than 2 per cent of issued shares of the same class in a company and acquires and disposes of them in a prescribed period of one month through a stock exchange or the Automated Real-Time Investments Exchange, then they are identified with each other in preference to other shares held by the company. If the disposal is not through such a stock exchange or investments exchange the prescribed period is six months. For shares acquired before the disposal, shares should be identified on a LIFO basis and for those acquired after the disposal, on a FIFO basis: s106(5) and (10).

iii) Shares (other than relevant securities) acquired and disposed of within a period of ten days: s107(3).

iv) If more shares (other than relevant securities) are acquired within the ten-day period than are disposed of then they are identified with the s104 holding on a first-in-first-out (FIFO) basis: s107(4).

v) Securities not treated as part of the s104 holding are treated as 'relevant securities' and are subject to a special set of identification rules: ss107(6) and 108.

vi) Shares forming part of the section 104 holding: ss107(8) and 104.

vii) Any excess shares over and above the s104 holding are matched with the 1982 holding and on a last-in-first-out (LIFO) basis: s107(9).

viii) Any excess shares over and above the 1982 holding to be matched with quoted shares held on 6 April 1965 on a last-in-first-out basis (LIFO) basis: para 4(3) Sch 2 TCGA.

Exemptions from the charge s263 etc

The Act allows for several otherwise chargeable assets and transactions to be exempted from the ambit of the charge:

a) Section 263: private motor cars and vehicles for normal private carriage use.

b) Section 268: decorations for gallantry.

c) Section 269: foreign currency gains from private use on return from holiday etc.

d) Section 51(1): gambling winnings (or losses).

e) Section 51(2): compensation for personal injuries, cf ss31 and 43.

f) Section 251: first transfer of debts.

g) Sections 222–223: private residences:

It must have been the taxpayer's principal or only residence during the period of ownership. Land up to 0.5 hectare, unless the house is a large residence, is also included. Houses occupied by dependent relatives (if occupied pre 6 April 1988 only) are exempt. Where a house is occupied by tenants or licensees as well as the taxpayer, strictly the exemption is lost. In practice a time and proportion calculation is accepted giving a partial exemption. The final three years of ownership count as occupation, as do other defined periods of absence: s223(1)–(3);

See *Lewis* v *Lady Rook* [1992] STC 171 and as applied in *Honour* v *Norris* [1992] STC 304.

h) Section 262: tangible moveable property is not brought to charge where the consideration for the disposal is less than £6,000. Where the consideration is over £6,000 a five-thirds calculation is used to exempt a partial amount.

i) Section 258: works of art.

j) Section 256: a charity may be subject to a gain on the disposal of a donated asset.

k) Section 257: gifts to charities may attract roll-over relief.

The effect is to reduce the allowable expenditure of the new asset by the amount of the chargeable gain realised on the disposal of the old asset.

Sections 152–158: replacement of business assets

Where a trader sells a qualifying business asset and replaces it with a new qualifying asset then relief against the charge is afforded. To qualify the trader must have used the asset through his ownership for the purposes of the trade.

The relief is as follows:

a) A qualifying asset must be land, buildings, plant and machinery, ships, aircraft, satellites, space stations and spacecraft, hovercraft, goodwill or milk quotas.

b) The relief is that he is treated as having disposed of the outgoing asset for a sum equal to its allowable expenditure, and the consideration afforded to the new asset is reduced by the roll-over gain.

c) The new asset must be purchased one year before or three years after (subject to an HMIT written extension) the disposal of the old asset.

d) The trader must take the new asset into use immediately on its acquisition unless the asset is not ready for use on its acquisition (see Revenue interpretation RI 7 of November 1991). However this will presumably not apply if it is let: see *Campbell Connolly & Co Ltd v Barnett* [1994] STC 50.

e) Gains made by one member of a group of companies may be rolled over if the replacement asset is purchased by another of the group's companies: s175(2A) and (2B).

f) Under self-assessment s141 FA 1996 introduced a new s153A into the TCGA provisions. The taxpayer making a chargeable gain is able to make a declaration, when submitting a tax return for self-assessment, to the effect that the proceeds from the sale of the chargeable asset are to be reinvested in a qualifying asset within the three year time limit. Such a declaration remains in force until it is withdrawn, superseded by an actual claim to rollover relief or (for companies) on the fourth anniversary of the accounting period in which the disposal occurred or (for individuals, partnerships and others) on the third 31 January following the year of assessment in which the disposal occurred.

Retirement relief

Schedule 6 TCGA 1992, Sch 7 paras 1 and 2 FA 1993.

Note: Relief being phased out beginning 1999–2000 following introduction of taper relief: see p157.

Relief is afforded where a trader has reached 50 years of age or is suffering from ill-health and wished to cease trading, ie he wants to make a 'material disposal' of the business or the shares in a family business. Relief is given against the charge on a sliding scale of the period of ownership.

The 'family business' (or 'family company') concept has been replaced by the 'personal company' as defined in FA 1993 Schedule 7 – being one in which not less than 5 per cent of the voting rights is exercisable by the individual.

The gains up to £250,000 are exempt. Half of the gains between £250,000 and £1,000,000 are also exempt: para 13 Sch 6 TCGA 1992 as amended by s92 FA 1994.

Clarke v *Mayo* [1994] STC 570: the issue of whether for retirement relief purposes a time gap between the sale of the business property and the disposal of the shares meant that the latter disposal ceased to be an associated and material disposal for ss163 and 164 TCGA 1992 purposes was decided in favour of the taxpayer.

Phasing out of retirement relief

The provisions described above are being gradually withdrawn following the introduction of taper relief, which includes specific additional relief for business assets – see p157. Relief as described above is allowed in full for a relevant disposal during 1998–99 but the following limitations apply for the years 1999–2000 to 2002–03. No relief under these provisions will be due for disposals after 5 April 2003.

Year 1999–2000 100% relief on gains up to £200,000: 50% relief £200,001 – £800,000

Year 2000–01 100% relief on gains up to £150,000: 50% relief £150,001 – £600,000

Year 2001–02 100% relief on gains up to £100,000: 50% relief £100,001 – £400,000

Year 2002–03 100% relief on gains up to £50,000: 50% relief £50,001 – £200,000

Jarmin v *Rawlings* [1994] STC 1005: a successful attempt to claim retirement relief where the several disposals together amounted to the disposal of 'part of a business'.

Mannion v *Johnston* [1988] STC 758 and *Atkinson* v *Dancer* [1988] STC 758: both unsuccessful attempts to show that disposals of assets had amounted to disposals of at least part of a business.

Barrett v *Powell* [1998] STC 283 concerned the surrender of an agricultural tenancy which was followed by period of farming under temporary licence. The court had to consider whether the surrender for which the consideration giving rise to the gain was paid, constituted disposal of part of a business under what is now s163(2)(a) TCGA 1992. The Court held that the Commissioners had misdirected themselves in finding that the taxpayer's business was in a wholly different position after the surrender of the tenancy. The judge ruled that the Commissioners had applied an incorrect statutory test and that the correct test was to compare the farming business position before and after the disposal. Only if it could be found that a part or all of the business had ceased as a result of the disposal, could the relief be applied. In fact only the asset comprising the tenancy agreement had been disposed of and this in itself was insufficient to qualify for the relief.

Relief for re-investment in shares: Sch 7 Part II FA 1993

This part of Sch 7 inserted new ss164A–164N into TCGA 1992 and gave a form of roll-over relief to an individual on a 'material disposal' of a 'qualifying investment' after 16 March 1993. It is referred to as 'reinvestment relief'. The relief is now merged into the Enterprise Investment Scheme (EIS) relief – see Chapter 3 – so that deferral of gains is restricted to reinvesting in qualifying EIS companies with effect from 6 April 1998: s165 FA 1998.

Allowable expenditure: s38

Where work has been carried out on an asset some expenditure may be allowed so as to increase the base cost of the asset, thereby lowering the gross gain. Section 38 only allows expenditure on the improvement of the asset and which is still reflected in the asset when disposed: s38(1)(b).

Section 59: partnerships

Where two or more people carry on a trade or business they are deemed to act as partners. Their liability to CGT is joint and several. It is presumed prima facie to be an equal liability but will be eventually assessed on their equity share as expressed in the partnership document. Partners are connected persons within the meaning of ss18 and 286, and therefore market value is substituted for disposals of assets between partners or within the partnership.

Where there is a change of partnership membership and consequently a change in equity shares then the Inland Revenue generally treat the reallocation of partnership assets (a deemed disposal) as taking place at neither a loss nor a gain. The same treatment is extended by s59A to limited liability partnerships under the Limited Liability Partnerships Act 2000.

18.3 Key cases and statute

- *Batey* v *Wakefield* (1981) 55 TC 550
  Capital gains tax – exemptions and reliefs – private residences

- *Campbell Connelly & Co Ltd* v *Barnett* [1994] STC 50
  Roll-over relief

- *Goodwin* v *Curtis* [1998] STC 475
  Capital gains tax – exemptions and reliefs – main residence

- *NAP Holdings UK Ltd* v *Whittles* [1994] STC 979
  Acquisition cost on inter-group disposals/reorganisation

- *O'Brien* v *Benson's Hosiery (Holdings) Ltd* [1979] STC 735
  Capital gains tax – assets – property brought into charge

- *Zim Properties* v *Proctor* [1985] STC 90
  Capital gains tax – disposal of assets

- Taxation of Chargeable Gains Act 1992, ss1(1), 21–22, 104–114 (as amended by FA 1988), 152–158, 222–223, 251, 263, 268 and 269.

18.4 Questions and suggested solutions

Note: you should also refer to the questions in Chapters 20–22 which deal with both capital gains tax and inheritance tax – a common occurrence.

QUESTION ONE

Advise F on the CAPITAL GAINS TAX consequences of the following events and transactions:

a) In May 1998 F bought a valuable modern impressionist painting for £2,300. He sold it in February 1999 for £6,500.

b) In June 1998 F bought a second hand hearse at an auction for £2,000. He sold it in January 1999 to the Bloggs Vintage Car Museum for £8,000.

c) In March 1998 F contracted to sell Blackacre to G in fee simple for £150,000. The conveyance was completed in May 1998. F had bought Blackacre for £60,000 in 1985. Blackacre, a country cottage, was the only property F owned at the time of the sale. He used Blackacre at weekends only. During the week F lived in rented flat in London close to his place of work.

d) In December F loaned H £10,000. In March 1999 F sold the debt which H owned him to J for £5,000. In May 1999 H paid J £8,000 in full and final settlement of the debt, £8,000 being the most that H could at that time afford.

University of London LLB Examination
(for External Students) Revenue Law June 1999 Q9

General Comment

This question illustrates the principles of capital gains tax, focusing particularly on exemptions and reliefs.

Skeleton Solution

Painting: chattel exemption; s262 – hearse: s263; relief for private motor vehicles – Blackacre: timing of disposal (s28(1)); application of s222 (principal residence relief) – sale of debt: s22(1); *Marren* v *Ingles*; s251.

Suggested Solution

a) Disposal of 'chattels'

The charge to capital gains tax arises on the disposal of assets (s1 Taxation of Chargeable Gains Act (TCGA) 1992), which includes all forms of property: s21(1) TCGA 1992. Certain assets are however subject to exemption or relief from the tax charge. Under the provisions of s262 of the 1992 Act where 'tangible moveable property' is disposed of for consideration of less than £6,000, any gain arising from the disposal is exempt from tax and is not regarded as a chargeable gain: s262(1) TCGA 1992. This exemption would apply to the painting which F bought since it is tangible moveable property and was sold for a consideration of only £3,700.

b) Sale of car

The sale of the hearse would fall within the exemption for private motor vehicles under s263 TCGA 1992.

c) Sale of Blackacre

F's disposal of Blackacre incurs a liability to capital gains tax since, under s21, all forms of property and assets are liable to capital gains tax, and reliance has to be placed on other provisions of TCGA or any exemptions from the general charge. Ordinarily, an asset will deemed to have been disposed of when consideration is given. However, where a contract precedes the conveyance, such is the case with real property, the time of disposal is the time the contract is made. Therefore, F disposed of Blackacre for CGT purposes in March 1998 rather than May 1998.

Under s222 an exemption is available in respect of the disposal of a private residence which an individual has, at any time during his period of ownership, occupied as his only or main residence. If a person has two residences (eg a flat in town and a country house), both of which could qualify, he may nominate one or other exemption as being his main residence even though he spends relatively little time there. The only restrictions are that both must actually be residences of his, and that, unless the election is made within two years of the period for which exemption is claimed, the inspector is given power to decide which in fact was his main residence. Provided that F makes the proper election, he will probably be able to use the principal residence relief exemption.

d) Sale of debt

Section 22(1) extends the meaning of 'disposal' beyond cases where an asset is transferred from one party to another. In particular, this covers capital sums received in return for forfeiture or surrender of rights, or for refraining from exercising rights. *Marren* v *Ingles* [1980] STC 500 shows that s22 applies whether or not the payer acquired an asset. It would appear that the sale of a debt would fall within s22(1).

However, under s251, debts do not give rise to chargeable gains or allowable losses, at least as far as the original creditor is concerned. Therefore, F will not be able to claim the £5,000 as an allowable loss. Second-hand debts are, however, chargeable assets. Thus, when a person purchases a debt at a discount and either sells it on at a profit, or obtains satisfaction of it, he will make a chargeable gain on his 'turn'. Therefore, J will be liable for CGT on the £3,000 profit from the debt.

QUESTION TWO

Howard is in the retail business. In recent years his profits have diminished owing to the recession. He decided not to curtail his business activities but to realise some of his personal assets. He sold some cuff links which he had inherited from his father. At the date of his father's death they were valued at £500. The price Howard received on selling them was £1,000. Howard's daughter had always admired a painting belonging to Howard. They agreed that she would buy it from him for half the current market value. Howard sold some publicly quoted shares. On most of these he realised a gain but on one property development company, he made a loss.

Howard owned a small estate in the country and lived in the main house. He sold the freehold of a cottage in the grounds of the estate for £600,000. The whole estate had cost him £300,000 when he purchased it. The value of the estate after the sale of the cottage is £500,000.

Advise on the capital gains tax consequences of the above.

For the purposes of this question ignore inflation.

University of London LLB Examination
(for External Students) Revenue Law June 1994 Q9

General Comment

This question illustrates the principles of capital gains tax, focusing particularly on exemptions and reliefs.

Skeleton Solution

Chattel exemption: s262; £6,000 – non-arms length sale; connected persons; s18; market value substitution; no-loss relief s18(3) – set-off of loss against chargeable gain: s2(2) – part disposal of property: s42 – relief for trading losses: s380 ICTA 1988.

Suggested Solution

Note: All references are to the Taxation of Chargeable Gains Act (TCGA) 1992 unless stated otherwise.

Disposal of 'chattels'

The charge to capital gains tax arises on the disposal of assets (s1), which includes all forms of property: s21(1). Certain assets are however subject to exemption or relief from the tax charge. Under the provisions of s262 of the 1992 Act where 'tangible moveable property' is disposed of for consideration of less than £6,000, any gain arising from the disposal is exempt from tax and is not regarded as a chargeable gain: s262(1). This exemption would apply to the cuff links which Howard inherited from his father since they are tangible moveable property and of only £1,000 in value. Therefore, no charge to tax arises on the gain of £500.

Sale of painting at less than full value

If Howard disposes of the painting to his daughter at less than market value the transaction will be subject to the provisions of s18 which reconstructs transactions between 'connected persons', defined in s286(2) and (8) as including descendants. On the normal application of the principles for calculating gains and losses Howard would have made a loss equal to half of the value of the painting. Section 18 however provides that in transactions between connected persons the consideration must be treated as being equal to the market value of the asset. Market value is what the asset might be expected to fetch on a sale on the open market. Howard may therefore be making a taxable gain if the current market value is greater than his original cost or other acquisition value for capital gains tax purposes. His daughter will acquire the painting at market value for the purpose of any future disposal. If the current market value is less than Howard's CGT base cost, there is no relief for the loss which he is making – s18(3) – unless another transaction with his daughter gives rise to a gain. The loss may not be set against other gains from transactions with other persons.

Since a painting is also tangible moveable property it may also come within the chattel exemption of s262 if the value is less than £6,000. Beyond £6,000 there is tapering relief under s262(2) to reduce the amount chargeable to tax.

Sale of shares

On the disposal of quoted shares the amount realised on the sale, after relevant expenses of the disposal, is compared with Howard's acquisition cost to give the amount of chargeable gain arising. From the resulting gain, an indexation allowance will be deductible by applying the movement in the retail prices index between acquisition and disposal dates, to the cost figure: s54. However, the loss-producing shares will not have the loss increased by the indexation allowance as a result of the changes made to s53 by the s93 Finance Act 1994 for disposals after 30 November 1993. The loss calculated by reference to the normal comparison of consideration against cost will be deductible from the gain on the other shares.

Part disposal of estate property

By disposing of the cottage within his estate Howard is deemed to be making a part disposal of his estate and special provisions apply to calculate the gain which he is considered to have made. These provisions apply where, on a disposal of property, any part of the property remains undisposed of. Under s42 the acquisition cost to be deducted from the sale consideration is to be apportioned pro rata between the part disposed of and the part retained. The ratio is arrived at by use of the respective sale price of the part disposed of in the ratio of itself plus the market value of the part remaining and applying the result to the original cost to give the acquisition cost element of the part sold: s42(2). In Howard's case, the ratio for the apportionment is £600,000 to £600,000 plus £500,000 = $\frac{6}{11}$ths of £300,000, giving a deductible cost of £163,636 and a gain of £136,264.

Trading loss relief

We are told that Howard's business is becoming less profitable. If he does in fact incur trading losses he may claim relief for these losses under s380 ICTA 1988 against his capital gains and hence some of the above chargeable gains may be relieved in this way to minimise the tax which would otherwise become payable.

In addition, Howard may claim to use the annual exemption of £5,800 to reduce his capital gains tax – under s3.

QUESTION THREE

'Capital gains tax has become too complex and should be abolished.'

Do you agree with this statement?

University of London LLB Examination
(for External Students) Revenue Law June 1993 Q6

General Comment

This question explores the drawbacks of the capital gains tax system.

Skeleton Solution

The concept of a 'capital' gain – short-term and long-term gains – identification of asset being disposed of – meaning of a disposal – problems associated with different types of assets: eg private residences – problems associated with certain types of transactions: company reorganisations.

Suggested Solution

Capital gains tax was initially introduced to tax the profits arising out of short-term acquisition and disposal of assets. Since 1965 the tax has been charged on all gains arising from the disposal of 'chargeable assets'. For administrative reasons various assets have been left out of the definition of chargeable assets, and equally the tax has been extended to include gains arising from 'all forms of property ... including ... incorporeal property generally' (s21 Taxation of Chargeable Gains Act (TCGA) 1992), as well as certain occasions when no asset is disposed of but a sum is received in respect of an asset. The tax is therefore chargeable on disposals and theoretical disposals and losses in value: s24 TCGA 1992.

If complexities arise on the meaning of the basic concept of what capital gains tax is meant to charge, then it is not difficult to conceive that the further provisions relating to the administration of the tax will themselves have become extremely complex.

Under s1(1) of TCGA 1992 tax is charged 'on the disposal of assets'. Neither of the words 'disposal' and 'asset' is defined in the Act. In the absence of such a definition a disposal will assume its ordinary natural meaning in that a disposal of an asset occurs when its ownership changes or the owner divests himself of the right over, or interest in, an asset. This will include a gift, sale, exchange and other transfers, whether actual or 'deemed' to have occurred.

The capital gains tax legislation brings in the concept of a 'deemed' disposal which is beyond the normal meaning of 'disposal': for example, on the occasion (under s71) of trustees being said to have disposed of and immediately reacquired assets on an occasion when a beneficiary becomes absolutely entitled to settled property. Where a life interest in settled property ceases there is deemed to be a change of ownership, and the trustee is deemed to dispose of the assets and immediately reacquire them at market value before the transfer to the beneficiary occurs. The growth in value is chargeable to capital gains tax in the hands of the trustees, except that where the occasion is on the death of the tenant no gain or loss is deemed to be made by the trustees.

Further, in ss144–147 the grant of an option is the disposal of an asset. Similarly, part disposals are disposals for capital gains tax purposes and occur where 'any description of property derived from the asset remains undisposed of'. A part disposal also occurs if a right over or an interest in is created in relation to an asset, such as in the case of the grant of a restrictive covenant over the use of land. To understand the concept of ownership one has to regard ownership as relating to a bundle of rights, some or all of which may be given away in favour of another person.

The statutes also require that a distinction be drawn between the disposal of a part of an asset and the part disposal of the full rights over an entire asset.

Equally important are occasions in which a 'disposal' is deemed not to have taken place:

a) the receipt of a capital sum where an asset is not lost or destroyed if the sum is used to restore the asset (s23);

b) giving of a mortgage or charge over property (s26);

c) in particular, relief is given from a charge to corporation tax on capital gains to facilitate various reorganisations, reconstructions, amalgamations and take-overs: ss126–137. Since these involve the disposal of existing shares or other securities and the issue of other shares or securities either by the same company or by a third company concerned in the transaction, a capital gains tax charge would normally arise on the initial disposal. The legislation dictates that in certain circumstances a 'disposal' will be regarded as not taking place, and therefore the initial transaction is regarded as being outside the scope of a charge to capital gains tax.

It will be plain from the foregoing that even the fundamental area of a charge to tax on a disposal of an asset is in itself far from straightforward and at times extremely complex. Furthermore, the legislation caters in detail for transactions involving specific assets and it is not surprising to find further complexities within those areas, having regard to the difficult nature of the basic concept.

Specific transactions

a) *Private residence relief*

An illustration of the complexities of capital gains tax legislation can be demonstrated from the examination of a relief from the tax on the disposal of a private residence, set out in the provisions of s222 TCGA 1992. The relatively simple concept of an exemption on the disposal of a taxpayer's private dwelling has exercised the courts on a number of occasions without, it must be said, arriving at a formula which can be easily and safely applied with certainty. A number of cases have considered what is a 'residence' for the purpose of this relief and whether this can include other buildings in the vicinity.

The principle case of *Batey* v *Wakefield* [1981] STC 521 determined that more than one building can qualify. In *Williams* v *Merrylees* [1987] STC 445 the 'residence' qualified together with a distant lodge house sold separately and later. However, in *Green* v *IRC* [1982] STC 485 and *Markey* v *Sanders* [1987] STC 256 relief for additional and more adjacent buildings was denied through the inability to disturb the finding of facts before the Commissioners. In *Lewis* v *Lady Rook* [1992] STC 171 it was decided that the Commissioners should have been looking for an 'entity' which in its entirety would qualify, and as a result nearby cottages were included in the relief for capital gains tax on the disposal of the entire 'residence' of the taxpayer.

b) *Shares and securities*

Much of the difficulty surrounding capital gains tax is traceable to the legislation surrounding the calculation of a gain arising from the disposal of shares of securities. Complex identification rules became necessary in what is now ss107–112 of TCGA 1992. The introduction of an indexation allowance was intended to remove the inflation element from a gain before it was charged to tax. The application of this allowance was dependent upon proper identification of the shareholdings etc being disposed of. The complex pooling arrangements were generally regarded as unworkable and certainly not productive when compared with the relatively small amount of tax being collected. The current rules, although an improvement on the original, still do not eliminate all of the complexities to be found in a charge to CGT on share disposals.

In relation to the disposal of other securities or debts, the existing capital gains tax legislation was not constructed for easy application to a rapidly changing financial world. The rapid growth in the production of new financial instruments consistently raised the question as to whether the security concerned was within existing definitions of exempt assets for capital gains tax purposes. Accordingly, there followed a series of provisions which were still being overtaken by new financial instruments which have culminated in, virtually, a blanket exemption for most corporate securities.

The alignment of the income tax and capital gains tax rates, by charging gains of individuals at their income tax rates and for companies at the corporation tax rate, has made the distinction between capital and income profits less important. Many of the remaining complexities involve the necessity of establishing an 'acquisition cost' for any asset disposed of in order to calculate a gain. There is undoubtedly a wide divergence between the rules for calculation of income for income tax purposes and gain for capital gains tax purposes, and any abolition of the capital gains tax regime through its inclusion in the income tax regime is likely to be burdened with the same complexities of real income and gains and deemed income and gains, which have given rise to much of the complex legislation designed to ensure that capital profits are not deferred indefinitely through tax avoidance arrangements.

Indeed, much of the early case reports were devoted to distinguishing between capital and income receipts. If capital gains tax were abolished this problem, which capital gains tax to a great extent eliminated from fiscal planning, would be resurrected.

QUESTION FOUR

Advise on the capital gains tax consequences of the following transactions which took place in 2001–02:

a) The sale by Martin for £300,000 of his house and grounds which he purchased in 1976. At the time of purchase the grounds were half a hectare. Martin lived in the house until 1994. He then spent two years living abroad. On his return to the United Kingdom he took up residence the house again. At that time he purchased an extra hectare of land which adjoined his garden. The solicitors acting for Martin in connection with the sale of the house this year were negligent. He should have received £320,000 for the sale. The solicitors paid him £20,000 by way of compensation.

b) The settlement by Norman of property on trustees to hold for A until he qualifies as a doctor, then for B for life then to C on attaining the age of 25. A qualified as a doctor in January 2002 and B was killed in a car crash in March 2002 when C was aged 24.

c) The sale by Olivia of jewellery. She received £7,000 for the jewellery which she had acquired for £5,000 in 1986.

d) The gift of a valuable painting by Paula to her brother, Oswald, on the occasion of his 21st birthday.

Adapted from University of London LLB Examination
(for External Students) Revenue Law June 1996 Q7

General Comment

This question illustrates the principles of main residence relief with the capital gains tax system.

Skeleton Solution

Disposal of main residence potentially chargeable: s21 TCGA 1992 – relief under ss222 and 223 – extent of exemption for 'garden or grounds': s222(1)(b) – proportional exemption for 'periods of occupation' as main residence – but extension for periods of non-residence: s222(2) and (3) – bought land not 'required' for enjoyment of the house as a residence – implications of receipt from 'right to sue' solicitor: *Zim Properties Limited v Procter* – revenue statement of practice following *Zim* case: underlying asset – CGT on transfer to trust: a disposal: s70 – implications of termination of interests: death of life tenant: s72 – sale of chattels: s260 scaled charge – gift of valuable painting: a disposal at market value: s17.

Suggested Solution

Note: all references are to the Taxation of Chargeable Gains Act (TCGA) 1992 unless stated otherwise.

a) Martin's disposal of his house and grounds during 2001–02 incurs a liability to capital gains tax since, under s21, all forms of property and assets are liable to capital gains tax, and reliance has to be placed on other provisions of TCGA or any exemptions from the general charge.

Under s222 exemption is available in respect of the disposal of a private residence which an individual has, at any time during his period of ownership, occupied as his only or main residence. The exemption extends to land up to one half of a hectare which he has for his own occupation and enjoyment with the residence as its gardens or grounds: s222(1)(b).

Under s223 a proportion of any chargeable gain is excluded based on a fraction of the years of actual occupation and other specified periods over the full period of ownership of the residence in question. A period of absence not exceeding three years is treated under s223(3) as a continuing period of occupation of the property, providing it has been occupied as the main residence both before and after the period of absence in question. For this purpose, therefore, Martin will have no restriction on the amount of the gain for which exemption is available. Since the original grounds amounted to half a hectare the exemption is extended to any gain corresponding to this garden. An apportionment of the sale price would need to be made corresponding to the value of the house and the half hectare of original garden. The remaining proportion relating to the additional piece of ground would be chargeable to capital gains tax, with a deduction for the acquisition cost of this additional piece of land. It is unlikely, in the circumstances outlined, that the exemption may be extended. Section 222(3) does make provision for such an extension where the land is required for the reasonable enjoyment of the dwelling-house as a residence. Since, however, the land was acquired at a later date, it can be concluded that it was not 'required' for the reasonable enjoyment of the house at that time.

The gain on which Martin is chargeable on the additional land will be reduced by indexation relief for the period of ownership, and it is open to him to claim reinvestment roll-over relief under s164A et seq if he reinvests an amount corresponding to the chargeable gain in a qualifying company.

The disposal price of the property for the purpose of the charge to capital gains tax will be £320,000. Although the additional £20,000 would not fall within the provisions of s22 since it does not relate to damage or injury to the assets or for the loss, destruction, depreciation, etc, of the property, the sum is derived from the right to sue his solicitor, and such a right is not beyond the scope of capital gains tax. For this purpose the exemption under s51(2) as a wrong or injury suffered by an individual in his personal capacity cannot be relied upon. As a result of the decision in *Zim Properties Limited* v *Procter* [1985] STC 90 compensation arising from the right to sue is a chargeable gain, since in that case it was held that the right to sue was in itself an asset for capital gains tax purposes. The Inland Revenue, following that decision, indicated that the right to sue would only be a chargeable gain where there was an underlying chargeable asset. In this situation, the disposal of the residence is a chargeable asset, although potentially giving rise to no gain, and therefore the application of the *Zim* concession has to be considered.

b) The transfer of the property to trustees is a disposal for capital gains tax purposes under the provisions of s70. This applies whether the settlement is revocable or not. Norman would therefore be liable to tax based on the value of the assets at the date of transfer, with a deduction for the original acquisition cost and any indexation allowance for the period from date of acquisition to the date of creating the settlement. The valuation is taken at market value under the provisions of s17(1)(a) on the basis that a transfer into a settlement is a transaction otherwise than by way of a bargain at arm's length. Norman is, therefore, treated as disposing of the assets to the trustees for a consideration equal to the market value of the relevant assets. The trustees' acquisition cost for any future capital gains tax charge is the said market value. However, under s260 Norman may claim to hold over the liability to capital gains tax, since his disposal is potentially one into an accumulation and maintenance settlement for the benefit of a beneficiary on obtaining the age of 25. Under s260(3) the amount of any held over gain would be deducted from the acquisition cost, to be used by these trustees in respect of any future occasion of charge to capital gains tax on the settled property assets.

There is no adjustment or charge for capital gains tax when A's interest comes to an end on qualification as a doctor. As of that date B acquires his life interest in the settlement. On the occasion of his death two months later s72 provides that no charge will be made in respect of any capital gain accruing to the date of death of the life interest beneficiary, providing the settled property in question remains within the settlement. However, on this occasion since the residual beneficiary C has not yet attained the age of 25, it is possible that the terms of the settlement would provide that the settlement comes to an end at that date with the property reverting to the settlor. In view of the hold-over relief position from the original transfer of property into the settlement. Norman would reacquire the assets at their original cost.

However, if the terms of the settlement provide that the property continues to be held for C, s72(1)(b) would ensure that, although the property is taken over by the trustees at the market value at that date, no actual chargeable gain would arise at that point.

c) The sale of jewellery by Olivia would be taxed according to the chattels provisions of s262. Under that section any asset sold for less than £6,000 is exempt from any charge to capital gains tax, while for assets sold in excess of £6,000 only five-thirds of the difference between the consideration and £6,000 is a chargeable gain. On this occasion the chargeable gain would amount to £1,667 (being £1,000 x ⅗rds). Any unused annual exemption could be deducted from this figure.

d) The gift of a valuable painting by Paula is a disposal for capital gains tax purposes under the general provisions of s21. If the asset in question is not a chattel for the purposes of s262, then there will be a charge to tax based on the current value of the painting. This arises from the rules of s17 which imposes market value as the consideration in cases where the disposal takes place otherwise than by way of a bargain at arm's length. However, as a result of s260, an election could be made to hold over the chargeable gain by deducting the relevant gain from the market value which Paula would otherwise have as her initial acquisition cost. This arises from the fact that the gift is an occasion of charge for inheritance tax purposes, albeit that it is within the s3A potentially exempt regime and therefore leads to the possibility of s260(1)(b) being applied to enable an election for hold over under s260(3) to be made.

QUESTION FIVE

Discuss the meaning of the words 'disposal' and 'assets' in the context of the capital gains tax legislation.

University of London LLB Examination
(for External Students) Revenue Law June 1992 Q8

General Comment

This question explores the meaning of the words 'disposal' and 'assets' in the context of the capital gains tax legislation.

Skeleton Solution

Ordinary meaning of disposal: change of ownership – meaning of ownership – extended tax meaning of 'disposal', 'deemed' – occasions when extended meaning applicable – part disposals, disposals of part – implications of part disposal: acquisition cost etc – each ownership right is an asset – reorganisation provisions: no disposal – *Zim Properties Ltd* v *Procter*; *Drummond* v *Austin Brown*; *Davis* v *Powell* – exempt assets.

Suggested Solution

Note: all references are to the Taxation of Chargeable Gains Act (TCGA) 1992.

Under s1(1) of the Taxation of Chargeable Gains Act 1992 (TCGA 1992), tax is charged 'in respect of capital gains, that is to say chargeable gains ... accruing to a person on the disposal of assets'. Neither the word 'disposal' nor the word 'assets' is defined in the Act.

In the absence of a definition, disposal will, unless otherwise provided for, assume its ordinary natural meaning in that a disposal of an asset occurs when its ownership changes or the owner divests himself of the rights over, or interest in, an asset. This will include gift, sale, exchange and other transfers deemed or actual.

The CGT legislation brings in the concept of a 'deemed' disposal which is beyond the normal meaning of 'disposal' (s71), for example, on the occasion of trustees being said to have disposed of and immediately reacquired assets on an occasion when the beneficiary becomes absolutely entitled to settled property. When a life interest in settled property ceases there is deemed to be a change of ownership, and the trustee is deemed to dispose of the assets and immediately reacquire them at market value before the transfer to the beneficiary occurs. The growth in value is that of the trustee, and the beneficiary takes on the market value as his acquisition cost. If this occurs on the death of the tenant no gain or loss is deemed to be made by the trustees.

On other occasions of disposals by trustees the normal rules apply to disposals of chargeable assets by trustees.

Gains made by trustees on their disposals are charged on them as a single and continuing body of persons. Therefore on a change of trustees there is no change of ownership, and accordingly no disposal of the trust assets.

Without a 'disposal' taking place there can be no chargeable gain arising, hence the importance of determining what is a disposal for capital gains purposes. In ss144–147 the grant of an option is the disposal of an asset, and part disposals are declared to be included in the concept of a disposal, s21(2), and determine when a part disposal has taken place. Generally there is a part disposal where 'any description of property derived from the asset remains undisposed of'. In addition, if a right over or interest in is created in relation to the asset, a part disposal will have taken place, such as in the case of the grant of a restrictive covenant over the use of land.

The concept of ownership, in relation to this change of ownership giving rise to a charge, is derived from the property law concept of ownership being a bundle of rights in or over property. Disposal takes place either in whole or in part when one or more of those rights is disposed of or created in favour of another person.

The purpose of recognising the distinction between a disposal and a part disposal is in identifying and ascertaining the appropriate acquisition cost for the calculation of the chargeable gain.

A part disposal occurs where one or more of the rights to or interests in an asset are disposed of and one or more remain. For example, the grant of a lease over property is the part disposal of the freehold rights over it.

On the other hand the disposal of a part occurs where an identifiable part is disposed of to the extent of all of the rights over it.

Other occasions on which a disposal of assets takes place are:

a) on the receipt of a capital sum derived from the asset (s22);

b) where assets are lost, destroyed or become of negligible value (s24);

c) in the acquisition of an asset on certain hire purchase contracts (s27).

Equally important are occasions on which a 'disposal' is deemed not to have taken place:

a) the receipt of a capital sum where an asset is not lost or destroyed if the sum is used to restore the asset (s23);

b) giving of a mortgage or charge over property (s26);

c) in particular, relief is given from a charge to corporation tax on capital gains to facilitate various reorganisations, reconstructions and amalgamations and take-overs: ss126–137. These involve the disposal of existing shares or other securities in companies and the issue of other shares or securities either by the same company or another company concerned in the transaction. The relief is given so that no chargeable gain becomes chargeable to tax as a result of the 'disposal' of the old shares or securities. Section 127 provides that 'a reorganisation shall not be treated as involving any disposal of the original shares or any acquisition of the new holding'.

In the transactions which are not 'reorganisations' the same provisions are applied with the necessary adaptations to cover reconstructions, conversions of securities etc: ss132 and 135. Because no disposal takes place no chargeable gain can arise: s1(1).

Assets for capital gains

Section 21(1) provides that 'all forms of property shall be assets' including rights, options and currency other than sterling.

The case of *Zim Properties Ltd* v *Procter* [1985] STC 90 held that the right to sue for compensation was itself an asset. It therefore looked at the value or acquisition cost of such a right in relation to the gain chargeable on the receipt of compensation or damages. This has led to the issue of an Inland Revenue extra statutory concession exempting such compensation from tax unless there was another underlying 'asset' involved other than the right to sue.

In *Drummond* v *Austin Brown* [1984] 3 WLR 381, although a capital sum was received on the termination of a tenancy it was held that it was not 'derived from the asset' – the lease – as the lease was no longer in existence.

Similarly in *Davis* v *Powell* [1977] STC 426, which was followed in *Drummond* v *Austin Brown*, the receipt of the capital sum was held to have derived not from the asset but from the statute providing for the payment.

Tangible moveable property is an asset for capital gains purposes, but s262 provides an exemption where the disposal proceeds do not exceed £6,000. Motor cars (s263) and foreign currency for personal expenditure (s269) also escape capital gains, cars not being regarded as assets for this purpose, and currency, although an asset, being exempt on its disposal where held for personal expenditure.

It should be noted that transactions carried out in foreign currency will involve not only the acquisition and disposal of the asset bought and sold but also the acquisition and disposal of foreign currency at UK values on acquisition and again the receipt and conversion of currency at UK values on the disposal of the asset.

Chapter 19

Death and Settled Property in CGT

19.1   **Introduction**

19.2   **Key points**

19.3   **Key cases and statute**

19.4   **Questions and suggested solutions**

19.1 Introduction

There is no charge to CGT on the increase in value of assets held by an individual at the date of death. There is no charge to CGT on assets passing to legatees and other beneficiaries for increases in value between death and distribution. Actual disposals during the administration of an estate are liable to CGT in the normal way by reference to any value realised in excess of the value as at death. If assets are put in trust after death or passed to legatees, the trust or legatee takes the assets over at their market value at the date of death.

Similarly, where assets have been held in an interest in possession trust, but not a discretionary trust – s72(3) – the death of the life tenant does not give rise to a charge to CGT on the increased value of the trust property which has arisen during the life tenancy: ss72(1)(b) and 73 TCGA 1992. The beneficiary in an interest in possession trust is deemed to have an interest in the underlying trust property similar to that which there would be if the property were not held in such a trust.

19.2 Key points

Death

a) On the death of an individual, the chargeable assets are treated as passing to the personal representatives at market value without a charge to tax on the increase since acquired: s62(1) TCGA 1992.

b) Assets passing to a legatee do so with no chargeable gain to personal representatives, and the market value 'cost' passes to the legatee: s62(4).

c) TCGA 1992 s62(6): post-death variation within two years is treated as if made by deceased, not a disposal by recipients. It also means that if settled on trust, the settlor is the deceased: *Marshall* v *Kerr* [1994] STC 638, dealing with s62(6) TCGA

1992. UK beneficiary under will of a Jersey resident failed to utilise the post death variations to treat deceased as settlor of offshore trust.

d) (For death of beneficiary see below.)

Settlement for CGT purposes

Under s60 TCGA 1992 'settled property' is any property held in trust other than property held as nominee or bare trustee or as trustee for infants or disabled persons absolutely entitled to the property.

Trustees

A change in the composition of the trustees of a trust does not give rise to any 'disposal of assets'. Trustees are regarded as a single and continuing body of persons: s69.

The rate of CGT charged on gains made by personal representatives was increased by s120 FA 1998 from 6 April 1998 to the 34 per cent 'rate applicable to trusts' under s686 ICTA 1988. The rate now applies to disposals by all UK resident trusts, where prior to the above date it applied only to trustees of discretionary trusts.

Transfers into and out of trust

TCGA 1992 s70: transfer of property into settlement is a chargeable disposal for CGT purposes.

TCGA 1992 s71: property leaving trust at end of trust or on passing to beneficiary is liable to CGT by reference to market value.

Currently, an anomaly exists in regard to the hold-over relief available when the beneficiary of an accumulation and maintenance settlement becomes absolutely entitled to capital as this will only apply when entitlement to capital occurs at the same time as the entitlement to income occurs. Under s31 Trustee Act 1925, income entitlement will occur on reaching majority at 18. Entitlement to capital will commonly be provided for at age 25. The charge to tax therefore will arise in these circumstances.

Other disposals by trustees

Disposals of trust assets by way of sale etc are charged to CGT on the trustees in the normal way. TCGA 1992 Sch 1: annual exemption for most trustees is one half of that for individuals – currently £3,750.

Disposal of interest in settled property

Under s76 CGT is not normally charged where a beneficiary makes a disposal of his interest under a settlement, but where that interest was acquired for money or money's worth, then the disposal is chargeable. The exemption does not apply to disposals on or after 6 March 1998 where the settlement has at any time been a non-resident settlement or the settled property is derived directly or indirectly from such a settlement: s76(1A) – (1B) TCGA 1992.

Death of life tenant

TCGA 1992 ss72–73: termination of life interest on death – uplift in value for trustees without CGT charge (except for gains held over on transfer of property into trust). If assets revert to the settlor, settlor takes over the trustees' original acquisition values: s73.

Termination of life tenancy other than on death

Termination of life interest other than on death – eg on marriage or for reasons of attaining vesting age – deemed disposal of relevant assets by trustees at market value: s71 TCGA 1992.

In *Begg-MacBrearty* v *Stilwell* [1996] STC 413, beneficiaries were held to become absolutely entitled to the trust property as against the trustees at new age of majority of 18 and not as originally provided for under the settlement.

Settlor retaining interest

TCGA 1992 ss77–79: settlor retaining an interest – trustee's gains are those of the settlor.

No taper relief for gains attributed to settlor under these provisions: s77(6A) TCGA 1992.

Non-UK settlements – charge on settlors and beneficiaries

Under the old FA 1981 system gains of non-resident settlements made by UK settlors were attributed to and taxed on UK beneficiaries in proportion to the amount of capital payments which they received from the trust. This 'matching' of gains to capital payments is subject to the 1991 provisions below.

Under the FA 1991 system (now s86 TCGA 1992), the gains made by non-resident settlements are chargeable to CGT on the settlor if he has an interest in the settlement. Under other non-resident settlements ss87–89 apply to charge gains on UK beneficiaries. Section 87 applies where the gains of the settlement have not been attributed to the settlor under s86 when they arose. Gains chargeable on beneficiaries are matched with capital payments made to them: s87(5) TCGA 1992.

a) Section 86(4) deems gains made by trustees of non-resident 'settlor with an interest' settlements to be chargeable on the settlor. See Sch 5 TCGA 1992 for detailed provisions and definitions and Sch 5A for the information provisions.

b) The amount is chargeable without attracting any taper relief: s86(4A) TCGA 1992.

c) Section 86 liability may also be triggered by a settlor becoming a UK resident after a period of non-residence – see s10A charge on 'temporary non-residents' – described in Chapter 18, effective from 17 March 1998.

d) Where a settlor is chargeable in these circumstances on gains made by a non-resident settlement, any gains which in the interim period have been attributed and assessed on beneficiaries under s87 are left out of account: s86A TCGA 1992.

e) From 6 April 1999 the provisions take into account gains in most non-resident settlements which were set up before 19 March 1991 when the provisions first came into effect. Gains made between 17 March 1998 and 5 April 1999 are treated as arising on 6 April 1999 and as taxable on the settlor for 1999–2000: Sch 5 para 9 TCGA 1992 as amended by s132 FA 1998.

f) Certain settlements remain 'protected' from the s86 provisions, even after the FA 1998 changes mentioned above. These are where the beneficiaries, whether actual or potential, are restricted to:

   i)   children of the settlor or spouse who are under 18 at the beginning of the tax year;

   ii) unborn children of the settlor or spouse;

   iii) future spouses of the settlor or of the settlor's children;

   iv) persons other than the settlor or spouse, child or step-child of the settlor or spouse or the child's spouse, companies (and their associated companies) controlled by any of the foregoing persons.

g) In addition, settlements created prior to 17 March 1998 where the grandchildren of the settlor are the sole, actual or potential beneficiaries are protected from the charge and gains made to 5 April 1999 are not taken into account in the manner described above: Sch 5 para 2A TCGA 1992.

h) Gains from 6 April 1999 will not be attributed as long as the settlement remains a grandchildren settlement: Sch 5 paras 2 and 2A TCGA 1992, amended by s131 FA 1998.

In *De Rothschild* v *Lawrenson (Inspector of Taxes)* [1995] STC 623, the Court of Appeal confirmed that gains realised in 1988–89 by non-resident trustees of a settlement under which the UK resident settlor enjoyed a life interest were to be treated as trust gains for the purposes of s80 FA 1981 (currently s87 TCGA 1992).

Transfer of trusts abroad etc

Sections 80–85 apply to charge CGT on unrealised gains on the transfer of trusts out of the UK or on the trustees ceasing to be treated as UK resident (eg under double tax treaty).

19.3 Key cases and statute

- *Begg-MacBrearty* v *Stilwell* [1996] STC 413
  CGT – death and settled property – termination of life interest

- *Marshall* v *Kerr* [1994] STC 638
  CGT – death and settled property – s62(6) TCGA 1992

- Taxation of Chargeable Gains Act 1992, ss62, 70–71, 76(1A)–(1B) (amended by Finance Act 1998, s120) and 86

19.4 Questions and suggested solutions

QUESTION ONE

In May 1998 C settled shares worth £1 million on Tim and Tania as trustees on trust 'for himself (C) for life, remainder to D for life, but if D fails her final examination for the London LLB at her first attempt and after her death in any event to E absolutely.'

What are the CAPITAL GAINS TAX consequences of the creation of such a settlement?

What are the CAPITAL GAINS TAX consequences of each of the following events?

a) In June 1998 D fails her final examinations at the first attempt;

b) In August 1998 the trustees appoint shares worth £10,000 to E;

c) In September 1998 C dies.

University of London LLB Examination
(for External Students) Revenue Law June 1999 Q8

General Comment

A question relating to the CGT regime for settled property.

Skeleton Solution

CGT consequences of creation of settlement – termination of life interest in remainder: s72 – appointment of shares by trustees to capital beneficiaries – death of life tenant in possession: s73(1); no chargeable gain on disposal; 'free uplift'.

Suggested Solution

Sections 68–79 TCGA 1992 provide a special regime for the CGT of settled property and settlements. Trustees are liable to pay CGT at the rate applicable to trusts, currently 34 per cent under s4(1AA). Further, under s77, if the settlor retains an interest in the settlement then the chargeable gains of the trust are treated as accruing to him. Consequently he has to pay tax on those chargeable gains at his marginal rate of income tax. C retained an interest in the property as he was a life tenant of the trust, thus making him liable for CGT on any chargeable gains.

D's failing of her final examinations did not cause the settlement to come to an end. Therefore, no charge to CGT arises; instead the trustees held the assets on the following trusts 'To C for life, then to E'. On C's death s72 applies: there is no charge to CGT, but rather a 'free uplift'. The trustees' base value increases to the current market value. Any sale of trust assets will not give rise to a charge to CGT unless they are sold for a sum in excess of the new base value.

The appointment of shares to E, the holder of the remainder interest, means that a beneficiary has become absolutely entitled to property. The assets representing that property will be treated as disposed of by the trustees at market value, and capital gains tax will be due from the trustees: s71.

On the death of C, the life tenant, s73(1) applies to avoid a charge to capital gains tax arising on the termination of that interest in possession of the trust assets, so that no gain or loss arises. E acquires the assets at their value at the date of death.

QUESTION TWO

a) Consider the meaning and significance of the phrase 'absolutely entitled as against the trustee' for the purposes of capital gains tax.

b) In 1985 Susan sold a house which she owned in America to her son Peter for £20,000 when its market value was £50,000. She had acquired it for the equivalent of £15,000 in 1983. In November 1988 Peter transferred the house, together with a large number of other properties, to trustees to hold upon trust for Wanda for life remainder to Belinda contingently upon attaining the age of 25. In 1990, when Belinda was aged 24, Wanda died.

Advise on the capital gains tax implications of these events. For the purposes of this question assume a static retail prices index.

University of London LLB Examination
(for External Students) Revenue Law June 1990 Q9

General Comment

This question explores the capital gains tax implications on settled property.

Skeleton Solution

Absolute entitlement – s60 TCGA 1992 – transactions between trustee and beneficiary ignored for CGT – consider *Saunders* v *Vautier, Stephenson* v *Barclays Bank* – co-ownership – *Booth* v *Ellard, Jenkins* v *Brown* – *Cochrane* v *IRC* – beneficiary not entitled during period of administration of estate – minor beneficiary – *Tomlinson*.

Suggested Solution

a) The phrase 'absolutely entitled as against the trustee' (AEAT) is to be found in s60

TCGA 1992. In s60(1) it is provided that if a person is so absolutely entitled, or would be absolutely so entitled but for (a) being an infant, or (b) being under another disability, the acts of the bare trustee or nominee in relation to the trust property are to be treated as the acts of the absolutely entitled beneficiary, and that transactions between the bare trustee or nominee and the beneficiary are to be disregarded.

Thus where a resident bare trustee disposes of trust property, realising a gain, the gain will escape CGT if, for example, the absolutely entitled beneficiary is non-resident. Further, if a bare trustee realises a gain the beneficiary may set his or her annual exempt amount against it (rather than using the trustee's reduced AEA). Conversely, where a non-resident bare trustee realises a gain on behalf of a resident absolutely entitled beneficiary the gain will fall into charge, rather than escaping tax.

The meaning of the phrase 'AEAT' is not entirely clear. Section 60 attempts some clarification. Section 60(2) says that a beneficiary is absolutely entitled as against a trustee where the beneficiary has the exclusive right, subject only to satisfying any outstanding charge, lien or other right of trustees to resort to the asset for the payment of duty, taxes, costs or other outgoings, to direct how that asset shall be dealt with. A number of points may be made in connection with s60(1) and (2):

i) Under the rule in *Saunders* v *Vautier* (1841) 4 Beav 115 an absolutely entitled adult beneficiary has the right to terminate the bare trust, but not to instruct the trustees how to deal with the settled property whilst the trust is on foot. Nevertheless it seems that a beneficiary who satisfies the rule in *Saunders* v *Vautier* satisfies s60(1).

ii) If the settled property in question is subject to a prior equitable interest or annuity then the requirements of s60 are not met: *Stephenson* v *Barclays Bank* [1975] 1 All ER 625.

iii) Co-owners of personal property may satisfy the conditions of s60 and consequently qualify as 'AEAT': *Booth* v *Ellard* [1980] STC 555.

iv) Co-owners of land, however, differ from co-owners of personalty since they cannot call for the land itself because of the statutory trust for sale. Nevertheless co-owners of land seem likely to be treated as satisfying s46: *Crowe* v *Appleby* (1975) 51 TC 374; *Jenkins* v *Brown* [1989] STC 577.

v) The form of co-ownership is irrelevant: s60 may apply both to joint tenants in equity and to tenants in common.

vi) For there to be a bare trust in a case of co-ownership the interests of the co-owners must be co-existent and of the same 'quality': *Booth* v *Ellard*. Thus successive owners never fall within s60 even if they could, together, apply the rule in *Saunders* v *Vautier*.

vii) A residuary legatee does not hold absolutely as against the PRs during the administration of the estate: *Cochrane* v *IRC* [1974] STC 335.

viii) Where the sole reason for a beneficiary's inability to give a good receipt is minority, the conditions of s60 may still be met. This is contemplated in s60(1) itself. Where, however, a gift is made contingently upon a beneficiary's attaining the age of majority then s60 is not satisfied and the property is settled property: *Tomlinson* v *Glyn's Executor and Trustee Co* [1970] Ch 112.

b) The sale by Susan to Peter of the US house will attract CGT provided that:

i) Susan is UK resident (this seems to be so on the facts); and

ii) the house is a chargeable asset (this is so, since land wherever situate is a form of property and therefore an asset: s21); and

iii) a chargeable disposal has occurred: this is so, sale being the classic example of a chargeable disposal; and

iv) a gain has resulted.

Item (iv) requires further investigation on these facts. Were the US house Susan's principal private residence, so that the conditions of ss222–223 were satisfied, then any gain, however calculated, would be exempt. This does not appear to be the case on the facts.

The gain on the sale of the house (leaving aside incidental costs and enhancement and title expenditure under s38) appears to be £5,000. This gain would be covered, it seems, by Susan's £5,000 annual exempt amount. However Susan and Peter are connected persons within s286, and therefore s18 provides that the bargain is deemed to be otherwise than at arm's length so s17 applies and Susan is treated as disposing of the asset for market value. The gain is therefore £50,000 – £15,000 = £35,000. Peter's deemed acquisition cost is Susan's deemed disposal consideration, ie £50,000. Holdover relief under s79 FA 1980 would have been available in 1985 on this sale at an undervalue, to the extent of the undervalue only: s79(3) FA 1980 (now repealed).

The creation of the settlement by Peter in 1988 was a disposal: s70. The disposal is otherwise than by bargain at arm's length. Peter is therefore treated as disposing of all the properties in question for their market values. Since s79 FA 1980 was repealed by s124 FA 1988 no holdover relief is available on the creation of the settlement. The trustees' acquisition cost is the market value of the properties at the date of the disposal into settlements. The trust is clearly an example of the 'settled property' regime under s68. Section 60 does not apply, since property is held in trust for persons entitled in succession: *Booth* v *Ellard*.

When Wanda dies Belinda's interest in the capital of the fund is still contingent since she has not yet reached 25, the age specified in the trust. The property remains settled property, therefore, since she cannot rely on her *Saunders* v *Vautier* right until her interest ceases to be contingent.

QUESTION THREE

What is settled property for the purposes of capital gains tax? Why is the definition important?

University of London LLB Examination
(for External Students) Revenue Law June 1991 Q9

General Comment

This question defines 'settled property' for purposes of capital gains tax.

Skeleton Solution

Settled property: ss60 and 68 TCGA 1992 – look at consequences of property being declared to be trust property.

Suggested Solution

Note: all references are to the Taxation of Chargeable Gains Act 1992.

A definition of settled property is given in s68 TCGA 1992: 'Settled property means any property held in trust, other than property to which s60 above applies.'

Section 60 applies to nominees and bare trustees, ie to property which is not settled property. It states:

> 'In relation to assets held by a person as nominee for another person, or as trustee for another person absolutely entitled as against the trustee, or for any person who would be so entitled but for being an infant or other person under disability (or for two or more persons who are or would be jointly so entitled), this Act shall apply as if the property were vested in, and the acts of the nominee or trustee in relation to the assets were the acts of, the person or persons for whom he is the nominee or trustee (acquisitions from or disposals to that person or persons being disregarded accordingly).'

Therefore any property held in trust, other than bare or nominee property, is settled property. The Act places special emphasis on the assets being 'settled property' rather than on the assets being held in a settlement. This is because it is possible, in the same settlement, for some assets to be 'settled property' and some assets to be 'nominee property'.

a) Nominee property is not settled property, so one treats all disposals by the trustees as disposals by the beneficiary, and the beneficiary is charged with capital gains tax under the usual CGT rules including the rule giving him or her exemption from tax on his or her first £5,500 of chargeable gains (ie the trustee's annual exemption does not apply).

b) Any disposal by the trustee to the beneficiary is ignored, because the beneficiary is already notionally in possession of the asset.

c) Trustees will ordinarily pay tax at their marginal rate of income tax. For 2001–02 this is 25 per cent. However, under s5 the trustees of an accumulation and maintenance trust are required to pay CGT at 35 per cent, ie basic rate of 25 per cent plus the additional rate of 10 per cent.

The transfer of property by the settlor to the trust is a disposal of assets, and this is so irregardless of whether the settlement is revocable or irrevocable or whether the settlor or his or her spouse is capable of benefiting under the trust. Where the settlor transfers chargeable assets to the trust, there will be either a resultant chargeable gain or an allowable loss.

Note: the settlor and his trustees are connected persons within s18(3) and, in the event of an allowable loss arising from the transfer into settlement, such a loss will only be deductible from a subsequent disposal of the trust assets by the trustees. However, on a transfer into settlement, the settlor can claim holdover relief under s165 or s260 if the requirements of either of those sections are satisfied.

When the trustees dispose of property, that will constitute a disposal for CGT purposes. However, a change in the body of the trustees will not result in a disposal of the trust property for CGT purposes (s69) when the trust assets vest in the new trustees.

The rate of CGT will depend on the type of trust that the settlor creates. In the case of an interest in possession trust, the rate of CGT is 25 per cent. However, in the case of a discretionary trust, the trustees would be liable to 35 per cent tax on disposals.

The trustees' annual exemption for 2001–02 is £4,535. When a beneficiary disposes of his interest, there will be no charge to CGT so long as that beneficiary did not acquire his interest for a consideration in money or money's worth, other than another interest under that settlement: see s76. If the interest has been purchased for a consideration, then any disposal will result in there being a charge to CGT.

Note: where a beneficiary with a life interest disposes of his interest, this will bring the wasting asset rules into operation on any subsequent disposal of that interest by the purchaser.

In some cases, the termination of a settlement may lead to the trust property passing to the purchaser for the remainder interest. That purchaser will dispose of his interest in consideration for receiving the trust property in the settlement: s76. This charge will not affect the deemed disposal by the trustees under s71.

Finally, where beneficiaries under a settlement exchange interests, this will not be treated as a purchase, and therefore any later disposal of either of the interests exchanged will not be subject to CGT.

QUESTION FOUR

T1 and T2 hold a wide range of assets on trust for L for life and then to M absolutely.

In this year various transactions were effected with the trust assets.

The trustees sold for £150,000 a flat in London which had been purchased for £100,000. The flat had been occupied by L. Following the sale the trustees purchased another flat for £180,000.

Shares which had been purchased in 1990 were sold at a large profit.

Under a power in the trust deed £5,000 was paid to L.

The trustees sold a valuable stamp collection and also received compensation from the stamp dealers for negligent advice about valuation of the collection.

L died in January 2002. The trustees sold more shares and made a chargeable gain of £5,000.

Advise T1 and T2 of the capital gains tax consequences of these events.

> Adapted from University of London LLB Examination
> (for External Students) Revenue Law June 1992 Q9

General Comment

This question illustrates the capital gains tax implications of transactions concerning property held in trust.

Skeleton Solution

Interest in possession trust: rate of CGT 25 per cent – sale of flat: private residence exemption? – shares sale: rebasing and indexation – capital distribution: assets taken by beneficiary s71 – sale of stamp collection: chargeable asset – compensation: *Zim Properties* v *Procter* – death of life tenant: no gain/no loss – share sale: trustee annual exemption.

Suggested Solution

Note: all references are to the Taxation of Chargeable Gains Act 1992.

T1 and T2 are trustees of a life interest trust and liable for capital gains tax on disposals of assets and in other circumstances provided for in the capital gains tax legislation.

Under s69, the trustees are treated as a single continuing body of persons so that changes in trustees are ignored and do not give rise to disposal of assets between them.

As an interest in possession trust, the rate of tax applicable to gains is 34 per cent. There is no 'additional rate' to tax for interest in possession trusts.

On the sale of the flat a capital gain of £50,000 arises, but since the flat has been occupied by the life tenant there is a probability that private residence relief will be due under s225. The condition that must be fulfilled is that the arrangement under which the flat is occupied must be under the terms of the settlement and not, for example, by permission of the trustees. The flat must constitute the only or main residence of the beneficiary: *Sansom* v *Peay* [1976] 1 WLR 1073.

The shares were acquired in 1990, and for the purpose of the capital gains tax computation the acquisition cost will be replaced by the value at March 1992. In addition the re-based cost will be increased by indexation allowance reducing the gain to any amount in excess of inflation increases since March 1992.

The distribution of £5,000 paid to the life tenant means that a beneficiary has become absolutely entitled to property. The assets representing that property will be treated as disposed of by the trustees at market value, and capital gains tax will be due from the trustees: s71.

The sale of the stamp collection is the disposal of a chargeable asset if the value exceeds the 'chattels exemption' limit of £6,000. Any gain will be taxable, subject to indexation allowance reduction.

The case of *Zim Properties Ltd* v *Procter* [1985] STC 90 determined that the right to sue was itself an asset which would give rise to a gain on receipt of a sum by way of compensation or damages. As the right will generally have been acquired for no cost, the strict position is that the whole amount of the receipt is taxable. However, in an Inland Revenue extra-statutory concession published in a press release following the case, the receipt was declared to be taxable only if there was also an underlying asset involved – in this case the stamp collection. Hence the full amount received will be brought into account as consideration for the disposal of the collection.

On the death of L, the life tenant, s72 applies to avoid a charge to capital gains tax arising on the termination of that interest in possession of the trust assets, so that no gain or loss arises. M acquires the assets at their value at the date of death.

Share sale: if the sale took place after the death of the life tenant, the remainderman had already been deemed to have acquired the assets and a disposal by the trustees would be one done as bare trustees only. The gain would be exempt for M as it was less than the annual exemption limit for individuals, £5,500. For disposals by the trustees prior to the date of death an annual exemption of one-half the individual's rate is available.

QUESTION FIVE

'The concept of being absolutely entitled as against the trustees is central to an understanding of the problems of applying capital gains tax to settled property.'

Discuss.

University of London LLB Examination
(for External Students) Revenue Law June 2002 Q7

General Comment

This question explores the capital gains tax implications on settled property.

Skeleton Solution

Absolute entitlement – s60 TCGA 1992 – transactions between trustee and beneficiary ignored for CGT.

Suggested Solution

The phrase 'absolutely entitled as against the trustee' (AEAT) is to be found in s60 TCGA 1992. In s60(1) it is provided that if a person is so absolutely entitled, or would be absolutely so entitled but for (a) being an infant or (b) being under another disability, the acts of the bare trustee or nominee in relation to the trust property are to be treated as the acts of the absolutely entitled beneficiary, and that transactions between the bare trustee or nominee and the beneficiary are to be disregarded.

Thus where a resident bare trustee disposes of trust property, realising a gain, the gain will escape CGT if, for example, the absolutely entitled beneficiary is non-resident. Further, if a bare trustee realises a gain the beneficiary may set his or her annual exempt amount against it (rather than using the trustee's reduced AEA). Conversely, where a non-resident bare trustee realises a gain on behalf of a resident absolutely entitled beneficiary the gain will fall into charge, rather than escaping tax.

The meaning of the phrase 'AEAT' is not entirely clear. Section 60 attempts some clarification. Section 60(2) says that a beneficiary is absolutely entitled as against a trustee where the beneficiary has the exclusive right, subject only to satisfying any outstanding charge, lien or other right of trustees to resort to the asset for the payment of duty, taxes, costs or other outgoings, to direct how that asset shall be dealt with. A number of points may be made in connection with s60(1) and (2):

a) Under the rule in *Saunders* v *Vautier* (1841) 4 Beav 115 an absolutely entitled adult beneficiary has the right to terminate the bare trust, but not to instruct the trustees how to deal with the settled property whilst the trust is on foot. Nevertheless it seems that a beneficiary who satisfies the rule in *Saunders* v *Vautier* satisfies s60(1).

b) If the settled property in question is subject to a prior equitable interest of annuity then the requirements of s60 are not met: *Stephenson* v *Barclays Bank* [1975] 1 All ER 625.

c) Co-owners of personal property may satisfy the conditions of s60 and consequently qualify as 'AEAT': *Booth* v *Ellard* [1980] STC 555.

d) Co-owners of land, however, differ from co-owners of personalty since they cannot call for the land itself because of the statutory trust for sale. Nevertheless co-owners of land seem likely to be treated as satisfying s46: *Crowe* v *Appleby* (1975) 51 TC 374; *Jenkins* v *Brown* [1989] STC 577.

e) The form of co-ownership is irrelevant: s60 may apply both to joint tenants in equity and to tenants in common.

f) For there to be a bare trust in a case of co-ownership the interests of the co-owners must be co-existent and of the same 'quality': *Booth* v *Ellard*. Thus successive owners never fall within s60 even if they could, together, apply the rule in *Saunders* v *Vautier*.

g) A residuary legatee does not hold absolutely as against the PRs during the administration of the estate: *Cochrane* v *IRC* [1974] STC 335.

h) Where the sole reason for a beneficiary's inability to give a good receipt is minority, the conditions of s60 may still be met. This is contemplated in s60(1) itself. Where, however, a gift is made contingently upon a beneficiary's attaining the age of majority then s60 is not satisfied and the property is settled property: *Tomlinson* v *Glyn's Executor and Trustee Co* [1970] Ch 112.

Chapter 20

Inheritance Tax: General

20.1   Introduction

20.2   Key points

20.3   Key cases and statutes

20.4   Questions and suggested solutions

20.1 Introduction

Inheritance tax is governed by the Inheritance Tax Act (IHTA) 1984 which has been effective since 25 July 1986. The Act may be loosely divided into two parts: (a) lifetime transfers and (b) transfers on death.

IHT operates when there is a chargeable transfer. The transfer however may be potentially exempt or chargeable immediately. All references are to IHTA 1984 unless otherwise stated.

20.2 Key points

Scope of the 1984 Act

Section 1: IHT is charged on the value transferred by a chargeable transfer.

Section 2(1): a chargeable transfer is any transfer of value made by an individual which is not exempt.

Section 3(1): a transfer of value is any disposition which reduces the value of the transferor's estate to include certain deemed transfers of value.

Section 3(2) provides that no account is taken of 'excluded property' as defined by s6 (foreign property of non-UK domiciles (see s267 for meaning of non-UK domicile)), and ss48, 53, 153, 158 for specific excluded property provisions.

'Disposition' means any transfer of property by sale or gift, the creation of a settlement and the release, discharge or surrender of a debt. Section 3(3) omissions to exercise a right are also included.

Where market value has been received by the transferor then there will be no reduction in the value of his estate. Thus open market sales are not chargeable, but gifts are potentially liable: s3A IHTA 1984.

Section 10 permits circumstances where transfers have been made by non-connected persons in commercial situations but constitute a bad bargain ie at an undervalue. No IHT charge arises in these circumstances.

Section 11: where a transfer is made by the transferor for the maintenance of his family, ie spouse or child, there is no chargeable transfer.

Sections 12–16 describe circumstances where there is no transfer of value, eg retirement benefits, close company transfers to trustees, waiver of remuneration and grant of agricultural tenancy.

Section 5(1): estate is defined as 'the aggregate of all the property to which he is beneficially entitled'. Note time of valuation and value of part of sets.

Rates of tax

Schedule 1 IHTA 1984 (as amended by current year's Finance Act): for transfer on and after 6 April 2002 no IHT is charged for cumulative transfers up to a total of £255,000, and transfers above this figure are charged at 40 per cent. Lifetime transfers are charged at half this rate, ie nil or 20 per cent. From 18 March 1986 cumulative transfers are calculated over a seven-year period: s7 IHTA 1984.

Grossing up

Sections 199–201 dictate who is liable to pay IHT: for lifetime transfers the transferor, the recipient of the transfer whose estate has been increased by the transfer, a tenant with an interest in possession, the beneficiary of income or property from settled property.

Section 204(6): the transferor is primarily liable to pay the tax, and the section limits the transferee's liability.

Where a transfer has been made, the value is grossed up to take account of the tax payable. Tables are used to calculate grossing up figures.

Death

Section 4(1): 'On the death of any person tax shall be charged as if immediately before his death he had made a transfer of value and the value transferred by it had been equal to the value of his estate immediately before his death'.

a) This deemed transfer of value at death must be cumulated with lifetime transfers made in the seven preceding years. On death the estate does not include excluded property although it does include property with a reservation of benefit prior to death.

b) Reservations of benefits create a partial IHT nullity for the donor. He or she is deemed to retain a beneficial enjoyment or title up to his or her death. The reservation of benefit rules apply where the gift is completed and also where only partial consideration has been given wherein there is an element of bounty. Compare rules for bad bargains: see s10 above.

c) Post-death variations (deeds of family arrangement)

Provision is made in ss17(a) and 142 to treat rearrangements of the deceased's wishes made within two years of death as having been made by the deceased, including the disclaimer of benefits.

See *Russell* v *IRC* [1988] STC 195: redirection of property and s142.

See also s144 for redistribution within two years of property settled by will of the deceased and s143 for transfers in compliance with the deceased's requests.

Marshall v *Kerr* [1994] 3 WLR 299; [1994] STC 638: a House of Lords' decision in CGT case, where property settled by a legatee following a variation of the deceased's intentions was held to be a settlement created by the UK resident legatee and not a settlement made by the deceased who had been non-UK domiciled.

Valuation, related property and associated operations

Section 160: property is valued at 'the price which the property might reasonably be expected to fetch if sold in the open market at that time'.

Related property

It is important to note the 'related property' valuation provisions of ss161 and 176 with particular reference to unquoted shares, fragmentation of assets and potential aggregation of husband and wife property.

Associated operations

Under s268 two or more transactions which affect the reduction in value of a person's estate through the same assets are effectively amalgamated to assess the full extent of the reduction. Also applicable where the earlier transfer is exempt (eg inter-spouse and onward to another donee by prior arrangement).

Liabilities

Section 5(5): mortages, charges and unpaid taxes are generally the only liabilities to reduce the value of an estate. Section 103 FA 1986 introduced a further restriction as to debts created by the deceased.

Transfers within seven years of death: s7(4)

Where death occurs within seven years of transfer of property the lifetime cumulation is recalculated using the full tax rates (on a sliding scale); therefore inheritance tax may be payable.

For example, where the transfer is made:

a) more than three but not more than four years before the death: 80 per cent;

b) more than four but not more than five years before the death: 60 per cent;

c) more than five but not more than six years before the death: 40 per cent;

d) more than six but not more than seven years before the death: 20 per cent.

Gifts with reservation of benefit

Section 102 FA 1986 and Sch 20 deal with gifts of property over which the donor retains some rights or from which the donor continues to derive benefit, such as occupation of gifted property. Section 102(3) treats the property as part of the deceased donor's estate, and s102(4) establishes the date of 'potentially exempt' if the reservation of benefit ceases.

Schedule 20 para 6(1)(a) relieves the potential charge where the donor pays full value (such as rent) for the continuing use, and para 6(1)(b) relieves where the benefit is from occupation of property which is necessary for the proper care and maintenance of the donor. For interpretation of statutory meanings see *St Aubyn* v *Attorney-General* [1952] AC 15 and *Commissioner of Stamp Duties* v *Perpetual Trustee Co Ltd* [1943] AC 435. See also *Ingram's (Lady) Executors* v *IRC* [1999] STC 37. The central point argued in *Ingram* was at what point the leasehold or other interest in favour of Lady Ingram arose. The outcome was that Ferris J concluded that the trustees never held the properties without their being subject to Lady Ingram's interest, that there had been no other intention on her part when the transfers were made and that there was therefore no benefit returned to the donor which could be held to be a benefit reserved out of the gift once made. Although the Court of Appeal disagreed with Ferris J, his decision was upheld by the House of Lords. Following the House of Lords ruling, s104 Finance Act 1999 was enacted to effectively close the loophole in future cases.

The Finance Act 2003 further changed the IHT provisions in order to prevent taxpayers exploiting the reservation of benefit rules by 'Eversden schemes'. In *Eversden* v *IRC* [2003] STC 822, the Court of Appeal held that the reservation of benefit provisions contained in s102(5) of the Finance Act 1986 does not apply to the extent that the gift is exempt by virtue of the spouse exemption. If one spouse gives the other an interest in possession (however brief) that is equivalent in inheritance tax terms to giving the property itself. The Court reasoned that there is then no room for the reservation of benefit rules to apply.

The effect of the new provisions is that the gift with reservation position is now to be considered at the time that the donor spouse's interest in possession comes to an end. This means that, for gifts with reservation purposes only, the initial interest of the spouse is disregarded. The donor will be regarded as having made a gift with reservation at that time if he can actually or potentially have enjoyment of the assets. The assets gifted will in these circumstances continue to form part of the donor's estate.

Specifically, s185 FA 2003 disapplies the current exception from s102(5) of the Finance Act 1986, for gifts to a spouse where gifts are made:

a) on or after 20 June 2003; and

b) into a trust in which the donor's spouse enjoys an interest in possession; and

c) the interest in possession comes to an end (whether on the donee's death or otherwise); and

d) the subsequent use of the gift is such that it will count as a taxable 'gift with reservation' if the gift is made at the time the interest in possession comes to an end.

Duty to account

Primary responsibility for the tax remains with the transferor or settlement trustees, with the donee or beneficiary of a trust only liable in the event that the tax remains unpaid. However for PETs which become chargeable on death, the donee becomes primarily responsible because s204(7) and (8) limit the personal representatives' liability to assets within their control. The value of the property attributed to a PET which becomes chargeable is the value at the time the gift was made and not of the property at the date of death.

The deceased's personal representatives are generally under a duty to deliver an account to the Inland Revenue within 12 months from the end of the month of death. This account should detail the property of the estate and also beneficial interests in possession and property over which he had a general power of appointment. Excepted estates fall under SI 1981/880, SI 1989/1078. In general the PRs of the estate must offer up the tax, and their liability is personal in so far as it relates to the assets they received in their capacities as PRs.

20.3 Key cases and statutes

- *Eversden* v *IRC* [2003] STC 822
  Inheritance tax – gifts in reservation of benefit

- *Ingram's (Lady) Executors* v *IRC* [1999] STC 37
  Inheritance tax – gifts with reservation of benefit

- *Marshall* v *Kerr* [1994] 3 WLR 299; [1994] STC 638
  Inheritance tax – post-death variations

- Finance Act 1999, s104

- Finance Act 2003, s185

- Inheritance Tax Act 1984

20.4 Questions and suggested solutions

Note: you should also refer to the questions in Chapter 18 which deal with both capital gains tax and inheritance tax – a common occurrence.

QUESTION ONE

What are the inheritance tax consequences of the following dispositions made by M, who died in May 2000.

a) In January 2000 M transferred £200,000 to Tim and Tina the trustees of a discretionary trust M set up to benefit her nephews and nieces;

b) In February 2000 M gave her son, H, £5,000 as a birthday present;

c) In March 2000 M gave her daughter, O, £5,000 on the occasion of her marriage; and

d) In January 1992 M transferred her house to R, her favourite nephew, but continued to live in it rent free after the transfer had been completed.

University of London LLB Examination
(for External Students) Revenue Law June 2000 Q9

General Comment

This question explores the inheritance tax consequences of lifetime transfers of property.

Skeleton Solution

IHT: value transferred by chargeable transfer; measure of charge; potentially exempt transfers – transfer to discretionary trust – lifetime transfer – gift in consideration of marriage – gift with reservation.

Suggested Solution

Inheritance Tax (IHT) was introduced by the FA 1986 as a replacement for capital transfer tax (CTT). In fact is is little more than a heavily altered form of CTT. The CTT legislation was consolidated in the Capital Transfer Tax Act 1984 which, since FA 1986, has (retrospectively, as it were) been known as the IHTA 1984.

IHT is chargeable on the value transferred by a chargeable transfer: s1 IHTA 1984. A chargeable transfer is any transfer made by an individual other than an exempt transfer: s2 IHTA 1984. The value transferred by a chargeable transfer is the amount by which a person's estate is reduced by the transfer: s3 IHTA 1984. Where an otherwise chargeable transfer is made inter vivos by gift by an individual to either:

a) another individual; or

b) an interest in possession settlement; or

c) an accumulation and maintenance settlement; or

d) a disabled trust;

then the transfer is potentially exempt: s3A IHTA 1984. If the transferor survives the PET by seven years the transfer becomes exempt. Where the transferor dies within that period the transfer becomes chargeable retrospectively and is taxed on the footing that it was chargeable when made (rather than being treated as part of the notional transfer on death). Thus, these consequences follow:

a) The amount of tax applicable to a PET which becomes chargeable is determined by the transferor's cumulative total in the seven years prior to the transfer (not the seven years prior to death). The rates of tax however are those in force at death.

b) Any chargeable transfers made after the PET may require to be reopened and looked at again, since the tax originally payable in respect of such a chargeable transfer will have been calculated on the footing that it was preceded by an exempt transfer rather than a chargeable one.

It should be noted that where the transferor dies less than seven but more than three years after the PET a tapering provision will apply to reduce the tax payable proportionately to the period of time elapsed. Finally, when a PET becomes chargeable, grossing up will not normally apply in the calculation of tax due at death rates, and the donee or transferee will primarily suffer liability thereon, though the Revenue may proceed against the PRs instead.

a) *Discretionary trust*

The transfer of £200,000 into a discretionary settlement is a chargeable disposition for inheritance tax purposes. M would, therefore, have made a chargeable transfer of this amount and a charge to inheritance tax at the lifetime rate of 20 per cent would be made on the value transferred less the nil rate band deduction. The transfer represents a real change in the ownership of the assets or monies transferred; it is not a transfer between individuals but to trustees and as a result is outside the exemption provided by s3A for PETs. The amount of tax applicable to this transfer would be revised in the light of M's death five months later.

b) *£5,000 to H*

The gift of £5,000 to H appears to satisfy the terms of ss1–3 IHTA 1984 and therefore appears to be a chargeable transfer. However, s19 (the annual exemption) may operate to exempt the first £3,000 of this sum. If M has not used up the previous year's £3,000 exemption then this may be rolled forward. Hence, the gift exceeds £250 and s20 (small gifts not exceeding £250 to any one person) is unavailable. Further there are no facts from which we can deduce that the other exemptions apply: ss21–29A IHTA 1984. Nor do the provisions deeming certain dispositions not to be transfers of value at all: ss10–17 IHTA 1984. To the extent that the transfer is a transfer of value and not an exempt transfer it will qualify as a PET under s3A

IHTA 1984, since it is a transfer, otherwise chargeable, to an individual. As M died within one year of the transfer the PET will be retrospectively chargeable at death rates.

c) *£5,000 to O*

Under s22(1) a gift by a parent on the occasion of a child's marriage is an exempt transfer up to £5,000. Therefore, M's gift to O will be exempt from IHT.

d) *House to R*

By conveying the house to her nephew for no consideration M was potentially liable to IHT on the value transferred, but it qualified as a potentially exempt transfer under s3A. Survival until the year 2000 would, under the PET rules, normally have lead to the value of the house dropping out of M's chargeable estate since more than seven years would have elapsed since the time of the gift. However, since M has continued to live there she has retained an interest in the property so that it cannot be said to have been wholly disposed of. The recipient of her gift, the nephew, did not take possession of the gift. M was therefore within the 'reservation of benefit' rules of Finance Act (FA) 1986 s102 and Sch 20 under which the value of such gifts is not excluded from the estate after seven years but would be part of the chargeable estate on death, since M did not wholly divest herself of it 'virtually to the entire exclusion' of the donor as the provisions dictate.

QUESTION TWO

William, a wealthy industrialist, has recently attained the age of sixty and has a large cash sum which he wants to settle on one or more trusts in order to avoid inheritance tax. His family consists of his wife, two children and five grandchildren. He would like to benefit his family and also have the possibility of charitable gifts being made from a trust.

Advise him on the inheritance consequences of creation and operation of:

a) interest in possession trusts;

b) accumulation and maintenance trusts;

c) discretionary trusts.

> University of London LLB Examination
> (for External Students) Revenue Law June 1995 Q9

General Comment

This question illustrates the inheritance tax consequences of creating various forms of trusts.

Skeleton Solution

IHT planning; transfers to spouse not chargeable lifetime or on death: s18 IHTA 1984 – use of interest in possession trusts; meaning of 'in possession': *Gartside* v *IRC* – accumulation and maintenance trusts; benefits – discretionary trusts; ten-year charge – transfer into trust – relevant property – interim charge – rate of tax – charitable purpose trusts.

Suggested Solution

Note: all references are to the Inheritance Tax Act (IHTA) 1984 unless stated otherwise.

Inheritance tax is chargeable on transfers of capital and arises when that transfer is a 'transfer of value' as defined by the inheritance tax legislation. Under s1 IHTA 1984 'tax shall be charged on the value transferred by a chargeable transfer'. Section 2 defines a 'chargeable transfer' as one which is not an exempt transfer. Section 3 defines a 'transfer of value' as a disposition made by a person as a result of which the value of his estate immediately after the disposition is less than it would be but for the disposition.

Transfers between married couples are not chargeable transfers of value by virtue of the special provisions of s18 which provides for exemption to be accorded to any transfer of value between spouses where property becomes comprised in the other spouse's estate. This exemption is afforded to both lifetime transfers and transfers on death.

Therefore, to the extent that any property is transferred to William's wife either during his lifetime or on his death, no charge to tax will arise. It is also prudent to consider such transfers especially where a spouse's own estate is small, so that further advantage can be taken of other exempt gifts and the 'nil rate band' which apply equally and independently to either spouse.

Interest in possession trusts

Transfers of property between spouses are exempt transfers under s18. However, this does not include property settled upon discretionary trusts for the benefit of the surviving spouse. Property in a discretionary trust is not treated as part of a deceased person's estate as the beneficiaries have no interest in the underlying property, but interests in interest in possession trusts are included in the taxable estate, as the life tenant is deemed to have an interest in the underlying trust assets. Transfers for the benefit of his wife could therefore be done by setting up an interest in possession trust. Initially, the transfer is regarded as a potentially exempt transfer (PET) and if the husband survives the full term of seven years after the transfer, there will be no IHT charge when he dies. Similarly, if the wife, as beneficiary of such a trust were to die, the underlying property is treated as part of her estate for IHT purposes.

The term 'interest in possession' is not formally defined in the inheritance tax legislation. For an understanding of its meaning reference can be made to the explanation of Lord Reid in *Gartside* v *IRC* [1968] AC 553 when he said '"in possession" must mean that your interest enables you to claim now whatever may be the subject of your interest'. Entitlement does not therefore depend on the actions or discretion of another party as it would in the case of a discretionary trust where the beneficiary's entitlement depends on the trustees exercising their powers to make an appointment of income or capital to the beneficiary. Until that occurs the beneficiary has no legal claim upon the income or assets.

In *Pearson v IRC* [1981] AC 753 the House of Lords held that 'interest in possession' means a 'present right to present enjoyment' of income.

Accumulation and maintenance trusts

Accumulation and maintenance trusts, although essentially discretionary trusts at the outset, do not bear the full impact of the tax regime for such trusts. Although similarly treated in most respects for income tax purposes, their inheritance tax treatment is more lenient.

A gift into trust which is an accumulation and maintenance trust is treated as a gift made to an individual and it therefore comes within the PET regime of s3A, the reasoning being that the capital and accumulated income will with certainty vest in an individual on the happening of a contingency. These trusts are well suited for settling part of the funds on the children, without incurring the IHT penalties of an ordinary discretionary trust.

Discretionary trusts

A special tax regime applies for inheritance tax purposes to settlements in which no qualifying interest in possession exists: ss58 et seq. In these cases the interest of the beneficiary is at the discretion of the trustees and, unlike interest in possession trusts, the beneficiary cannot be said to be the beneficial owner of the underlying settled property. On putting property into a discretionary trust, the settlor is charged to tax on the value transferred. This is only one of the occasions when a tax charge arises.

In the absence of beneficial ownership of the underlying assets no charge to tax would normally arise while the settled property remains in a discretionary trust and therefore a special regime was enacted to make a periodic charge to tax. Unlike the interest in possession trust, the variation of the beneficiary's interest in the trust would give rise to no change in the ownership of the property and accordingly to no chargeable transfer of value.

The discretionary trust charges are based on 'relevant property' (s58(1)) which is property in which there is no qualifying interest in possession other than (inter alia) accumulation and maintenance trusts. The tax charge is based principally on a ten-year charge to tax on each tenth anniversary of the setting-up of the settlement. If all or part of the trust terminates, there is an interim charge. This also applies if the trust is converted into a non-discretionary trust and is based on the reduction in value of the fund. The interim charge, when applicable, is based on the commencement value of the trust and on the settlor's previous transfers.

The ten-year rate of tax is 30 per cent of the lifetime rate, ie currently a charge of six per cent of the trust assets. A charge arises on the occasion of property being added to the trust (s67(3)), on which the current rather than the commencement value of the settled property is used, if higher. Discretionary trusts set up by will or intestacy are treated as commencing on the date of death.

The interim charge referred to above will most commonly arise when settled property ceases to be 'relevant property' either on leaving the settlement or remaining settled after a transfer to an interest in possession or accumulation and maintenance trust. Further occasions of charge are when depreciatory transactions reduce the value of the property (s65(1)(b)), unless this results from a commercial transaction. There are exclusions for reductions in value arising from the payment of expenses relating to relevant property or where an income tax charge arises on the recipient.

The exit charge on property leaving the trust is charged at the lifetime full rate on actual or deemed capital distributions.

If there is an acceptable alternative under one of the other types of trust already considered, the discretionary trust route should not be adopted because of the IHT liabilities.

Charitable purpose trusts

Property settled in trust for charitable purposes does not attract a charge to tax under the discretionary regime outlined above. For these purposes such property is not 'relevant property' for s58 charge purposes and unless it is disposed of by trustees and used for non-charitable purposes, no charge will arise when the property leaves the trust. The desire to benefit charities can be achieved in this way.

QUESTION THREE

Using examples to illustrate your answer consider the associated operations provisions in s268 Inheritance Tax Act 1984.

University of London LLB Examination
(for External Students) Revenue Law June 1991 Q7

General Comment

This question focuses on the 'associated operations' provisions in s268 IHTA 1984.

Skeleton Solution

Purpose of associated operations provisions – definition: s268 IHTA 1984 – section is very wide – no guidelines from IR – example: *IRC* v *MacPherson*.

Suggested Solution

The 'associated operations' provision have been enacted mainly to prevent a taxpayer from reducing the value of a gift or the inheritance tax chargeable.

'Associated operations' are defined in s268 Inheritance Tax Act (IHTA) 1984 as:

> '(1) ... any two or more operations of any kind, being:
> (a) operations which affect the same property, or one of which affects some property and the other or others of which affect property which represents, whether directly or indirectly, that property, or income arising from that property, or any property representing accumulations of any such income; or
> (b) any two operations of which one is effected with reference to the other, or with a view to enabling the other to be effected or facilitating its being effected, and any further operation having a like relation to any of those two, and so on;
> whether those operations are effected by the same person or different persons, and whether or not they are simultaneous; and "operation" includes an omission.
>
> (2) The granting of a lease for full consideration in money or money's worth shall not be taken to be associated with any operation effected more than three years after the grant, and no operation effected on or after 27 March 1974 shall be taken to be associated with an operation effected before that date.
>
> (3) Where a transfer of value is made by associated operations carried out at different times it shall be treated as made at the time of the last of them; but where any one or more of the earlier operations also constitute a transfer of value made by the same transferor, the value transferred by the earlier operations shall be treated as reducing the value transferred by all the operations taken together, except to the extent that the transfer constituted by the earlier operations but not that made by all the operations taken together is exempt under s18 (spouse exemption).'

On a reading of s268, we can conclude that this section is extremely wide and can be used on a multitude of occasions. The IR have not issued any statements or given any guidelines as to when they will invoke s268. Neither is the operation of s268 and its relation to the 'new approach' as postulated in *Ramsay v IRC* [1982] AC 300 etc, clear.

For an example of a case where the 'associated operations' provision was used, see *IRC v MacPherson* [1989] AC 159. There trustees entered into an agreement which reduced the value of the trust property. They later appointed the property in favour of the beneficiary. This was held to be an associated operation. Lord Jauncey identified the boundaries of the associated operations provisions as follows:

> 'If an individual took steps which devalued his property on a Monday with a view to making a gift thereof on Tuesday, he would fail to satisfy the requirements of s20(4) [now s10(1)] because the act of devaluation and the gift would be considered together. The definition in s44 [now s268] is extremely wide and is capable of covering a multitude of events affecting the same property which might have little or no apparent connection between them. It might be tempting to assume that any event which fell within this wide definition should be taken into account in determining what constituted a transaction

for the purposes of s20(4). However, counsel for the Crown accepted, rightly in my view, that some limitation must be imposed. Counsel for the trustees informed your lordship that there was no authority on the meaning of the words "associated operations" in the context of the capital transfer tax legislation but he referred to a decision of the Court of Appeal in Northern Ireland, *Herdman* v *IRC* (1967) 45 TC 394, in which the tax avoidance provisions of ss412 and 413 of the Income Tax Act 1952 had been considered. Section 412(1) provided that a charge to income tax arose where the individual had by means of a transfer of assets either alone or in conjunction with associated operations acquired rights whereby he could enjoy a particular description of income. Lord MacDermott CJ upheld a submission by the taxpayer that the only associated operations which were relevant to the subsection were those by means of which, in conjunction with the transfer, a taxpayer could enjoy the income and did not include associated operations taking place after the transfer had conferred upon the taxpayer the power to enjoy income. If the extended meaning of "transaction" is read into the opening words of s20(4) the wording becomes:

> "A disposition is not a transfer of value if it is shown that it was not intended, and was not made in a transaction including a series of transactions and any associated operations intended, to confer any gratuitous benefit ..."

So read it is clear that the intention to confer gratuitous benefit qualifies both transactions and associated operations. If an associated operation is not intended to confer such a benefit it is not relevant for the purposes of the subsection. That is not to say that it must necessarily per se confer a benefit but it must form a part of and contribute to a scheme which does confer such a benefit.'

The associated operations provision in s268 IHTA 1984 allows the IR to tax any number of transactions including omissions as one single transaction. The transactions can be carried out by different persons at different times. For example, suppose that Andy wishes to make a gift of a parcel of land to Ben. If Andy transferred that land directly to Ben, it would result in there being a disposition subject to IHT. Rather, Andy could grant a lease of the land to Ben and Andy could later transfer the reversion to Ben, thereby paying IHT on the then reduced value of the reversion. Note, this type of device is still effective if transfer of the reversion to Ben occurs more than three years after the initial grant of the lease: see s268(2) IHTA 1984.

QUESTION FOUR

Agnes is a wealthy woman who owns many assets. In September 1995 she conveyed her home to her son Thomas. At that time Agnes moved out of the house and Thomas and his wife and children moved into the house. Agnes regularly visited Thomas in the house and stayed there for a period at Christmas.

In November Agnes settled £500,000 on discretionary trust for a wide range of beneficiaries, including members of her family.

Agnes owned a valuable pair of vases. Each vase alone is worth £10,000 but as a pair they are worth £30,000. At Christmas Agnes gave her other son, Richard, a painting worth £8,000 and also sold him one of the pair of vases for £10,000.

In February 1996 Agnes died unexpectedly. Under her will Richard inherited all her assets.

Advise on the inheritance tax position.

University of London LLB Examination
(for External Students) Revenue Law June 1996 Q9

General Comment

This question explores the IHT consequences of lifetime transfers of property.

Skeleton Solution

Conveyance of property; initially a potentially exempt transfer (PET): s3A IHTA 1984 – reassessment of PET following death – transfer to discretionary trust immediately chargeable; not a PET; not within s3A provisions – availability of annual exemption: s19 – reassessment of IHT charge on trust assets on death.

Suggested Solution

Note: all references are to the Inheritance Tax Act (IHTA) 1984 unless stated otherwise.

Inheritance tax is chargeable in respect of any reduction in an individual's estate. Agnes, therefore, in conveying her home to her son Thomas in September 1995, has reduced her estate by the value of the property. However, under the potentially exempt transfer (PET) provision of s3A, the transfer incurs no immediate liability to tax. In normal circumstances if Agnes had survived for a period of seven years from the date of the conveyance of the property, there would be no charge at any future date to inheritance tax.

One possible exception to this rule would occur if she is deemed to have made a transfer but reserved to her the benefit of use of the property concerned. This would lead to the property being treated under s102 and Sch 20 FA 1986 as still being part of her estate until the benefit reserved to her came to an end. Only then would the period of seven years for the purpose of obtaining full exemption begin to run. However, the information provided suggests that her son and family have taken bona fide occupation of the property and the exposure to s102 would not therefore apply.

Discretionary trust

The transfer of £500,000 into a discretionary settlement is a chargeable disposition for inheritance tax purposes. Agnes would, therefore, have made a chargeable transfer of this amount and a charge to inheritance tax at the lifetime rate of 20 per cent would be made on the value transferred less the nil rate band deduction of £250,000 for 2001–02. The transfer represents a real change in the ownership of the assets or monies transferred; it is not a transfer between individuals but to a body of trustees and as a result is outside the exemption provided by s3A for PETs. The amount of tax applicable to this transfer would be revised in the light of her death three months later.

Sale and gift of other assets

The gift of the painting worth £8,000 would initially be treated as a PET to the extent that it exceeds the annual exemption limit of £3,000 under s19. In addition, by selling a part of a set of vases, Agnes has effectively reduced the value of her estate by £10,000. The sale of a single vase has reduced her assets from £30,000 to £10,000 and she has in turn received £10,000, for the sale. Since this does not arise from a commercial transaction at arm's length, the provisions of s3 apply.

On Agnes's death in February 1996, her estate is subject to inheritance tax based on the value of the asset retained. In addition, tax is recalculated in respect of the chargeable transfers made within the previous seven years and this will lead to a revision of the tax charged on the payment into the discretionary trust. Tax will be recalculated at the 40 per cent rate applicable on death, with credit being given for the tax already charged. The value of the house as at September 1995 will also be brought into account based on the value at that date, and the other assets previously chargeable will be re-taxed at the 40 per cent rate. In addition to the nil rate band, a reduction would be due in respect of the annual exemption for the current year and any unused amount for the previous year before arriving at the 'cumulative chargeable total'.

The assets comprised in the discretionary trust will be subject to the ten-year periodic charge under s58(1) on each tenth anniversary of the setting up of the settlement. The rate of tax applicable to each charge is currently 30 per cent of the lifetime rate which would provide a charge of 6 per cent based on the current year's rate.

QUESTION FIVE

In September 1996 Danielle gave six of her set of valuable china cups to her daughter and the other six to her son. She also gave £3,000 to her son and the same amount to her daughter. Danielle's daughter is an unemployed solicitor but her son is employed in a good job. In December she paid for the wedding reception of her son and gave him £6,000 on the occasion of his marriage.

At Christmas Danielle gave £250 to her good friend Esther and the next day Danielle gave another £250 to her brother on the understanding that he would give the money to Esther.

As Danielle was worried about the future security of her daughter she conveyed her house to her daughter in March and agreed that she, Danielle, would continue to live in the house with her daughter but from the date of the conveyance she would pay rent to her daughter.

Advise on the inheritance tax position on the alternative assumptions that:

a) Danielle lives until the year 2004;

b) Danielle dies in 1998.

Adapted from University of London LLB Examination
(for External Students) Revenue Law June 1993 Q9

General Comment

This question explores the inheritance tax consequences of lifetime transfers of property.

Skeleton Solution

IHT is charged on reduction of estate and gifts within seven years of death: IHTA 1984 ss3A and 131 – IHT on transfer of a set of assets: valuation: s3(1) – annual exemption: s19: £3,000 – potentially Exempt Transfers (PETs): s3A – gifts in consideration of marriage: s22 – small gifts exemption: s20: £250 per person – reservation of benefit and payment of rent: FA 1986 s102 and Sch 20 para 6(1)(a).

Suggested Solution

Note: all references are to the Inheritance Tax Act (IHTA) 1984 unless stated otherwise.

Under s1 IHTA 1984 inheritance tax is chargeable on the value transferred by a chargeable transfer, which is – s2(1) – any transfer of value which is not exempt. Accordingly, for IHT to be imposed there has to be (1) a transfer of value, (2) a transfer which is not exempt from IHT and (3) value has to be transferred out of a person's estate.

The essence of IHT is the reduction in the transferor's estate, and the value of that reduction provides the key to the amount on which IHT is imposed. Since a sale produces a compensating increase in the estate by the injection of the sale proceeds of the departing asset, there is normally no net loss to the estate and no IHT is imposed. The main incidence of IHT therefore is on gifts, since they lead to a reduction in the value of the estate and the amount of that reduction is the amount on which IHT is imposed: s3(1). Inheritance tax is imposed when the value of the actual chargeable transfers accumulated during the previous seven years exceeds £150,000, the current amount of the 'nil rate band'.

Gift of set of china

When Danielle disposes of her set of china in two separate transactions the value which each receives will be what the appropriate half-set is worth. However, for IHT purposes, under s3(1) the value by which Danielle's estate has been reduced is the value of the complete set, which is most probably greater than the sum of the two halves. In normal circumstances that would be attributed to being a chargeable transfer which would be taken into account in her accumulated chargeable transfers for the purposes of a charge to IHT. However, it is also a qualifying PET under s3A, so that no immediate charge to tax arises.

If she dies in 1998, the full value will be included in her estate chargeable to IHT.

If, however, she survives until the year 2004, the PET rules under s3A(4) will give full exemption to the transfer and it will be excluded from her estate, on the grounds that more than seven years have elapsed since the making of the gift.

Gifts to son and daughter

In each year Danielle can give away up to £3,000 and claim her annual exemption under s19 in respect of that amount. The excess of the second £3,000 is a chargeable and accountable transfer which would be added to her cumulative lifetime total of chargeable gains.

If she dies in 1998, only the excess £3,000 will be included in her estate chargeable to IHT.

If, however, she survives until the year 2004, the PET rules under s3A(4) will give full exemption to the transfer and it will be excluded from her estate.

Gift in consideration of marriage

Under s22(1) a gift by a parent on the occasion of a child's marriage is an exempt transfer up to £5,000. The £1,000 excess is a PET and the normal seven-year rule of survival applies to it. The payment of the wedding reception cannot be said to be a gift to any individual nor is it intended to confer any gratuitous benefit on the recipients. It would therefore be excluded under s10.

Small gifts relief

Gifts of up to £250 to any number of individuals are exempt under the small gifts relief provisions of s20. Therefore the gift direct to Esther will be an exempt transfer, but the second indirect gift would be a chargeable transfer since its destination is predetermined and it is therefore not an outright gift to Esther's brother.

Gift of house

By conveying the house to her daughter for no consideration Danielle is potentially liable to IHT on the value transferred, but again it qualifies as a potentially exempt transfer under s3A, and if Danielle were to die in 1998 the value of the house would count as part of her chargeable estate and would be accumulated with the other transfers which were previously potentially exempt but are now chargeable transfers.

Survival until the year 2004 would, under the PET rules, normally lead to the value of the house dropping out of her chargeable estate since more than seven years would have elapsed since the time of the gift. However, since Danielle has continued to live there she has retained an interest in the property so that it cannot be said to have been wholly disposed of. The recipient of her gift, the daughter, has not taken possession of the gift. Danielle would therefore be within the 'reservation of benefit' rules of the Finance Act (FA) 1986 s102 and Sch 20 under which the value of such gifts is not excluded from the estate after seven years but would be part of the chargeable estate on death, since Danielle will not have wholly divested herself of it 'virtually to the entire exclusion' of the donor as the provisions dictate. However, the possible application of these rules is over-ridden by the provision of FA 1986 Sch 20 para 6(1)(a) where the benefit reserved by occupation is in return for a full market value consideration. If therefore the rent is a full market rent for the property, the PET rules will exclude the value of the property from Danielle's chargeable estate if she survives until the year 2004.

Chapter 21

IHT Reliefs and Related Provisions

21.1   Introduction

21.2   Key points

21.3   Key cases and statutes

21.4   Question and suggested solution

21.1 Introduction

The most significant change made to the operation of inheritance tax (IHT) was the introduction from 18 March 1986 (Budget day) of the concept of the 'potentially exempt transfer'(PET). The effect of this was to take out of a charge to tax most dispositions between individuals either at the time of the disposition or on the subsequent death of the disponer, provided that occurred more than seven years later. As a result, IHT is mostly a tax on death or on gifts within seven years of death. The remaining heads of charge are subject to other specific exemptions and reliefs, governed either by the nature of the property disposed of (business property, national heritage) or by the identity of either of the parties to the transaction (married couples, charities, political parties).

21.2 Key points

All references are to IHTA 1984 unless stated.

Potentially exempt transfer

Section 3A(1) FA (No 2) 1987: must be made by an individual after 18 March 1986 and must otherwise be a chargeable transfer. PETs include outright gifts, accumulation and maintenance settlements for the disabled and interest in possession settlements.

The PET, where made within seven years of death, becomes a chargeable transfer and is subject to IHT and cumulated with the taxpayer's estate.

Sections 36–42: partially exempt transfers

This involves a complex recalculation of the IHT payable according to the gross values involved, by double grossing up.

Exemptions and reliefs

Section 19: within each tax year £3,000 may be transferred free of IHT. This allowance may be rolled forward where unused to the next year only.

Section 21: normal and regular expenditure by the transferor out of his income is exempted. There must be however sufficient income remaining to maintain his 'usual standard of living'. See *Bennett* v *IRC* [1995] STC 54: an 87-year-old lady directed the trustees of a life interest trust from which she benefitted to pay any income which was surplus to her requirements, to her three sons. They made payments in February 1989 and February 1990 before she died later that month. It was held that, despite the actual short period over which the payments were made, the pattern of normal expenditure had been sufficiently established, that it had been intended, barring unforeseen circumstances, to continue for a sufficient period to become regarded as the transferor's normal expenditure out of income.

Section 20: small gifts of any number up to £250 may be made by the donor as long as they are to different donees. In addition the gifts must be absolute and not conditional.

Section 22: gifts in consideration of marriage must be made at the time of the marriage. A parent may gift £5,000 and a more distant relative up to £2,500.

Section 11: maintenance payments to former spouses and children do not fall within the IHT charge. Under s11(6) transfers associated with the dissolution of a marriage are still covered by the exemption. Therefore for IHT purposes the s18 provisions continue until divorce and include the divorce arrangements.

Exemptions in paras 19–22 apply to lifetime transfers only.

Exemptions and reliefs in paras 18, 23–28 and 103–122 apply also on death.

Section 18: inter-spouse exemption. This is an important exemption, and there is no limit placed upon the amounts of transfers between spouses unless one is not UK domiciled, when there is a limit of £55,000.

Sections 23–28 exempt gifts to charities, political parties, national benefit etc. The national benefit relief applies only to gifts made prior to 17 March 1998, when the provisions were withdrawn by s143 FA 1998.

Section 30 et seq: conditional exemption for works of art and national heritage property accessible to the public. See also s142 and Sch 25 FA 1998, which imposed further obligations on the donor, including the measure of public access, in order to benefit from this relief.

Section 36 et seq: allocation of exemptions on a subsequent occasion of charge.

Business and agricultural property reliefs: ss103–124

Both reliefs are available for lifetime transfers, transfers on death and transfers into and out of settlements.

a) Time limit for relief

Whatever the category of business property, the relief is conditional upon the property being owned by the transferor for a minimum period of two years immediately preceding the transfer: s106. Sections 113A and 113B allow relief where relevant property has been replaced by 'replacement property', eg when a transferee disposes of property received and reinvests the proceeds in other property.

b) Categories of relevant business property

The changes made by s184 FA 1996 and Schedule 41 simplified the range of relief which previously applied to differing ranges of property and in particular to differing levels of shareholding in unquoted trading companies. Following the FA 1996 changes, 'relevant business property' means:

For 100 per cent business property relief

i) Property consisting of a business or an interest in a business: includes life tenant's beneficial interest in trust assets.

ii) Unquoted securities which taken either on their own or combined with any other unquoted securities or unquoted shares gave the transferor control of the company immediately before the transfer. All must be owned by the transferor.

iii) Any unquoted shares in a company – providing the company does not carry on a business of dealing in securities, stocks or shares, land or buildings or making or holding investments: s105(3).

For 50 per cent business property relief

i) Shares or securities in a company which are listed on a recognised stock exchange and which either on their own or when taken together with other shares or securities owned by the transferor, gave the transferor control of the company immediately before the transfer.

ii) Land or buildings, machinery or plant used in the business of a company which the transferor controls or in a partnership of which the transferor is a member.

In considering whether 'control' exists for the purposes of the relief mentioned above, all shares and securities giving rise to voting rights must be considered, irrespective of whether they are exercisable or exercised in practice. See *Walding* v *IRC* [1996] STC 13: it was claimed that a holding of 45 per cent gave control because 24 per cent of the shares in the company were in the name of an infant. It was held that personal capacity did not detract from the requirements of s269 which for this purpose looks at the total shares in which voting rights are 'capable of being exercised'.

Agricultural property relief

i)   Agricultural land or pasture in the United Kingdom, the Channel Islands and the Isle of Man. This includes farms held by tenants under tenancies commencing after 31 August 1995, including a tenant succeeding to a pre-31 August 1995 tenancy on the death of the existing tenant: s185 FA 1996.

ii) Woodlands.

iii) Buildings used in connection with the intensive rearing of livestock or fish if the occupation of each is ancillary to that of agricultural land or pasture.

iv) Cottages, farm buildings and farmhouses as are of a character appropriate to the farm property. See *Starke and Another (Brown's Executors) v IRC* [1994] STC 295: property on a medium-size farm, consisting of a large farmhouse and outbuildings was declared not to be agricultural property within the meaning of s115(2).

21.3 Key cases and statutes

* *Bennett v IRC* [1995] STC 54
  Inheritance tax – exemptions to reliefs – recurring payments

* *Parke (Deceased) (No 2), Re* [1972] Ch 385
  Inheritance tax – exemptions and reliefs – gifts in consideration of marriage

* *Starke and Another (Brown's Executors) v IRC* [1994] STC 295
  Inheritance tax – agricultural property relief – character of property

* Finance Act (No 2) 1987, s3A

* Finance Act 1998, ss142–145

* Inheritance Tax Act 1984, ss36–42 and 103–124

21.4 Question and suggested solution

In February 1994 Jamie was told by his doctors that he was seriously ill and had probably less than seven years to live. He made the following gifts later that month:

a) £10,000 to Old College, his former college in Oxford;

b) £100,000 to T1 and T2 on trust for his former wife Karen for life, with remainder to his children Larry and Monica; and

c) £200,000 to T3 and T4 on discretionary trust for such of his nephews and nieces as they should see fit.

Jamie died in March 1997. By his will he made the following legacies and devises:

a) His house in France, 'Chez Jamie', to his mistress, Norma;

b) His house in London to his wife, Ophelia; and

c) His residue to his son, Philip.

At the time of his death, 'Chez Jamie' was worth £200,000, the London house was worth £350,000 and his residue was worth £50,000.

What are the IHT consequences of these facts? Assume that Jamie died resident and domiciled in the UK for IHT purposes.

University of London LLB Examination
(for External Students) Revenue Law June 1997 Q6

General Comment

A practical examination of the lifetime and death rules under which inheritance tax liability can arise.

Skeleton Solution

The charge to IHT – potentially exempt transfers (PETs): s3A – charity exemption: s23, charitable purposes; *Special Commissioners* v *Pemsel* – gift to interest in possession trust: s3A PET – gift to discretionary trust: no s3A treatment; immediately chargeable transfer – discretionary trust regime: ss58 et seq – IHT on death: no exclusion for foreign based property; s6(1) – spouse exemption: s18 – recalculation of IHT on death for earlier transfers and PETs now chargeable.

Suggested Solution

Note: all references are to the Inheritance Tax Act (IHTA) 1984 unless stated otherwise.

Inheritance tax (IHT) impacts on both lifetime transfers and dispositions or transfers on death. Certain lifetime transfers are exempt from IHT entirely and others, referred to as potentially exempt transfers (PETs), if the transferor survives for seven years after the transfer: s3A. Transfers of property between spouses, whether made during lifetime or passing on death, are unconditionally exempt (s18) with no limit on value unless the recipient spouse is non-UK domiciled. The transfers which remain exempt only under the seven-year rule under s3A are 'potentially exempt transfers' (PETs) and the treatment is confined to transfers between individuals or to interest in possession trusts in which the individual beneficiary will have an interest in the underlying property of the trust or on a transfer to an accumulation and maintenance trust. Certain gifts, such as gifts to charities, are exempt from IHT.

These various elements of IHT charge, reliefs and exemptions are relevant to Jamie's inheritance tax position, the treatment of which would be as follows.

Dispositions in February 1994

Gift to Old College, Oxford

A gift to a charity is specifically exempt from IHT under s23(1). In order to qualify for this exemption the charity must be one established for 'charitable purposes' in the same manner as a charity seeking income tax exemption in ss505 and 506(1) ICTA 1988. 'Charitable purposes' is established by case law and includes 'the advancement of education': see Lord MacNaghten in *Special Commissioners* v *Pemsel* [1891] AC 531. The gift of £10,000 to the college has therefore no IHT implications either when made or at the time of Jamie's death.

Gifts to trusts – T1 and T2

A gift into a trust in which an individual has an interest in possession is within the scope of the PET treatment under s3A. The trust for Jamie's former wife for life with the remainder to his children satisfies this condition. The effect of this is that at the time when the gift is made no charge to IHT would arise, but on Jamie's death the transfer will have to be brought into account for the purpose of calculating IHT on it and the rest of Jamie's estate: s3A(4) and (5). Liability for any tax on the gifts rests with the recipient trustees.

Gifts to trusts – T3 and T4

Transfers into trusts which have no 'qualifying interest in possession' fall within the special regime of ss58 et seq. In these cases the interest of the beneficiary is at the discretion of the trustees and, unlike interest in possession trusts, the beneficiary cannot be said to be the beneficial owner of the underlying settled property. On a transfer of property into such a trust, a charge to IHT arises, being a chargeable transfer to which the statutes afford no specific exemption or relief. In addition to tax on the entry into the trust, the regime in ss58 et seq imposes a regular ten yearly charge on the trust property. Without this no charge to tax on such property would arise during the lifetime of the trust, whose body of trustees retain the ownership of the property irrespective of changes in their identities. The liability for the tax will normally rest with the transferee.

Dispositions on Jamie's death – March 1997

House in France – £200,000

The IHT charge which arises on Jamie's estate on his death will include property wherever situated. Foreign-based property is only excluded from the charge to IHT if owned by an individual who is domiciled outside the UK at the time when the charge arises: s6(1). The £200,000 value of the property left to his mistress will therefore be subject to an IHT charge.

House in London – £350,000

This property would normally form part of Jamie's chargeable estate and be regarded as a 'chargeable transfer' for IHT purposes. However, transfers between spouses are 'exempt transfers' under s18 for all purposes and the value of the property is therefore excluded from the calculation of IHT on Jamie's death. There is no upper limit for such exemption treatment.

Residue to son – £50,000

This amount forms part of the chargeable estate as at Jamie's date of death and is not subject to any reliefs nor exemptions. Tax will therefore be levied on it as shown below.

The calculations of IHT due at the relevant dates would proceed as follows:

February 1994

a) *Gifts to Interest in Possession trusts – T1 and T2 – £100,000 – PET – no charge s3A*

b) *Gifts to discretionary trusts – T3 and T4 –*

chargeable transfer –		£200,000	
Add: Total chargeable transfers in previous 7 years (s7)		nil	
Deduct: Annual exemptions (s19) 2 x £3,000	6,000		
Nil rate band 1993–94 Sch 1	150,000	156,000	
Amount charged to IHT Feb 1994		£44,000	Tax £17,600
Cumulative chargeable transfers carried forward		£200,000	

March 1997

Recalculation of tax on February 1994 transfers

PET of £100,000 to T1 and T2 becomes subject to tax. Tax position recalculated as follows:

Note: the annual exemption allocated previously to T3 and T4 remains: s19(3A). Both transfers are assumed to be made on the same date for the purpose of the nil rate band re-allocation.

Value of Transfer to T1 and T2	£100,000
Value of transfer to T3 and T4 (net of s19)	194,000
Add chargeable transfers in previous 7 years	nil
	£294,000

Deduct: nil rate band 1996–97	200,000
Tax due at 40% on	£94,000
IHT due	£37,600
The tax due by T1 and T2 – 100,000/294,000	£12,790
The tax due by T3 and T4 – 194,000/294,000	£24,810
Tax for T3/T4 limited under s7(4)(a) to 80%	£19,848
Less paid 1993–94	17,600
IHT now due T3/T4	£2,248

Tax on remainder of estate March 1997

Value of house in France	£200,000
London House exempt: s18	–
Residue to son	50,000
Add: Cumulative transfers in previous 7 years	294,000
	544,000
Deduct: nil rate band 1996–97	200,000
Tax due at 40% on	344,000
IHT due	£137,600
Less IHT paid as above	37,600
IHT now due	£100,000
Tax due on house to Mistress – 200/250 thereof	£80,000
Tax due on residue to sons – 50/250 thereof	£20,000

Chapter 22

IHT and Settled Property

22.1   Introduction

22.2   Key points

22.3   Key cases and statute

22.4   Questions and suggested solutions

22.1 Introduction

Settlements fall into three categories for IHT purposes:

a) with an interest in possession;

b) with no interest in possession – discretionary trusts;

c) special or privileged trusts – accumulation and maintenance trusts.

There is a potential liability to IHT on transfers to a trust while property remains in trust (the periodic charge) and when property leaves a trust (the exit charge).

22.2 Key points

Where a settlement is created in the life of the settlor it will be a PET where:

a) if the otherwise chargeable transfer creates an IIP trust;

b) if the trust is an accumulative and maintenance or trust for the disabled.

If these two categories of trusts are not created there will be an immediate chargeable transfer.

Interest in possession (IIP)

This has no clear definition, but see *Pearson* v *IRC* [1980] 2 WLR 872, where IIP was described as a present right to present enjoyment.

Section 49(1): where someone has an IIP he is treated as having a beneficial entitlement to that property as his estate is increased to the full value of the settled property.

Transfers to these trusts for the life of an individual are PETs since the life tenant has an interest in the underlying assets: see s3A. There is no periodic charge or exit charge on the death of the life tenant if the life tenant or the settlor takes the property. If property does not revert to the settlor or the settlor's spouse on the life tenant's death, it is chargeable to the estate of the life tenant: ss49, 51–54. Property may also revert to the settlor during lifetime or within two years of death, without charge: s53(4).

Section 53(1)

This states that no tax is to be charged under s52 if the property is excluded property: see s48 in this context.

Discretionary trusts

Property held in trust subject to the discretion of its trustees is subject to the 'discretionary trust regime' for IHT and attracts a charge on entry (not a PET), a further 'periodic charge' (ss58–85) during the life of the trust, plus on the occurrence of specific events (s65) and an 'exit charge' when property ceases to be settled property.

Discretionary trusts are charged via the periodic 'ten-yearly charge' or the ten-year anniversary at 30 per cent of the rates applicable to a chargeable transfer of settled property into a settlement. Currently this produces a 6 per cent charge (30% x lifetime rate of 20%). If the property enters the settlement between anniversaries then an apportionment is made.

Section 65: a charge arises when the property enters the settlement (or ceases to be relevant property: s68(6)). A charge will also arise when the trustees make a disposition.

Charitable purpose trusts

Section 58: does not include property in these trusts as relevant property.

Section 70: imposes a charge on exit when the property is no longer held for charitable purposes and where the trustees make a non-charitable disposition (s10(1)).

Section 71: accumulation and maintenance trusts

Property within these trusts is specially privileged and is not 'relevant property' for IHT purposes: see ss58 and 71. Transfers into such trusts are PETs. No periodic nor exit charge.

It is necessary that a beneficiary will become beneficially entitled at a specified age not being more than 25 years (s31(1)(ii) Trustee Act 1925). Section 71 charges on a disposition by the trustees (s10(1)). The charge is made in the same way as under s70.

Section 71(4): no charge is made on a beneficiary becoming entitled to an IIP or dying before entitlement or where the trustees advance capital for the benefit of the infant.

Section 144: two-year discretionary trust

The testator will make a will creating a trust without an interest in possession. Where the trust is ended within two years of his death the IHT usually charged 'shall not be charged but the Act shall have the effect as if the will had provided that on the testator's death the property should be held as it is held after the event'. IHT is therefore charged at the estate rate on the property at death, although a later calculation may be necessary.

See *Frankland v IRC* [1997] STC 1450, where the exemption provided for by s144(2) for transfers which would be chargeable but for rewriting the provisions of a will was held not be available for a transfer from a discretionary trust to one in which the deceased's husband had an interest in possession. The transfer was intended to achieve s18(1) inter-spouse exemption by avoiding a charge under s65 (by using s144) on the transfer out of the discretionary trust into an interest in possession trust in which the deceased's husband had an interest. This failed because the husband's interest did not arise under the will as the rewriting had occurred within the first three months, forbidden by s65(4). In effect the two year period is reduced at the start by three months for such transfers.

22.3 Key cases and statute

- *Melville* v *IRC* [2001] STC 1271 (CA)
  Inheritance tax – settled property – definition of 'property'

- *Pearson* v *IRC* [1980] 2 WLR 872
  Inheritance tax – settled property – interest in possession

- Inheritance Tax Act 1984, ss2(1), 53(1), 58–85 and 71

22.4 Questions and suggested solutions

QUESTION ONE

Compare the inheritance tax regime for taxing interest in possession trusts with that of discretionary trusts.

University of London LLB Examination
(for External Students) Revenue Law June 1992 Q6

General Comment

This question compares the taxation treatment of interest in possession trusts and discretionary trusts.

Skeleton Solution

An 'interest in possession': meaning: *Gartside* v *IRC*; *Pearson* v *IRC* – 'in possession' – interest in underlying property – IHT charge: death: termination: disposal of interest –

rate of tax – discretionary settlement: ten-year charge – transfer into trust – relevant property – interim charge – rate of tax.

Suggested Solution

Note: all references are to the Inheritance Tax Act (IHTA) 1984.

Interest in possession settlements are treated differently for Inheritance Tax (IHT) purposes from those in which no such interest exists, such as discretionary trusts.

The term 'interest in possession' is not formally defined in the inheritance tax statutes and in the provisions in ss58 et seq; what is known as the 'discretionary trust regime' is in fact referred to and relates to trusts 'without interests in possession': see s59.

The Inland Revenue, in a statement, gave their understanding of the meaning of the term as being:

> '... where the person having the interest has the immediate entitlement (subject to any prior claim by the trustees for expenses or other outgoings out of income) – to any income produced by that property as it arises; but that a discretion or power, in whatever form, which can be exercised after income arises so as to withhold it from that person, negatives the existence of an interest in possession. For this purpose a power to accumulate is regarded as a power to withhold it unless any accumulation must be held solely for the person having the interest or his personal representatives. On the other hand the existence of a mere power of revocation or appointment the exercise of which would determine the interest wholly or in part (but which so long as it remains unexercised does not affect the beneficiary's immediate entitlement to income) does not in the Board's view prevent the interest from being an interest in possession.'

In *Gartside* v *IRC* [1968] AC 553 Lord Reid explained that ' "in possession" must mean that your interest enables you to claim now whatever may be the subject of the interest ...'.

In *Pearson* v *IRC* [1981] AC 753 the Revenue argued, unsuccessfully in the lower courts but successfully in the House of Lords, that a power to accumulate negated the interest in possession. The House of Lords held that an 'interest in possession' means 'there must be a present right to present enjoyment' of income. In essence the House of Lords held that with a power to accumulate there was no right of anything, and the entitlement depended upon whether the power was exercised.

One must therefore distinguish between administrative powers and dispositive powers and recognise that the interest is in net income after administrative expenses properly chargeable to income. A dispositive power is a power to dispose of the net income after it arises.

An example of a settlement without 'interest in possession' is where income is being accumulated for persons with interests contingent on future events, eg on attaining his majority the beneficiary becomes entitled to income as it arises, and his interest is then 'in possession'.

The beneficiary in an interest in possession settlement is treated (ss49 and 50) as beneficially entitled to the whole of the settled property in which his interest subsists and the settled property as part of his estate: s5(1). The same applies to one with a part interest and to an annuitant entitled to a fixed income.

On the death of a life tenant or on the lifetime transfer of his or her interest for less than full value, there is a chargeable transfer of value. The creation of a settlement on one's self is not a transfer of value since no reduction in estate occurs.

In interest in possession settlements the inheritance tax regime which applies relates to the occasions on which the underlying interest in the property changes. This produces two occasions of chargeable events:

a) the death of the person entitled to the interest (ss4(1) and 49(1)); and

b) the termination of beneficial enjoyment during life, for example on an assignment of part or all of the interest.

The disposal of an interest to a third party is treated as terminating it, notwithstanding that the interest actually remains in existence until the death of the life tenant. An assignment is a transfer of value equal to the value of the settled property. The transfer of value can, if the normal conditions are satisfied, be a potentially exempt transfer (PET).

There is an exemption where on the termination the property reverts to the settlor: s53(6).

The rate of tax applicable to settlements with interests in possession is the same as for any other individual's lifetime or death transfer.

Quick succession relief applies where settled property with interest in possession is subjected to two chargeable transfers within five years.

The treatment of discretionary trusts for IHT purposes applies equally to all settlements without an interest in possession.

The tax charge is based principally on a ten-year charge to tax on each tenth anniversary of the existence of the settlement. If all or part of the trust terminates, there is an interim charge (which similarly applies if the trust is converted into a non-discretionary trust) and is charged on the reduction in value of the fund.

On putting property into a discretionary trust, the settlor is charged to tax on the value transferred.

The interim charge, when applicable, is based on the commencement value of the trust and on the settlor's previous transfers.

The discretionary trust charges are based on 'relevant property' (s58(1)) which is property in which there is no qualifying interest in possession other than, inter alia, accumulation and maintenance trusts.

Discretionary trusts set up by will or intestacy are treated as commencing on the date of death.

A charge arises on the occasion of property being added to the trust (s67(3)) on which the current rather than the commencement value of the settled property is used if higher.

The interim charge referred to above will most commonly arise when settled property ceases to be 'relevant property' either on leaving the settlement or remaining settled after a transfer to an interest in possession or accumulation and maintenance trust. Further occasions of charge are when depreciatory transactions reduce the value of the property (s65(1)(b)), unless this results from a commercial transaction. There are exclusions for reductions in value arising from the payment of expenses relating to relevant property or where an income tax charge arises on the recipient.

For the above purposes 'excluded property', being property not chargeable to inheritance tax, is not relevant property.

The ten year rate of tax is 30 per cent of the lifetime rate, ie currently a charge of 6 per cent of the trust assets.

The exit charge on property leaving the trust is charged at the lifetime full rate on actual or deemed capital distributions.

QUESTION TWO

Discuss the inheritance tax consequences of the creation and operation of a discretionary trust.

University of London LLB Examination
(for External Students) Revenue Law June 1993 Q8

General Comment

This question focuses on the inheritance tax consequences of discretionary trusts.

Skeleton Solution

Discretionary settlement: ten-year charge – transferred into trust – relevant property – interim charge – rate of tax.

Suggested Solution

Note: all references are to the Inheritance Tax Act (IHTA) 1984.

A special tax regime applies for inheritance tax purposes to settlements in which no qualifying interest in possession exists. In these cases the interest of the beneficiary is at the discretion of the trustees and, unlike interest in possession trusts, the beneficiary cannot be said to be the beneficial owner of the underlying settled property. For interest in possession settlements, where there is a change in that beneficial ownership a charge to inheritance tax is made on the basis that the individual is deemed to have made a lifetime chargeable transfer equivalent to the value of the settled property,

In the absence of beneficial ownership of the underlying assets no charge to tax would normally arise while the settled property remained in a discretionary trust and therefore a special regime was enacted to make a periodic charge to tax. Unlike the interest in possession trust the variation of the beneficiary's interest in the trust would give rise to no change in the ownership (or no deemed transfer) of the property and accordingly to no chargeable transfer of value.

The treatment of discretionary trusts for IHT purposes applies equally to all settlements without an interest in possession. The discretionary trust charges are based on 'relevant property' (s58(1)) which is property in which there is no qualifying interest in possession other than inter alia accumulation and maintenance trusts. The tax charge is based principally on a ten-year charge to tax on each tenth anniversary of the existence of the settlement. If all or part of the trust terminates, there is an interim charge (which similarly applies if the trust is converted into a non-discretionary trust) which is charged on the reduction in value of the fund.

On putting property into a discretionary trust, the settlor is charged to tax on the value transferred. The interim charge, when applicable, is based on the commencement value of the trust and on the settlor's previous transfers. Discretionary trusts set up by will or intestacy are treated as commencing on the date of death. A charge arises on the occasion of property being added to the trust (s67(3)), on which the current rather than the commencement value of the settled property is used, if higher.

The interim charge referred to above will most commonly arise when settled property ceases to be 'relevant property' either on leaving the settlement or remaining settled after a transfer to an interest in possession or accumulation and maintenance trust. Further occasions of charge are when depreciatory transactions reduce the value of the property (s65(1)(b)), unless this results from a commercial transaction. There are exclusions for reductions in value arising from the payment of expenses relating to relevant property or where an income tax charge arises on the recipient.

For the above purposes 'excluded property', being property not chargeable to inheritance tax, is not relevant property.

The ten-year rate of tax is 30 per cent of the lifetime rate, ie currently a charge of 6 per cent of the trust assets. The exit charge on property leaving the trust is charged at the lifetime full rate on actual or deemed capital distributions.

QUESTION THREE

Compare the meaning of the term 'disposal' as used in the Taxation of Chargeable Gains Act 1992 with the term 'disposition' as used in the Inheritance Tax Act 1984.

University of London LLB Examination
(for External Students) Revenue Law June 1995 Q8

General Comment

This question provides guidance on the meaning of the terms 'disposal' as used in the TCGA 1992 and 'disposition' as used in the IHTA 1984.

Skeleton Solution

CGT: 'disposal' of assets; not defined in s1 TCGA 1992 – inclusion of 'deemed disposal'; eg s71 TCGA 1992 – grant of option a disposal: ss144–147 – part disposals included: ss21(2) and 42 – occasions not giving rise to a 'disposal' – capital sum derived from assets: s22(1) – IHT: 'disposition' not defined: see ss3, 10(3) and 272 IHTA 1984 – disposition extended to include 'arrangements' in ordinary meaning of the word.

Suggested Solution

The terms 'disposal', as used in the capital gains tax (CGT) legislation, and 'disposition', as used in inheritance tax (IHT) legislation, would appear to be similar and to reflect the same basic intentions. An examination of their respective effects in bringing about a charge to tax within each tax illustrates that the two cannot be taken to be synonymous with each other.

The two taxes are intended to operate under vastly differing conditions. While both can come into effect on the transfer of property, only CGT can operate where full value is given in return.

Capital gains tax 'disposal'

Note: all references are to Taxation of Chargeable Gains Act (TCGA) 1992 unless stated otherwise.

Under s1(1) tax is charged 'on the disposal of assets'. Neither of the words 'disposal' nor 'asset' is defined in the Act. In the absence of such a definition a disposal will assume its ordinary natural meaning in that a disposal of an asset occurs when its ownership changes or the owner divests himself of the right over, or interest in, an asset. This will include a gift, sale, exchange and other transfers whether actual or 'deemed' to have occurred.

The capital gains tax (CGT) legislation brings in the concept of a 'deemed' disposal which is beyond the normal meaning of 'disposal' for example, on the occasion (under s71) of trustees being said to have disposed of and immediately re-acquired assets on an occasion when a beneficiary becomes absolutely entitled to settled property. Where a life interest in settled property ceases there is deemed to be a change of ownership and the trustee is deemed to dispose of the assets and immediately re-acquire them at market value before the transfer to the beneficiary occurs. The growth in value is chargeable to capital gains tax in the hands of the trustees except that where the occasion is on the death of the tenant no gain or loss is deemed to be made by the trustees.

Further, in ss144–147 the grant of an option is the disposal of an asset. Similarly, part disposals are disposals for CGT purposes and occur where 'any description of property derived from the asset remains undisposed of': s21(2) TCGA 1992. A part disposal also occurs if a right over or an interest in an asset is created, such as in the case of the grant of a restrictive covenant over the use of land. To understand the concept of ownership one has to regard ownership as relating to a bundle of rights, some or all of which may be given away in favour of another person. The deduction for allowable expenditure on a part disposal is catered for by apportioning the cost of the whole to the part disposed of according to the formula in s42.

The statutes also require that a distinction be drawn between the disposal of a part of an asset and the part disposal of the full rights over an entire asset.

Equally important are occasions in which a 'disposal' is deemed not to have taken place:

a) the receipt of a capital sum where an asset is not lost or destroyed, if the sum is used to restore the asset (s23);

b) giving of a mortgage or charge over property (s26);

c) in particular relief is given from a charge to corporation tax on capital gains to facilitate various reorganisations, reconstructions, amalgamations and take-overs: ss126–137. Since these involve the disposal of existing shares or other securities and the issue of other shares as securities either by the same company or by a third company concerned in the transaction, a capital gain would normally arise on the initial disposal. The legislation dictates that in certain circumstances a 'disposal' will be regarded as not taking place and therefore the initial transaction is regarded as being outside the scope of a charge to CGT. It will be plain from the foregoing that even the fundamental area of a charge to tax on a disposal of an asset is in itself far from straightforward and at times extremely complex. Furthermore, the legislation caters in detail for transactions involving specific assets and it is not surprising to find further complexities within those areas, having regard to the difficult nature of the basic concept.

The meaning of disposal is extended beyond its ordinary meaning of a transfer or sale, to include cases where no asset is transferred but where a capital sum is said to be derived from the asset – ie to cases where no asset is in fact transferred. In *O'Brien* v *Benson's Hosiery (Holdings) Ltd* [1979] STC 735 it was held that any right which could be turned to account was an asset for capital gains tax purposes. *Zim Properties Ltd* v *Proctor* [1985] STC 90 held that a right to bring an action – the right to sue – was in itself a right capable of being dealt in or turned to account and was therefore an asset for CGT purposes.

Section 22(1)(a) also taxes sums which arise as compensation for the damage to, loss or destruction of, assets.

Inheritance tax 'disposition'

Note: all references are to Inheritance Tax Act (IHTA) 1984 unless stated otherwise.

The term 'disposition' is not defined in the inheritance tax legislation and occurs in s3 IHTA 1984 to explain the meaning of a 'transfer of value' upon whose value IHT is imposed. IHT therefore is not imposed on dispositions per se but on transfers of value which reduce a person's estate in value: s3(1); if the transfer does not consist of exempt property: s2(1).

Sections 10(3) and 272 elaborate on how the term is to interpreted only to the extent that it is to include deemed dispositions such as provided for as an occasion of charge in s3(3), where a person fails to exercise a right and by omitting to do so the estate of another is increased: s10(3). Section 272 includes within the meaning a disposition which is effected by 'associated operations' so that where by two linked transactions there is greater value transferred than if each had been conducted independently of the other and not in anticipation of the other taking place.

In the absence of any comprehensive definition, the term 'disposition' must be taken to have not less than its ordinary English meaning of any 'arrangement'. It has probably been the intention of the legislative draftsmen that the term be intentionally very general so as to include matters other than sales, gifts and other means by which a person can dispose of property. As seen in the general charging sections of the IHT legislation, the intention is to charge any occasion whereby value passes out of a person's estate and not only when property itself passes out of the control of the person.

By adopting the term 'disposition' for this purpose, charges to IHT will include the variation of the rights over the property concerned as well as the entire divestment of the property. Arrangements such as the granting of leases over property or the granting of similar rights of occupation or licence to use property will fall within the ambit of IHT if benefit is conferred on another by doing so – hence the use of the associated operations provisions of s272. Equally, however, these arrangements are taken out of the possibility of an IHT charge by s10(1) if they are conducted without the intention of conferring any gratuitous benefit on the recipient. Therefore normal commercial transactions do not fall within the charge to tax on the basis of being arm's length transactions: s10(1)(a).

Chapter 23

Administration, Assessment and Back Duty

23.1   **Introduction**

23.2   **Key points**

23.3   **Key cases and statute**

23.1 Introduction

The Commissioners of Inland Revenue, who collectively constitute the Board of Inland Revenue, are responsible for the administration and management of income tax, corporation tax, inheritance tax and capital gains tax. The statutory authority for administration of these taxes, the assessment and collection procedures, is conferred by the Taxes Management Act (TMA) 1970.

Self-assessment

Income tax

The Finance Act 1994 introduced into the Taxes Management Act 1970 – in ss178–199 and Sch 19 – provisions which fundamentally alter the management, assessment and collection of income tax from 1996–97 onwards. Each taxpayer liable to income tax now has the option to calculate a single amount of tax payable on his total income when submitting the annual tax return and to make payment of that amount as and when due, without involving the Inland Revenue in the process of calculating tax due on income under each schedule and issuing notices for payment. The deadline for submission of a tax return incorporating the calculation of tax is 31 January following the end of the year of assessment. The assessment process may still be put onto the Revenue but the tax return must be submitted by 30 September following the year of assessment to allow for this. These changes amend or add new provisions to the Taxes Management Act 1970. See in particular ss7–9, 12AA–12AB and ss59A–59C TMA 1970.

The changes noted throughout the preceding chapters also reflect changes to the basis of assessment which make the switch to self-assessment less complex. These changes are contained mainly in ss178–218 and Sch 20 Finance Act 1994, ss103–123 and Sch 21 Finance Act 1995 and Schs 19–25 Finance Act 1996 and amend the corresponding provisions of ICTA 1988.

Corporation tax

Companies are required to operate a full system of self-assessment for corporation tax purposes for accounting periods beginning on or after 2 July 1998. This extends the existing pay and file system by replacing the formal assessment issued by the Inland Revenue with the tax return and self-assessment submitted by the company. The provisions are contained in Sch 18 FA 1998.

Certain other changes are required to implement the self-assessment procedure, principally by replacing options currently available to the Inland Revenue to take action to raise an assessment to tax in certain circumstances, with an obligation on the company to report and account for tax in such situations. This will include an obligation to account for inter-company transactions (transfer pricing) on an arm's length basis and reporting profits which are subject to the UK's controlled foreign companies (CFCs) regime.

In addition, any liability to account for tax on loans to participators of close companies (see Chapter 17) must be included on the self-assessment tax return.

Changes to arrangements for group relief (see Chapter 15 for further discussion) will include the need to quantify and specify the amount of the claim on the tax return as well as the principal company in the group being able to submit a single 'joint amended return' containing all the relevant information regarding the allocation of group relief between the various group companies.

Claims for capital allowances (see Chapter 6 for further discussion) must be included on the self-assessment tax return form.

23.2 Key points

Administration of taxation

See the diagram on the following page which illustrates how taxation is administered.

Returns and assessments

a) Obligation on a person chargeable to tax to deliver a return or to notify liability to tax in the absence of receiving a return: ss7–10 TMA 1970 (companies), s12AA and 12AB (partnerships).

b) Inland Revenue may require completion of return and payment of tax under self-assessment, including trustees: ss8 and 8A.

c) Inland Revenue can require returns from third parties: ss15 and 20.

d) Power to amend self-assessment (ss28A–28C) or to make assessment: s29.

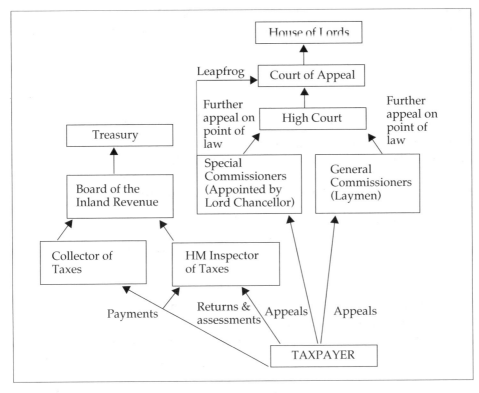

Note: decisions by either the special or the general commissioners on a point of fact are final. Appeals to the courts may only be made on a point of law.

e) Power to assess following 'discovery': see, from 1996–97 s29(1) – formerly s29(3). See limitation where assessments agreed by appeal procedure under s54. From 1996–97 amended provisions contained in s29(6) as a result of the *Cenlon* and *Scorer* cases: *Cenlon Finance Ltd* v *Ellwood* (1961) 40 TC 176, expanded by *Scorer* v *Olin Energy Systems Ltd* [1985] STC 218 and distinguished in *Gray* v *Matheson* [1993] STC 178.

f) Error or mistake relief: s33.

Power to obtain information

Wide powers to obtain information under ss19A, 20 and 20A–C – the 'section 20 notice'.

See *R* v *IRC, ex parte Ulster Bank Ltd* [1997] STC 832 in relation to s20 notices. The bank sought leave to bring judicial review proceedings, citing an earlier compromise of proceedings as giving rise to a legitimate expectation that no further enquiries would be made by the Inland Revenue. The Court of Appeal held that the notices were permitted under s20(3) and (8A) TMA 1970 and the description permissible in a s20(8A) notice included classes or categories of documents not known to exist or to be in the possession of the person upon whom the notice was served. In so holding, the court in part disapproved the decision reached by Ferris J in *R v O'Kane and Clarke, ex parte Northern Bank Ltd* [1996] STC 1249. The court, however, would appear to have confirmed Ferris J's view that a notice under s20(3), unlike a notice under s20(1) and (2), could not seek particulars or information but only documents.

Appeals

Notice of appeal within 30 days of issue of notice of assessment: s31.

Appeal from a decision of the Commissioners dealing with their findings of facts cannot normally be made except where unsustainable by way of unreasonable conclusion from the facts: see *Edwards* v *Bairstow & Harrison* [1956] AC 14; 36 TC 207. Appeals against findings based on point of law may be taken to a higher court.

Interest and penalties

Interest provisions s86 et seq operate to charge interest from the appropriate 'reckonable date' which is specified in s86(2) TMA 1970. Penalties subject to exercise of discretion: ss93–107.

The self-assessment provisions also impose surcharges on tax which remains unpaid for more than 28 days from the due date at a rate of 5 per cent of the payment due: s59C(2) TMA 1970. An additional 5 per cent surcharge is payable on tax remaining unpaid six months after the due date: s59C(3) TMA 1970. These surcharges are in addition to the interest payments under s86.

Back duty – investigations

Powers to assess beyond the normal time limits in cases involving 'neglect', 'wilful default' or 'fraud': ss29(1), 34 and 36.

Dates of payment of tax

Under self-assessment, tax becomes due on 31 January in the year of assessment for all tax other than from business income. This forms a payment on account for the year and the balance is paid on the following 31 January after the submission of the self-assessment return for the year. For business income, one half of the payment on account for the year is due on 31 January, the second on 31 July and any balance found to be due is payable on the following 31 January: see ss59A and 59B TMA 1970.

Statutory interpretation

Pepper v Hart [1992] STC 898: this Schedule E case erased the rule that reference to parliamentary material was inadmissible when interpreting the meaning of statutes. It established, where statutes were 'ambiguous or obscure or led to absurdity', that reliance could be placed on 'one or more statements by a minister or other promoter of the Bill together if necessary with such other Parliamentary material as is necesary to understand such statements' and where 'the statements relied upon are clear'. The case affects the interpretation of both tax and non-tax statutes equally.

See also *IRC* v *McGuckian* [1997] 1 WLR 991 [1997] STC 908 in Chapter 25 below regarding the House of Lords' apparent adoption of the 'purposive approach' to statutory interpretation (as opposed to the literal approach).

23.3 Key cases and statute

- *Pepper* v *Hart* [1992] STC 898
  Administration, assessment and back duty – statutory interpretation

- *R* v *IRC, ex parte Ulster Bank Ltd* [1997] STC 832
  Administration, assessment and back duty – power to obtain information

- Taxes Management Act 1970

Chapter 24

Value Added Tax

24.1   Introduction

24.2   Key points

24.3   Key cases and statutes

24.4   Question and suggested solution

24.1   Introduction

All references are to the Value Added Tax Act (VATA) 1994 unless stated.

Value added tax is charged on goods and on services supplied in the UK as well as on the acquisition of goods from EC member states and on importation of goods from non-member states: s1 VATA 1994. The principal Act is the Value Added Tax Act 1994. Much of the operation of VAT is provided for in the Value Added Tax (General) Regulations 1995 (SI 1995/2518) which consolidated the 1985 general regulations with all subsequent regulations. It should be noted that pre 1995 VAT orders, as opposed to regulations, are still in force and have not been affected by the consolidation of the regulations mentioned above.

VAT was introduced into the UK in the Finance Act 1972 and was consolidated into the Value Added Tax Act 1983 to comply with the European Community Sixth VAT Directive of 17 May 1977. It is administered and collected by HM Customs and Excise. Management of the tax is controlled by the Customs and Excise Management Act (CEMA) 1979 and Schedule 11 VATA 1994. The provisions of VATA 1983 and the VAT provisions of the subsequent Finance Acts were further consolidated into the new Value Added Tax Act (VATA) 1994.

The legislation at times distinguishes between goods and services, and therefore the liability for imposing or accounting for VAT on a transaction may rest on whether what is supplied is treated as a supply of goods or a supply of services. In addition one has to interpret whether what is supplied is in fact supplied 'in the UK' – exports will be supplied 'in the UK' but to an overseas person and vice versa.

In dealing with the foreign element of VAT from 1 January 1993 (the introduction of the 'Single European Market'), a further distinction has to be drawn between those supplies which concern an EC recipient or supplier and those which concern an overseas non-EC one. It should also be noted that the 'acquisition in the UK' aspects of s1(1)(b) and (c) relate to goods only and not to services, which are separately dealt with under what are termed the 'reverse charge' provisions of s8 for supplies of professional services and other services listed in Sch 9. Other international services are zero rated under Sch 8 Group 7.

Liability to register for VAT

a) Traders or intending traders must register with HM Customs and Excise before value added tax can be charged on taxable supplies: see s3 and Schs 1–3 VATA 1994. Intending traders' provision: see para 9 Sch 1. Makers of wholly non-taxable supplies are not liable to be registered.

b) Liability to register is imposed according to turnover or expected turnover of 'taxable supplies' – currently £56,000 per annum: para 1(1) and para 5 Schs 1 and 3 VATA 1994. Turnover for Sch 2 registration purposes (supplies received from other Member States of the EU) is £70,000.

c) Once registered, an obligation to submit quarterly or monthly returns arises: Sch 11 para 2 VATA 1994.

d) See Sch 11 VATA 1994 for administration, collection and enforcement provisions.

Finance Act 1996 introduced a new Sch 9A into VATA 1994 to counter the misuse of the inter-group supply rules. Customs now have power to direct that certain supplies will be subject to VAT or to bring an associated company into a VAT group in exceptional circumstances. These powers became necessary following schemes where input VAT was claimed on the supply of cars using companies leaving the group at an appropriate point in the chain of supply and payment and so utilising the non-charging of VAT between group members.

24.2 Key points

a) VAT (called 'output tax') is charged (s4) when the following elements exist:

   i) it is a supply of non-exempt goods or services,

   ii) made in the UK,

   ii) by a taxable person,

   iii) in the course or furtherance of business.

'Goods and services'

The distinction between supplies of goods and of services is governed by VATA 1994 Sch 4 paras 1–6, with paras 7–9 dealing with 'deemed supplies'. In all cases supplies which are exempt supplies are not subject to a VAT charge. Zero-rated supplies are treated as chargeable but at a nil rate of tax.

Empire Stores Ltd v *CEC* [1994] STC 623: the European Court of Justice held that free goods given by mail order firms for customer introductions were taxable supplies – tax to be levied on their value.

'In the UK'

VATA 1994 s1 charges tax on supplies in the UK, including anything treated as a supply. It also charges tax – s2(1)(b) – on acquisition of goods from another EC state (from 1 January 1993) and on the importation of goods from outside the EC. See 'place of supply' below. See *The Chinese Channel (Hong Kong) Ltd* v *CEC* [1998] STC 347 in which it was held that the company did not have a business establishment in the UK as a result of appointing a UK marketing company for its broadcasting activities.

Businesses based outside the EC which lease goods to non-business customers based in the UK are treated as making supplies of services in the UK: see s97A VATA 1994, introduced by s22 FA 1998. Non-EC providers of such services will be required to register for UK VAT if the value of their supplies exceeds the VAT registration threshold. Where such supplies are made by UK-based businesses they will not be treated as made in the UK if the leased goods are effectively used and enjoyed outside the EC.

'By a taxable person'

Supplies must be made by a taxable person (s1); 'taxable person' – s3 – is a person who 'is, or is required to be [VAT] registered'.

'In the course or furtherance of business'

The meaning of business: see s94. Non-business supplies, eg sales by private individuals, are 'beyond the scope' of VAT.

Polysar Investments Netherlands BV [1993] STC 222, a Dutch case before the European Court of Justice: restriction of input tax deduction for holding companies, on the basis of non-business activities.

b) Place of supply

Section 7 determines whether goods or services are supplied 'in the UK'. Subject to the reverse charge exception (s8), services are treated as being supplied where the supplier belongs (see s9):

i) goods not removed from the UK – supplied in the UK;

ii) goods not removed to the UK – supplied abroad;

iii) goods removed to the UK – UK supplied if supplier responsible for installation/ assembly in the UK;

iv) goods removed from the UK – supplied abroad if supplier responsible for installation etc abroad;

v) goods acquired from EC taxable person – UK supplied;

vi) goods removed to EC taxable person – supplied abroad;

vii) goods imported from non-EC – UK supplied.

For place of supply of warehoused goods: see s18. See also s11 for acquisition of goods from EC Member States.

Detailed regulations in the Value Added Tax (Supply of Services) Order 1992 (SI 1992/3121) cover the place of supply of certain services relating to land, transport and the services of intermediaries. In other areas of VAT law it is sometimes important whether what is supplied is a supply of services or a supply of goods. At times the VAT Act directs certain items to be a supply of services so that their place of supply and VAT treatment falls within the relevant general provisions for services or for goods.

c) Time of supply

The time of supply – s6 – is (for goods) the earlier of delivery of the goods/performance of the services *or* the issue of a tax invoice or receipt of payment: see *Customs and Excise Commissioners* v *Faith Construction Ltd* [1989] STC 539 and other payment-in-advance schemes for VAT avoidance – *Customs and Excise Commissioners* v *West Yorkshire Independent Hospital*; *Customs and Excise Commissioners* v *Dormers Builders (London) Ltd* [1989] STC 539.

d) Reverse charge

Section 8: for certain services – those standard rated services contained in Sch 5 – received by a UK taxable person from abroad, the recipient must account for the tax in the UK. A fully taxable person may deduct a corresponding amount as allowable input tax. Schedule 5 services relate to intellectual property, advertising, professional and financial services, supplies of staff and certain inter-EC services related to transport of goods.

e) Valuation and mixed supplies

Section 19: VAT is charged on consideration given for the supply: if for money, based on that amount; post 1 August 1992, if not wholly in money, the value of the consideration – not market value as before that date following *Boots Co plc* v *CEC* [1990] STC 387. Problems of determining the consideration or its value arise particularly in cases where mixed supplies take place. It is not always clear what the supply being made is or what the consideration received represents. In *Virgin Atlantic Airways Ltd* v *CEC* [1995] STC 341 the question at issue was whether free transport to the airport for its passengers was part of the zero rated supply of passenger transport under Sch 8 Group 8 or a separate and therefore standard rated supply. It was held that the passenger contracted for a single supply of transport from home to the destination and that the two elements of car and aircraft were therefore indivisible. Accordingly the zero rating under Sch 8 applied in its entirety.

See also the decision reached in *British Airways plc* v *CEC* [1990] STC 643 where in-flight meals were held to be an integral part of the supply of air transport and therefore similarly zero rated.

In the case of *CEC* v *Leightons Ltd*; *CEC* v *Eye-Tech Opticians* [1995] STC 458, it was held that in the supply of spectacles the dispensing activities were distinguishable from the supply of spectacles and that only the latter constituted a standard rated supply, the former being exempt. The consideration was therefore to be properly apportioned.

f) Recovery of input tax – making fully or partly taxable supplies

   i) Under ss24–26 a person who makes only taxable supplies (whether standard or zero rated) may recover the full amount of VAT incurred ('input tax') on the acquisition of goods and services by the business. See also Value Added Tax (General) (Amendment (No 2)) Regulations 1987 (SI 1987/510). *British Airways plc* v *CEC* [1996] STC 1127: British Airways supplied meal vouchers to passengers whose flights were delayed, meals being taken in a restaurant. The passengers paid the restaurant any excess of the cost of the meals over the face value of the vouchers. BA paid the restaurant the value of the vouchers redeemed and attempted to recover the VAT paid on the meals. It was held that BA were not the recipients of the supply of meals and could not therefore deduct the VAT incurred. The meals were held to have been supplied to the passengers by the restaurant and not to BA.

   ii) A person making wholly exempt supplies may not recover any input tax.

   iii) Those making mixed exempt and taxable supplies may recover 'input VAT' attributable to taxable supplies.

   iv) Capital goods: all businesses are subject to restrictions on deduction of input tax on capital items specified in reg 37B of Value Added Tax (General) Regulations 1985 – mainly computers and buildings.

The following changes took effect from 3 July 1997:

- The capital goods scheme has been extended to cover 'refurbishment works' and 'fitting out works' for existing properties and 'civil engineering works' (in addition to the land and buildings and computers which are already within the scheme).

- Rent was previously disregarded in determining the value of an acquisition of land and buildings for the purposes of the scheme so that only leases at a premium were capable of falling within the scheme. The value of rent on which VAT is charged is taken into account when it is paid or payable more than 12 months in advance, or is invoiced for a period in excess of 12 months. Where a capital item of £250,000 or more includes such rent, VAT incurred on such rent is to be taken as part of the total amount of VAT which is capable of being adjusted under the scheme.

- Anti-avoidance provisions now prevent the adjustment period being artificially reduced in circumstances where there are movements in or out of VAT groups or where a business is transferred as a going concern (except where the new owner is registered with the registration number of, and in substitution for, the transferor). In such circumstances, each 'year' for the purposes of the adjustment period will be a whole calendar year and the method of determining the extent of vatable use will have to be agreed with Customs.

- A test is imposed on the occasion of a disposal of a capital item before the end of the adjustment period, which may require further payment or repayment of VAT.

v) Recovery of input tax is also denied where the expenditure relates to business entertainment – as laid down in the Value Added Tax (Input Tax) Order 1992 (SI 1992/3222).

See *BMW (GB) Ltd* v *Customs and Excise Commissioners* [1997] STC 824. The company organised sporting theme days. It was held that the arrangements between the company and car dealers gave rise to a payment by car dealers for the right to invite customers to the events and was not a payment for the supply of the food and drink. Accordingly there was the free of charge supply of food and drink on all occasions and this was the hallmark of business entertainment which was to be disallowed under the VAT Order specified above.

The VAT Tribunal had relied upon the decision in *Customs and Excise Commissioners* v *Shaklee International* [1981] STC 776 in determining that the supply of free meals amounted to business entertainment. The court agreed that the decision of the VAT tribunal was in all respects the right one and declined to set aside the findings of fact which the tribunal had reached.

vi) SI 1992/3222 also contains provisions which denied input tax recovery in relation to VAT paid on motor car purchases even if used wholly for business purposes (see regulation 7(1)) as well as tax on secondhand goods, works of art etc (regulation 4), where tax is accounted for under a special scheme. From 1 August 1995 businesses purchasing cars wholly for business use may deduct the input tax on those which they elect to treat as 'qualifying cars'. Correspondingly there will be VAT on the full sale price when disposed of. See *Royscot Leasing Ltd and Royscot Industrial Leasing Ltd* v *Customs and Excise Commissioners; Allied Domecq plc* v *Customs and Excise Commissioners; Harrison T C Group Ltd* v *Customs and Excise Commissioners* [1996] STC 898 re cars purchased for part business and personal use and for leasing – the three cases, which were pre the August 1995 changes, were considered together and in each case input tax recovery was denied. The cases were referred by the Court of Appeal to the European Court of Justice, where in January 1999 the Advocate-General submitted an opinion (to be considered by the ECJ) recommending support for HM Customs' case that:

- UK VAT law restricting the right to deduct input tax on business cars, whether wholly or partly used for business, did not contravene art 11(4) of the Sixth VAT Directive;

- the original right to restrict such a deduction was not merely temporary;

- currently, such a restriction may be maintained even for cars which form the tools of the relevant trade.

vii) Bad debt relief is available for debts written off six months after the date of supply: s36 VATA 1994. Claims for bad debt relief can be made after 31 July 1998 where the consideration is not payable in money – ie where the expected consideration was a payment in kind: s36(1)(a) as amended by s23 FA 1998. This followed the European Court of Justice ruling in *Goldsmiths (Jewellers) Ltd v Customs and Excise Commissioners* [1997] STC 1073, that the UK's existing restriction to consideration in money under s36 was contrary to European law.

g) Zero rated supplies

Means taxable supplies chargeable at a nil rate of tax – ie rate could be varied at any time. Such supplies are as listed in Sch 8.

h) Exempt supplies

Section 31 and Sch 9: supplies within these categories are not taxable supplies (see reference to taxable supplies in s1).

Matters exempt under these categories include hire purchase and credit sale facilities and making arrangements for financial transactions.

In *Customs and Excise Commissioners* v *Lloyds TSB Group Ltd* [1998] STC 528 Customs and Excise had ruled that certain services being provided by the finance group in relation to hire purchase and leasing finance amounted to the management of credit and not the 'making of arrangements' as required by item 5 of the exemption. The VAT Tribunal decided that the main character of the supply was the arranging of new credit and on appeal the High Court supported the VAT Tribunal's findings.

Primback v *CEC* [1996] STC 757 concerned the VAT liability of what had become widely advertised as 'interest-free credit' retail sales. The transactions involved the customer entering into a finance agreement with a finance house to pay £x by instalments, corresponding to the retail sale price of the goods. The credit was arranged by the retailer, who therefore, by analysis was making a supply of both the goods and of the 'arranging of credit'. The supply by the finance house was that of the credit itself. The finance house in turn paid a lesser total sum to the retailer. The issue which arose therefore was the treatment for VAT purposes of the credit charge, which was not disclosed to the customer.

In the Court of Appeal it was held that the making of arrangements for the supply of credit remained exempt within what is now VATA 1994 Sch 9 group 5, irrespective of whether it was disclosed to the customer or not.

i) Special arrangements

Retail accounting schemes. See *Primback* v CEC [1996] STC 757 and noted at (h) above.

Group accounting and registration: s43 and 44. Group supplies treated as made by one company. Finance Act 1996 introduced a new Sch 9A into VATA 1994 to counter the misuse of the inter-group supply rules. Customs now have power to direct that certain supplies will be subject to VAT or to bring an associated company into a VAT group in exceptional circumstances.

Partnerships: s45.

Agents etc: s47 and 48. See also the case of *The Chinese Channel (Hong Kong) Ltd* v *CEC* [1998] STC 347 at section earlier in this chapter headed 'In the UK'.

Transfer of a going concern without VAT on the transfer: s49 and Value Added Tax (General) Regulations 1995 reg 6.

Farming flat rate scheme – from 1992: see s54.

j) Land

i) Schedule 8: zero rated if sale or lease (over 21 years) of a private dwelling or community home by the person constructing it: see *Customs and Excise Commissioners* v *Link Housing Association Ltd* [1992] STC 718.

See Sch 8 group 5, including construction related services.

Lubbock Fine v *CEC* [1994] STC 101: VAT liability on the payment by a landlord to a tenant to surrender a lease – the European Court of Justice held that the surrender was exempt.

ii) Schedule 9 group 1: exempt if the supply is

- 'The grant of any interest in or right over land'.

  Except: the freehold sale ('grant of the fee simple') of commercial buildings, whether partly or fully constructed, which will therefore be standard rated. Grant includes an assignment.

- Sporting rights, holiday accommodation, parking, caravan facilities, seats in a place of entertainment etc.

iii) Schedule 10: option to waive exemption

The exemption in Sch 9 may be waived by the supplier making an 'option to tax' the supply under Sch 10 – thus charging VAT and being able to recover input VAT incurred by him.

24.3 Key cases and statutes

- *British Airways plc* v *CEC* [1996] STC 1127
  Value added tax – taxable supplies – mixed supplies – recovery of input tax

- *Customs and Excise Commissioners* v *Lloyds TSB Group Ltd* [1998] STC 528
  Value added tax – exempt supplies – finance

- *Customs and Excise Commissioners* v *Redrow Group plc* [1999] STC 161
  Value added tax – recovery of input tax

- *The Chinese Channel (Hong Kong) Limited* v *Customs and Excise Commissioners* [1998] STC 347
  Value added tax – taxable supplies – place of supply of services

- *Wellcome Trust Ltd* v *Customs and Excise Commissioners* [1996] STC 945
  Value added tax – taxable supplies – meaning of 'business'

- Value Added Tax Act 1994

- Value Added Tax Act (General) Regulations 1995 (SI 1995/2518)

24.4 Question and suggested solution

a) Discuss the meaning of 'supply' for the purposes of VAT, distinguishing between 'goods' and 'services'.

b) Give three examples of supplies to a VAT registered business on which input tax cannot be recovered.

Written by the Author

General Comment

This question focuses on the meaning of 'supply' for purposes of VAT.

Skeleton Solution

VAT is levied on taxable supplies – meaning of supply: s4(2) VATA 1994 – supplies of goods or services – distinction may govern place of supply and allow regulations to affect deemed supplies of services – input tax recovery barred on certain assets.

Suggested Solution

a) A taxable supply for VAT is defined by s4(2) VATA 1994 as 'a supply of goods or services made in the UK other than an exempt supply'. The term 'supply' includes all forms of supply, but not anything done otherwise than for a consideration. Anything that is not a supply of goods, but is done for a consideration, is a supply of services. Thus VAT applies to all goods and services when supplied in the UK by businesses, other than exempt supplies. Exempt supplies are those given in Sch 9 VATA 1994

Schedule 4 gives a list of certain transactions which are to be treated as supplies, albeit done for no consideration. These include:

i) gifts costing over £10;

ii) goods appropriated from a business for the owner's use;

iii) loans of goods for private purposes.

The Treasury is also empowered to render free supplies of services chargeable to VAT but have not as yet made any such orders.

Deemed supplies of goods can occur when certain supplies are made by an exempt or partially-exempt person to himself. However, there are also certain transactions deemed not to be supplies for VAT purposes, and these include:

i) the transfer of a business between registered persons;

ii) supplies between companies within a group registration;

iii) goods which have been lost or destroyed.

Transactions which fall out of the scope of VAT altogether include wages and salaries of employees, although benefits in kind are taxable supplies and may give rise to a VAT liability.

b) Section 25(7) VATA 1994 empowers the Treasury to order that the input tax on specific goods and services cannot be recovered by the purchaser. Three examples of such an order are:

i) motor cars unless new and acquired for re-sale or fall within the scope of the Value Added Tax (Input Tax) (Amendment (No 3)) Order 1995 or the Value Added Tax (Cars) (Amendment (No 2)) Order 1995;

ii) business entertainment;

iii) goods bought secondhand, including antiques, books, firearms, horses, works of art etc, where VAT has only been charged on the profit margin of the dealer.

Chapter 25

Anti-Avoidance

25.1 Introduction

25.2 Key points

25.3 Key cases and statutes

25.4 Questions and suggested solutions

25.1 Introduction

Tax avoidance must be distinguished from tax evasion. The former may prove an acceptable means of reducing the taxpayer's liability whilst the latter is an offence.

It must be remembered that unless an examination question specifically requests only one tax to be covered then all avoidance provisions and procedures should be discussed, for each tax.

The legislation has been enacted piecemeal to react to certain situations and is found throughout the taxes acts, IHTA and TCGA. Case law is also important in this area. The courts now look at the 'substance' not only the form of each case.

25.2 Key points

Income tax

Most of the relevant legislation lies in Part XV ICTA 1988 and is designed to prevent successful alienation of income for higher rate band tax by the donor. The usual mechanism employed is for the donor to make some form of settlement away from himself.

Note: settlements have a much wider meaning than that found in the law of equity.

Anti-avoidance: income tax (references to ICTA 1988 unless otherwise stated)

Sections 660A–682: settlements – see Chapter 12 for details.

Transactions in securities – countering 'tax advantage' – ss703–709. See s73 FA 1997 extending meaning of 'tax advantage'. See *IRC* v *Universities Superannuation Scheme Ltd* [1997] STC 1.

Sections 739–742: transfer of assets to non-residents or non-domiciliaries: *Vestey* v *IRC* [1980] AC 1148 (noted (1980) BTR 4).

ICTA 1988 s739 applies only to transactions made while the individual is ordinarily resident in the UK: *IRC* v *Willoughby* [1997] STC 995. The House of Lords' decision to some extent supports their Lordships' views expressed in *McGuckian* (see below) that the section as enacted was intended only to catch ordinarily resident transferors. Post-Finance Act 1997 applies to income on or after 26 November 1996, irrespective of the residence status at the time of transfer and applies where avoidance of income tax is one of the motives: s81 FA 1997.

The section applies to:

a) transfer of assets or operation associated with transfer: s739(1)–(4), defined s742(1)–(3);

b) by virtue or in consequence of (a), income accrues to a person who is not resident or not domiciled at the time when income accrues: s739(1–4); and

c) transferor or wife has power to enjoy income defined: ss737–739; or

d) transferor or wife receives or is entitled to receive capital sum payment of which is in any way connected with transfer or association operation, s739(1)–(4), provided that:

e) transfer in (a) is made to avoid tax of individual ordinarily resident in UK, s741, then:

f) income of non-resident deemed to be that of transferor and charged under Schedule D Case VI: s739(1)–(4), s743.

Note the wide powers of IR to obtain information: s745.

In *IRC* v *McGuckian* [1997] 1 WLR 991 [1997] STC 908, the House of Lords dealt with an issue under what is now s739 ICTA 1988 in which there was a transfer of company shares to a non-resident trustee of a settlement followed by the rights to a dividend being assigned to a resident company for consideration. The UK resident company then paid an amount of dividend less commission to the trustee. The issue was whether this was a tax avoidance scheme and the House of Lords considered it was.

ICTA 1988, s740:

Where the same circumstances as outlined in (a) and (b) above apply, and an individual ordinarily resident in UK, who is not liable under s739 by reference to transfer in (a) receives, after 10 March 1981, a benefit provided out of assets which are available for the purposes by virtue or in consequence of transfer in (a) or any associated operations, then the amount of benefit, if not otherwise chargeable to income tax, is treated as that of individual.

Note

a) Remittance basis for non-domiciliaries: s740.

b) Section 741 applies mutatis mutandis.

c) If benefit paid exceeds relevant income available excess may be carried forward under s740 or may be charged to CGT under s87 TCGA 1992.

d) Where more than one beneficiary receives benefit from income, IR can apportion income between beneficiaries as is just and reasonable but cannot take income into account more than once.

Capital gains tax

In addition to legislation contained in the Taxation of Chargeable Gains Act (TCGA) 1992, there is a great deal of relevant case law. As no comprehensive clearance procedure exists with the Inland Revenue, avoidance schemes are usually put to the test in court. The courts have stated that their decisions act only as guidelines and not definitive answers to avoidance. Cases have shown, however, that the courts' attitudes as to what constitutes 'acceptable' avoidance is becoming more restrictive.

The courts have usually found that where there is a 'scheme' originally intended to be carried through to its end merely to avoid tax consequences then the scheme will be ignored.

CGT (references to TCGA 1992 unless otherwise stated)

Value – shifting provisions.

a) Section 29(2): where value passes out of shares in company or rights over them which are owned or exercisable by person exercising his control over them, then it is treated as disposal of shares or rights by him at consideration which could have been obtained in arm's length transaction: *Floor v Davies* [1979] 2 All ER 677

b) Section 29(4): transactions by which owner of land or other property becomes lessee; and

is an adjustment of the rights and liabilities under the lease which is on the whole favourable to the lessor; then

is treated as a disposal by lessee of an interest in the property.

c) Section 29(5): where an asset is subject to right or restriction; and

right or restriction is extinguished or abrogated (in whole or in part); then

is treated as a disposal by him of the right or restriction.

d) Section 30

i) disposal of asset other than between spouses or from personal representatives to legatee; and

ii) scheme effected or arrangements made; whereby

iii) value of asset been materially reduced; and

iv) tax-free benefit will be conferred on

v) person making disposal or person with whom he connected; or

vi) any other person provided that avoidance of tax was the or one of the main purpose(s) of the scheme or arrangements; then

vii) for purposes of calculation of loss or gain, consideration may be increased by such amount as appears to inspector to be just and reasonable. *Eilbeck* v *Rawling*, *Ramsay (WT) Ltd* v *IRC* [1982] AC 300.

Note: connected persons see Chapter 18 Capital gains tax. Reference ss18 and 286 TCGA 1992.

Case law

a) Form v substance: *IRC* v *Duke of Westminster* [1936] AC 1; *IRC* v *Plummer* [1979] 3 All ER 775; and *Floor* v *Davies* [1979] 2 All ER 677; [1978] 2 All ER 1079 (CA).

b) 'Fiscal nullity' doctrine: *Eilbeck* v *Rawling, IRC* v *Ramsay* [1981] 1 All ER 865; *IRC* v *Burmah Oil Co Ltd* [1982] STC 30; and *Cairns* v *MacDiarmid* [1983] STC 176.

c) 'Pre-planned scheme' doctrine: *Furniss* v *Dawson* [1984] 1 All ER 530, noted (1984) BTR 109; *Craven* v *White* [1988] STC 476; [1987] STC 297; *Young* v *Phillips* [1984] STC 520; *Magnavox Electronics Co Ltd* v *Hall* [1985] STC 260; *Sherdley* v *Sherdley* [1987] STC 217; *Piggott* v *Staines Investments* [1995] STC 114; *R* v *HM Inspector of Taxes, ex parte Fulford-Dobson* [1987] STC 344; *Commissioners of the Inland Revenue* v *Challenge Corporation Ltd* [1926] STC 848; *IRC* v *McGuckian* [1997] 1 WLR 991; [1997] STC 908; and *MacNiven* v *Westmoreland Investments Ltd* [2001] 2 WLR 377.

Cases and facts

a) *IRC* v *Duke of Westminster*

'Every man is entitled if he can to order his affairs so as to diminish the burden of tax. The limits within which this principle is to operate remain to be proved and determined judicially.' (Lord Tomlin)

b) *Floor* v *Davies*

i) Taxpayer and his sons-in-law hold majority of shares in IDM Ltd.

ii) They agree in principle to sell these shares to KDI for about £560,000.

iii) They then agree to sell the shares to a newly created company, FNW, in return for preference shares in FNW. FNW then sells the IDM shares to KDI for £560,889.

iv) A third company, Donmarco, subscribes for preference shares in FNW and, due to a rights issue which only Donmarco takes up, becomes the only ordinary shareholder in FNW. Under special provisions in its articles, FNW then goes into liquidation and six-sevenths of its assets go to Donmarco.

c) *IRC v Ramsay*

i) Taxpayer company acquires all of shares in C Ltd and then makes two loans to C Ltd each of £218,750 and each at 11 per cent for 30 and 31 years respectively.

ii) Taxpayer exercises the right (provided for in the loan) to make corresponding increase and decrease in rate of interest, the first loan being reduced to nil per cent and the second to 22 per cent.

iii) Taxpayer sells second loan and makes a profit of £172,731 and the first loan is repaid at par.

iv) Taxpayer makes a loss of £175,647 on sale of shares in C Ltd.

d) *Furniss v Dawson*

i) Taxpayers sell shares in their family companies, X Ltd and Y Ltd, to GJ Ltd, a newly incorporated 10M Co, in return for shares in GJ Ltd.

ii) GJ Ltd then sell the shares in X Ltd and Y Ltd to purchaser (who had originally agreed to buy direct from taxpayers) for £152,000.

iii) Taxpayers are left with shares in GJ Ltd, whose only asset is the £152,000 received from purchasers:

> '... appellate courts are concerned more to chart a way forward between principles accepted and not to be rejected than to attempt anything so ambitious as to determine finally the limit beyond which the safe channel of acceptable tax avoidance shelves into the dangerous shallows of unacceptable tax evasion. The law will develop from case to case.' (Lord Scarman)

e) *Craven v White*

Taxpayers arranged for shares to be sold to J Ltd after those shares had previously been transferred to M Ltd, a Manx company incorporated specifically for that purpose. The proceeds of the transactions were loaned to the taxpayers.

In the House of Lords decision in *Craven v White* [1988] STC 476 their Lordships took a stronger approach to limiting the effectiveness of the tax avoidance schemes. It appears that any pre-arranged scheme which attempts to defer, reduce or avoid tax falls within the *Ramsay* principle.

f) *IRC v Willoughby* [1997] STC 995

A case involving the application of s739 where the commercial aspects were fully explored and great stress was laid on the transactions being within a specific statutory framework provided for by Parliament. This has led to s81 FA 1997, referred to above.

g) *Piggott* v *Staines Investments* [1995] STC 114

This case involved a scheme to recover corporation tax paid by an acquired company by introducing it into a group whose parent company (BAT Group) had surplus ACT. A dividend was paid to Staines by another group company without ACT under a group election, followed by a dividend payment out of Staines to its parent company which could then pay a dividend to its shareholders. BAT did not have to account for ACT since the dividend it had received had borne tax (see Chapter 16). Despite the time delay of ten months in the respective 'steps', it was held that they were still within the *Furniss* v *Dawson* doctrine and had to be ignored as being for no purpose other than the avoidance of tax. This has taken the 'certainty' aspect of the steps further than before – to a stage of being caught unless the opposite was very unlikely to occur.

h) *IRC* v *McGuckian* [1997] 1 WLR 991; [1997] STC 908

The House of Lords dealt with an issue under what is now s739 ICTA 1988 in which there was a transfer of company shares to a non-resident trustee of a settlement followed by the rights to a dividend being assigned to a resident company for consideration. The UK resident company then paid an amount of dividend less commission to the trustee. The issue was whether this was a tax avoidance scheme.

The House of Lords held that s739 (formerly s478) applied to the facts and was aimed at the transfer of assets whereby income otherwise liable to tax in the United Kingdom became payable to a non-resident person where the transferor was ordinarily resident in the United Kingdom at the time of the transfer and the transferor or his wife could enjoy the income. The House or Lords held that the exemption from the section for transactions with no tax avoidance motive could not apply since steps inserted with no commercial or business purpose could be ignored under the *Ramsay* doctrine developed particularly under *Furniss* v *Dawson* [1984] 2 WLR 226 and [1984] STC 153. Accordingly the taxpayer was assessable on the dividend income.

The case raised some very substantial issues after the judgment was announced, not from the ruling that *Furniss* v *Dawson* applied but more from the comments of their Lordships in the course of reaching their conclusions. It was the apparent adoption of the 'purposive approach' to statutory interpretation (as opposed to the literal approach) which caused greatest comment and concern and the reaction that all tax avoidance and planning could be outlawed by the decision.

There have been different views since the judgment as to whether the *Ramsay* doctrine has been developed even further as a result of the case or whether it amounts to merely an affirmation of the *Furniss* v *Dawson* decision with an indication of how the House or Lords will view tax avoidance cases in the future.

Whichever view prevails, the judgment in *McGuckian* has been one of the most important decisions in recent years.

i) *MacNiven* v *Westmoreland Investments Ltd* [2001] 2 WLR 377

The Court of Appeal had to consider whether steps inserted in a transaction had no commercial purpose and whether the sole or main benefit of financing was the obtaining of tax relief for interest, denied under s787 ICTA 1988. The case involved the making of further loans to meet accrued unpaid interest. The Court of Appeal held inter alia that there was a distinction between tax avoidance and tax mitigation and that as the company had financed itself to take advantage of a statutory tax relief, this was an acceptable option since in the view of the judges, the company had incurred real economic outlay on real loans.

The House of Lords also took this view, but the problem for the future is to determine what the correct judicial approach to adopt is where a degree of anti-avoidance or mitigation has been followed.

In the light of the success of the Inland Revenue in *McGuckian*, this case to some extent restores the acceptable tax planning platform but it will require more cases to come before the House of Lords before it will be possible to see whether a different approach will be taken in this difficult area.

25.3 Key cases and statutes

- *Craven* v *White* [1988] STC 476; [1987] STC 297
  Tax avoidance – pre-arranged schemes – *Ramsay* principle

- *Floor* v *Davies* [1979] 3 All ER 677
  Anti-avoidance – form *v* substance

- *Furniss* v *Dawson* [1984] STC 153
  Tax avoidance – pre-ordained series of transactions – single composite transaction

- *IRC* v *Duke of Westminster* [1936] AC 1
  Anti-avoidance – form *v* substance

- *Ramsay (WT) Limited* v *IRC* [1981] STC 174
  Tax avoidance – single composite transaction – business effect

- Income and Corporation Taxes Act 1988, ss660A–682 and 739–742

- Taxation of Chargeable Gains Act 1992, ss29–30

25.4 Questions and suggested solutions

QUESTION ONE

'There is a need in the United Kingdom for a general anti-avoidance provision in the tax legislation. The present position leaves great uncertainty.'

Discuss.

University of London LLB Examination
(for External Students) Revenue Law June 1996 Q4

General Comment

This question explores the policy behind the UK anti-avoidance legislation.

Skeleton Solution

United Kingdom has no general anti-avoidance rule – ss703–787 deal with avoidance in specified circumstances – clearance procedure: not the effective tool it might be: s707 – bona fide commercial transaction exception: as in s703(1) – difficulty of phrasing legislation in anticipation of future developments – avoidance cases: approach of the courts: *IRC v Duke of Westminster; Ramsay (WT) Ltd v IRC; Furniss v Dawson;* pre-ordained series of transactions single composite transaction: *Craven v White; Shepherd v Lyntress Limited;* certainty of sequence of transactions: *Piggott v Staines Investments;* evolution of principles laid down by judges – difficulty of harnessing general rule to existing legislation and to specific transactions – pre-transaction rulings deemed not to be the solution – residual problems as exist at present for clearance procedures.

Suggested Solution

Note: all references are to the Income and Corporation Taxes Act (ICTA) 1988 unless stated otherwise.

The question poses the proposition that the absence of a general anti-avoidance rule in United Kingdom tax legislation leads to uncertainty in the operation of the tax system. It presupposes, therefore, that the introduction of a general rule as to what is and what is not tax avoidance will remove any uncertainty as to the tax treatment of specific tax transactions. In the light of this proposition, how would such a rule be framed and how in practice would it remove the perceived uncertainty in determining the taxing outcome of commercial transactions?

The current and historical position in the United Kingdom in the field of anti-avoidance has been to develop legislation aimed either at laying down the method of taxing specific transactions or in nullifying the tax benefit otherwise accruing in specified circumstances. Most of these provisions can be found in Part XVII ICTA 1988 – ss703–787 – including the cancellation of tax advantages from certain 'transactions in securities' (s703 et seq), the transfer of assets abroad (s739), the sale of income from personal activities (s775), taxation as income of certain capital gains from land related transactions (s776) and restriction on interest relief: s787.

Sections 703–709 cancel a tax advantage arising from 'transactions in securities' in prescribed circumstances. These include dividend-stripping operations and certain capital distributions. The tax advantages at which the sections are aimed include avoidance of liability for tax such as ACT on dividends and other distributions, but also the obtaining of tax deductions and reliefs. In operating the effects of this section, there remains the need to determine, either before or after the relevant transaction has taken place, whether a 'tax advantage' within the ambit of the sections has been obtained, whether this has occurred in any of the 'prescribed circumstances' of s704, and even if this has occurred, whether the transaction has been carried out for bona fide commercial reasons. The sections are not applicable to transactions proved to be for bona fide commercial purposes, with the further proviso that they do not have the obtaining of tax advantages as one of their main objects. The rules incorporate a procedure for clearance, in advance of the transaction, that the section will not apply to it.

It is clear from the above that despite the attempts to lay down specific rules to operate against tax avoidance in prescribed circumstances, there remains an uncertainty at each step as to what is intended to be within, and what is intended to escape, the operation of the sections. The interpretation of the precise wording of the legislation as set out remains the area where continuing uncertainty prevails despite the existence of a clearance procedure under s707. However, it may be assumed that the clearance procedure is sufficient to the extent that the taxpayer receives a favourable ruling. Only where the ruling is rejected is there likely to be a dispute as to the operation of the taxing provisions or the 'bona fide commercial' exemption from them.

The transactions in securities and other existing United Kingdom anti-avoidance measures were enacted over a period of years from the 1930s to 1960s in response to the growing incidence of tax avoidance. In particular, the aggressive marketing of tax-planning schemes to avoid particular taxing results under existing legislation highlighted the opportunities for doing so, and it followed that measures to counter the loss of revenue were necessary.

The present anti-avoidance legislation, enacted at the time when commercial tax planning was to some extent in its infancy, could not be phrased in such a manner as to keep pace with the increasing sophistication of commercial operations, whether devised for tax planning or otherwise. Being directed at specific targets leaves the door open for devising and tailoring commercial operations in a format which sidesteps the precise written word of the law. That may give rise to the need for further legislation which in turn may quickly become obsolete when a further new method of achieving the same tax advantage is developed. A general provision giving the Inland Revenue the power to act when the object of the legislation is defeated by commercial schemes or arrangements has not been successfully developed in the United Kingdom, and the difficulties and practicalities of enforcing such a power are enormous and wide ranging. The anti-avoidance decided cases of recent years give some indication of the difficulties encountered in successfully challenging and countering unacceptable tax avoidance.

In the absence of general anti-avoidance rules, other than the specific transaction cases referred to in Part XVII ICTA 1988, tax law is enforced on the basis of case law decisions, many of which relied upon the dictum in the case of *IRC* v *Duke of Westminster* [1936] AC 1 and the statement by Lord Tomlin that 'every man is entitled if he can to order his affairs so that the tax attaching under the appropriate Acts is less than it otherwise would be', which would seem to give taxpayers the right to arrange their transactions in any way they can, to avoid or lessen their liability to tax. In the *Duke of Westminster* case the deeds of covenant could not be disregarded for tax purposes as they were bona fide legal transactions. The House of Lords affirmed, however, that in construing the true legal effect of a transaction, regard may be had to all the surrounding circumstances. This element has been developed by the courts to provide the 'new approach' to the treatment of tax avoidance schemes.

Until the 1980s the extent to which this decision could be relied upon was largely unexplored, and only when the marketing of complex tax avoidance schemes became commonplace and available to a wider market than previously, were its implications challenged in order to prevent massive losses of tax revenues. In attempting to state the law as it stood, and in deciding how each case should be judged, the courts began to find it necessary to express views as to which types of transactions or arrangements should be found unacceptable if cases of similar structure came before them in the future. They began to try to be almost as specific as the anti-avoidance statutes themselves, but in their decisions they handed down a series of rules containing undefined concepts which in turn themselves gave rise to further litigation to determine the extent of the effects of what the courts had decided. In trying to clarify the *Westminster* principle the courts had embarked upon a 'new approach' as to what would and would not be found acceptable tax planning. In the absence of specific tax legislation to counter anti-avoidance, the courts had begun to establish themselves as quasi-law makers rather than confining their role to the interpretation of the statutes as laid down by Parliament. The series of rulings with new and undefined concepts, together with the change in the role being played by the courts, created an uncertainty for taxpayers through the necessity to try to apply these largely undeveloped concepts to very specific transactions or arrangements. Following the early cases it was unclear whether the courts would continue to counter tax planning with a general ruling as developed in *Furniss* v *Dawson* [1984] 1 All ER 530, or whether this position would be relaxed to set limits on its application, as did occur in the later decisions. In the interim period, however, the certainty expected under the tax system for the taxpayer and the Inland Revenue largely disappeared.

At the heart of any argument for a general anti-avoidance provision must be the need for both the Revenue and the taxpayer to proceed with certain knowledge as to what is and what is not acceptable tax planning or avoidance. In countries where there is a general anti-avoidance provision, as in Australia for example, the provision to some extent merely raises the problems highlighted above in countering avoidance under s703. The provision attacks 'schemes or arrangements' in certain prescribed circumstances and inevitably still leads to conflict and dispute where the meaning or purpose of the provisions is in doubt or conflicts with normal commercial purpose.

By nature, a general anti-avoidance provision has to be couched in broad terms, and the difficulty inevitably arises that the application of broad principles to the particular circumstances of a transaction does not always mean that only the intended offending transactions are caught by it. Generally speaking, commercial transactions are designed to meet a commercial purpose, and it would be an unacceptable consequence of a general rule if the opposite were to occur where the commercial transaction structure has to be foregone in order to avoid the unnecessary confinements of a general tax rule. Despite the exemption for 'bona fide commercial' transactions, that dilemma may still remain.

Ramsay (WT) Ltd *v* IRC

Apart from the statutory provisions there were, prior to the *Ramsay (WT) Limited* v *IRC* [1982] AC 300 case, no common law principles of general application to control tax avoidance. Prior to this the approach adopted by the courts in complex or 'multiple-step' transactions was to determine the outcome of each individual step of the transaction without regard to their overall purpose. Tax avoidance schemes were designed to create tax benefits by inserting other transactions or steps into genuine commercial deals. Therefore, an intended transaction between A and B which would have a tax liability attached to it would be carried out via C where the effect would be that the transaction from A to C and from C to B would reduce or extinguish the liability. Such schemes became increasingly artificial and led to the *Ramsay* decision that while a court could not treat otherwise than as genuine documents or transactions which were found to be genuine, the court could not be restricted to considering those documents or transactions in isolation from any context to which they properly belonged. Thus, the principle emerged that if a series of transactions were in reality part of a larger composite transaction, then the courts were entitled to look at the effect of that composite transaction and attach a tax liability which accorded with the result of the composite transaction. In doing so, the courts could disregard any transactions within that series, or steps introduced into transactions, whose sole purpose was the reduction or elimination of tax.

Furniss *v* Dawson

In *Furniss* v *Dawson* [1984] 1 All ER 530 the House of Lords, by means of two separate rulings, decided that the new approach to anti-avoidance could be applied to transactions which had 'enduring legal consequences', and not only to transactions which were self-cancelling. In addition, it ruled that steps in a composite transaction need not be contractually bound together to be regarded as composite. Lord Brightman indicated that:

'... no distinction is to be drawn for fiscal purposes because none exist in reality, between (1) a series of steps which are followed through by virtue of an arrangement which falls short of a binding contract, and (2) a like series of steps which are followed through because the parties are contractually bound to take each step seriatim.'

The new approach was to be applied to pre-ordained series of transactions and these would be regarded as a single composite transaction.

Pre-ordination

In the case of *Craven* v *White* [1988] STC 476 the Lords took the opportunity to consider in what circumstances transactions were considered to be 'pre-ordained', and in the majority ruled that the taxpayer had to be in a position to carry out the subsequent transactions when the first of the transactions is carried out. If not, then the likelihood of the subsequent transactions being carried out was insufficient to constitute pre-ordination. This is to be applied at the time when the 'inserted step' transaction is carried out.

It was also set out in the *Craven* v *White* judgment that the artificiality of a scheme is evidenced by the absence of any commercial or business purpose to a transaction. Therefore, if the taxpayer can show genuine commercial reasons for the inserted steps, the new approach to anti-avoidance may not be applied. In *Shepherd* v *Lyntress Ltd* [1989] STC 617 the taxpayer company was successful in avoiding the application of the principles arising from *Ramsay* and *Furniss* v *Dawson* to the extent that taking advantage of a fiscal privilege is not necessarily tax avoidance. *Shepherd* illustrated that the courts would be reluctant to apply the new approach with its punitive tax consequences if there are some other genuine reasons for carrying out the inserted steps, or if it can be shown that the taxpayer has merely acted to take advantage of a tax relief provided for by statute.

The cases subsequent to *Ramsay* refined its anti-avoidance doctrine and in doing so established for the first time some basic common law principles to be applied to transactions involving tax avoidance.

The case of *Piggott* v *Staines Investments* [1995] STC 114 involved a scheme to recover corporation tax paid by an acquired company by introducing it into a group whose parent company (BAT Group) had surplus ACT. This has taken the 'certainty' or pre-ordination aspect of the steps further than before – to a stage of being caught unless the opposite was very unlikely to occur.

The judges have evolved the law from where it stood before the series of cases in the 1980s, and there can be little doubt that substantial changes have occurred through what can only be described as judge-made law since it has gone beyond the previously accepted role of interpretation in laying down principles to be followed. It is clear that these principles will be followed and that their effect has been to change for all time the conduct of tax-planning activities without any additional provision being inserted into United Kingdom tax legislation.

The Inland Revenue issued a consultative document 'Pre-transaction Rulings' in late 1995, with a view to extending the existing opportunity for clearances to all transactions in advance of their taking place. Most other countries with a general anti-avoidance have a pre-transaction ruling procedure which includes ruling on anti-avoidance matters. The Revenue view was that the risks to the Exchequer of doing so were great and might lead to refusal to rule in certain circumstances or to rule in general terms, leaving the same process of settling the outcome by negotiation or appeal as is available at present. Similarly, alerting the Revenue at an early stage to a growing number of unacceptable transactions would lead to the need to counter these by further specific legislation.

In the end it appears that the traditional United Kingdom system of specific legislation, coupled with judicial interpretation, will remain as the fulcrum of the United Kingdom's anti-avoidance machinery for the foreseeable future. Other possible approaches do not appear to present less uncertainty than at present and do not remove the need for judicial interpretation. Given that commercial transactions will continue to evolve with further complexity, the current approach does at least have an element of certainty or at least the guidance of precedent handed down from the courts against which to measure the impact in given situations.

QUESTION TWO

Compare the approach of the courts to tax avoidance cases before the decision of the House of Lords in *IRC* v *Ramsay* with the approach today.

University of London LLB Examination
(for External Students) Revenue Law June 1993 Q5

General Comment

This question illustrates the development of anti-avoidance precedents in the courts.

Skeleton Solution

IRC v *Duke of Westminster* – statutory anti-avoidance provisions – absence of common law principles for controlling tax avoidance – *Ramsay (WT) Ltd* v *IRC* and *Eilbeck* v *Rawling* – *Furniss* v *Dawson* – composite transactions – pre-ordination – *Craven* v *White* – *Shepherd* v *Lyntress*.

Suggested Solution

In the case of *IRC* v *Duke of Westminster* [1936] AC 1 the statement by Lord Tomlin that 'every man is entitled if he can to order his affairs so that the tax attaching under the appropriate Acts is less than it otherwise would be' would seem to give taxpayers the right to arrange their transactions in any way in which they can, to avoid or lessen their liability to tax. This would not, however, extend to unlawful or criminal transactions. In the *Duke of Westminster* case the deeds of covenant could not be disregarded for tax purposes as they were bona fide legal transactions. The House of Lords affirmed, however, that in construing the true legal effect of a transaction, regard may be had to all the surrounding circumstances. This element has been developed by the courts to provide the 'new approach' to the treatment of tax avoidance schemes.

Statutory provisions

Until the development of the 'new approach' the ability to deny tax relief in tax avoidance schemes consisted entirely of specific statutory provisions. These provisions were introduced to counter specific types of transactions and set out the conditions under which a specific type on transaction would be caught by the provision. These are currently contained in ss703–787 Income and Corporation Tax Act (ICTA) 1988 and include the cancellation of any tax advantage gained through certain transactions in securities, the denial of tax reliefs in some circumstances, the bringing into charge to tax income which through arrangements outside the UK would avoid UK tax liability and the charging to income tax or corporation tax again which would be otherwise treated as capital.

Apart from these statutory provisions there were, prior to *Ramsay (WT) Ltd v IRC* [1982] AC 300, no common law principles of general application to control tax avoidance. Before this the approach of the courts in multiple step transactions was to determine the outcome of each individual step of the transaction without regard to their overall purpose. Tax avoidance schemes were therefore designed to create tax benefits by inserting other transactions or steps into genuine commercial deals. Therefore, an intended transaction between A and B which would have a tax liability attached to it would be carried out via C, where the effect would be that the transaction from A to C and from C to B would reduce or extinguish the liability. Such schemes became increasingly artificial and led to the *Ramsay* decision, that while a court could not treat otherwise than as genuine documents or transactions which were found to be genuine, the court could not be restricted to considering those documents or transactions in isolation from any context to which they properly belonged. The principle therefore emerged that if a series of transactions was in reality part of a larger composite transaction then the courts were entitled to look at the effect of that composite transaction and attach a tax liability which accorded with the result of the composite transaction. In doing so, the courts could disregard any transactions within that series, or steps introduced into transactions, whose sole purpose was the reduction or elimination of tax.

Furniss *v* Dawson

In *Furniss* v *Dawson* [1984] 1 All ER 530 the taxpayer would have incurred an immediate charge to capital gains tax on a sale of shares if carried out direct to the intended recipient. By diverting the transaction via another company in the Isle of Man the liability could be deferred. The scheme was countered by the House of Lords by means of two separate rulings. It decided that the new approach to anti-avoidance could be applied to transactions which had 'enduring legal consequences' and not only to transactions which were self-cancelling. In addition it ruled that steps in a composite transaction need not be contractually bound together. In other words, in the transaction involving A and B the use of a transaction involving C as intermediary would create a situation where there was no direct contract between A and B. Lord Brightman indicated that:

> '... no distinction is to be drawn for fiscal purposes because none exist in reality, between (1) a series of steps which are followed through by virtue of an arrangement which falls short of a binding contract, and (2) a like series of steps which are followed through because the parties are contractually bound to take each step seriatim.'

The new approach was to be applied to pre-ordained series of transactions and these would be regarded as a single composite transaction.

Pre-ordination

In the case of *Craven* v *White* [1988] STC 476 the Lords took the opportunity to consider in what circumstances transactions were considered to be 'pre-ordained' and, in the majority, ruled that the taxpayer had to be in a position to carry out the subsequent transactions when the first of the transactions is carried out. If he or she was not, then the likelihood of the subsequent transactions being carried out was insufficient to constitute pre-ordination. This is to be applied at the time when the 'inserted step' transaction is carried out.

Shepherd *v* Lyntress

It was also set out in the *Craven* v *White* judgment that the artificiality of a scheme is evidenced by the absence of any commercial or business purpose to a transaction. Therefore if the taxpayer can show genuine commercial reasons for the inserted steps, the new approach to anti-avoidance may not be applied. In *Shepherd* v *Lyntress* [1989] STC 617 the taxpayer company was successful in avoiding the application of the principles arising from *Ramsay* and *Furniss* v *Dawson* to the extent that taking advantage of a fiscal privilege is not necessarily tax avoidance and illustrated that the courts would be reluctant to apply the new approach, with its punitive tax consequences, if there were some other genuine reasons for carrying out the inserted steps or if it could be shown that the taxpayer had merely acted to take advantage of a tax relief provided for by statute.

The cases subsequent to *Ramsay* have refined the anti-avoidance doctrine of that case and in doing so have established for the first time some basic common law principles to be applied to transactions involving tax avoidance.

Revision Aids

Designed for the undergraduate, the 101 Questions & Answers series and the Suggested Solutions series are for all those who have a positive commitment to passing their law examinations. Each series covers a different examinable topic and comprises a selection of answers to examination questions and, in the case of the 101 Questions and Answers, interrograms. The majority of questions represent examination 'bankers' and are supported by full-length essay solutions. These titles will undoubtedly assist you with your research and further your understanding of the subject in question.

101 Questions & Answers Series

Only £7.95 Published December 2003

Constitutional Law
ISBN: 1 85836 522 8

Criminal Law
ISBN: 1 85836 432 9

Land Law
ISBN: 1 85836 515 5

Law of Contract
ISBN: 1 85836 517 1

Law of Tort
ISBN: 1 85836 516 3

Suggested Solutions to Past Examination Questions 2001–2002 Series

Only £6.95 Published December 2003

Company Law
ISBN: 1 85836 519 8

Employment Law
ISBN: 1 85836 520 1

European Union Law
ISBN: 1 85836 524 4

Evidence
ISBN: 1 85836 521 X

Family Law
ISBN: 1 85836 525 2

For further information or to place an order, please contact:

Mail Order
Old Bailey Press at Holborn College
Woolwich Road
Charlton
London
SE7 8LN

Telephone: 020 8317 6039
Fax: 020 8317 6004
Website: www.oldbaileypress.co.uk
E-Mail: mailorder@oldbaileypress.co.uk

Old Bailey Press

The Old Bailey Press Integrated Student Law Library is tailor-made to help you at every stage of your studies, from the preliminaries of each subject through to the final examination. The series of Textbooks, Revision WorkBooks, 150 Leading Cases and Cracknell's Statutes are interrelated to provide you with a comprehensive set of study materials.

You can buy Old Bailey Press books from your University Bookshop, your local Bookshop, directly using this form, or you can order a free catalogue of our titles from the address shown overleaf.

The following subjects each have a Textbook, 150 Leading Cases, Revision WorkBook and Cracknell's Statutes unless otherwise stated.

Administrative Law
Commercial Law
Company Law
Conflict of Laws
Constitutional Law
Conveyancing (Textbook and 150 Leading Cases)
Criminal Law
Criminology (Textbook and Sourcebook)
Employment Law (Textbook and Cracknell's Statutes)
English and European Legal Systems
Equity and Trusts
Evidence
Family Law
Jurisprudence: The Philosophy of Law (Textbook, Sourcebook and Revision WorkBook)
Land: The Law of Real Property
Law of International Trade
Law of the European Union
Legal Skills and System (Textbook)
Obligations: Contract Law
Obligations: The Law of Tort
Public International Law
Revenue Law (Textbook, Revision WorkBook and Cracknell's Statutes)
Succession (Textbook, Revision WorkBook and Cracknell's Statutes)

Mail order prices:	
Textbook	£15.95
150 Leading Cases	£12.95
Revision WorkBook	£10.95
Cracknell's Statutes	£11.95
Suggested Solutions 1999–2000	£6.95
Suggested Solutions 2000–2001	£6.95
Suggested Solutions 2001–2002	£6.95
101 Questions and Answers	£7.95
Law Update 2004	£10.95

Please note details and prices are subject to alteration.

To complete your order, please fill in the form below:

Module	Books required	Quantity	Price	Cost
		Postage		
		TOTAL		

For the UK and Europe, add £4.95 for the first book ordered, then add £1.00 for each subsequent book ordered for postage and packing.
For the rest of the world, add 50% for airmail.

ORDERING

By telephone to Mail Order at 020 8317 6039, with your credit card to hand.

By fax to 020 8317 6004 (giving your credit card details).

Website: www.oldbaileypress.co.uk
E-Mail: mailorder@oldbaileypress.co.uk

By post to: Mail Order, Old Bailey Press at Holborn College, Woolwich Road, Charlton, London, SE7 8LN.

When ordering by post, please enclose full payment by cheque or banker's draft, or complete the credit card details below. You may also order a free catalogue of our complete range of titles from this address.

We aim to despatch your books within 3 working days of receiving your order. All parts of the form must be completed.

Name

Address

Postcode

E-Mail

Telephone

Total value of order, including postage: £

I enclose a cheque/banker's draft for the above sum, or

charge my ☐ Access/Mastercard ☐ Visa ☐ American Express

Cardholder: ....

Card number

☐☐☐☐ ☐☐☐☐ ☐☐☐☐ ☐☐☐☐

Expiry date ☐☐☐☐

Signature: ....Date: ....